THE FREEDOM OF CORK

A Chronicle of Honour

THIS BOOK IS DEDICATED, WITH LOVE,
TO ALICE QUINLIVAN.
AND IT HAS BEEN WRITTEN IN MEMORY
OF CHARLES SCHÖN, TOM O'CONNOR
AND DICK HASLAM.

THE FREEDOM OF CORK

A Chronicle of Honour

AODH QUINLIVAN

The Collins Press

First published in 2013 by
The Collins Press
West Link Park
Doughcloyne
Wilton
Cork

© Aodh Quinlivan 2013
with research assistance from Pádraig Mac Consaidín

Commissioned by Cork City Council to commemorate the seventy-fifth anniversary of the
re-opening of Cork City Hall and the fiftieth anniversary of the awarding of the Freedom
of Cork City to John Fitzgerald Kennedy.

A catalogue record for this book is available from the British Library

ISBN: 9781848891890

Typesetting by Burns Design
Typeset in Goudy

Printed in Poland by Białostockie Zakłady Graficzne SA

CONTENTS

ACKNOWLEDGEMENTS

Toni Morrison once said, 'If there's a book that you want to read, but it hasn't been written yet, then you must write it.' This is a book that I would want to read and it has been a pleasure to research and write it. That pleasure has been enhanced by the support I have received from many individuals and organisations:

- Cork City Council commissioned this book and the organisation has been 100 per cent behind the project from the start. The book has straddled three mayoralties and I am eternally grateful to Councillors Terry Shannon, John Buttimer and Catherine Clancy. The Corporate Affairs Department oversaw the process and my thanks are offered to Valerie O'Sullivan, Tadhg Keating and Jo Gazely.

- The book required a lot of research in the Cork City and County Archives where I was treated very well, as always, by Brian McGee and his dedicated staff.

- The book has been beautifully published by The Collins Press. This is my second collaboration with them and they have been extremely professional, diligent and efficient.

- My thanks are also humbly offered to friends and colleagues who provided valuable feedback on different drafts of the book; on this list are Paul Moynihan, Margaret O'Brien, J.P. Quinn, Philip Murphy and Michelle Considine.

- To Dan Breen in the wonderful Cork Public Museum in Fitzgerald's Park, I say 'thank you' for your help and good luck with your own researching and writing.

- Photographer Tony O'Connell deserves much praise, not only for the quality of his work, but for being a gentleman. As a keen historian, I hope he is pleased by the end result.

- I am delighted to acknowledge Chris Carroll, the gifted silversmith, for being so generous with his time and for providing such rich history regarding the freedom caskets.

- In the miscellaneous category, I am grateful to the staff of Cork County Library, Cork City Library, National Gallery of Ireland, Historic Scotland, English Heritage Archive, Diocese of Cork and Ross, and the John F. Kennedy Presidential Library and Museum.

- This book would not have come to such splendid fruition without the loving support and guidance of my beautiful wife, Emmanuelle, and our gorgeous children, Adam (five), Lucie (three) and Alice (ten months). Thank you individually and collectively – you are my world.

- The final acknowledgment is reserved for Pádraig Mac Consaidín who has been a wonderful research assistant. Pádraig's high-quality research has enhanced this book and the information he skilfully unearthed adds colour, depth and vibrancy to *The Freedom of Cork: A Chronicle of Honour*.

Enjoy the book. If it contains any errors or omissions, I take full responsibility for them.

AODH QUINLIVAN

THE FREEDOM
OF THE CITY

The honour of receiving the freedom of the city is bestowed by many municipalities across the world in recognition of those who have distinguished themselves, contributed to the community or brought high esteem on a municipality through their works or actions. In the Republic of Ireland, for example, a national system to honour citizens does not exist and the freedom of the city conferred by local councils fills that void. Effectively, as the *only* way that an Irish local council can confer honours it has logically become *the highest* honour that a municipality can bestow. As such, it is symbolic of the esteem in which a particular city holds the person.

An example of a 'key to the city' commonly used in the United States.

In the United Kingdom and Ireland, the freedom award is one of the oldest surviving local traditions. For example, it is believed that the first freedom of the city of London was presented in 1237.[1] The medieval term 'freeman' meant someone who was not the property of a feudal lord and who enjoyed privileges such as the right to earn money and own land.[2] Historically, governance of incorporated towns and cities (essentially places with a municipal corporation) was entrusted to the mayor and officials elected by freemen and, more often than not, one had to be a freeman to stand for election in the first instance. There were other advantages of being a freeman, such as: the right to exercise the franchise (right to vote), practice a trade or engage in commerce without restrictive conditions.[3] Another concession often afforded to freemen was the right to enter and exit a city freely, without toll or the need to satisfy burdensome legal requirements.

This was the case in the city of New York, which in its early days was surrounded by walls, meaning that access to the city could be attained only by unlocking one of the city's many gates. A freeman of the city of New York therefore held a 'key to the city', which allowed him to unlock these gates and thus enter and exit at his leisure.[4] Hence, being a freeman did not just have a prestigious dimension but a practical one as well.

Accordingly, the tradition in New York and in the United States generally is to award the 'key to the city'; in essence, however, it is the same as the 'freedom of the city'. An interesting footnote about the freedom of the city of New York is that the first woman to receive the honour was Cork's Muriel MacSwiney (née Murphy) on 31 December 1920. Muriel was the widow of Terence MacSwiney, the famed Lord Mayor of Cork, who had died on hunger strike in Brixton Prison in London two months previously. Terence MacSwiney's death brought worldwide attention to the British presence in Ireland and ultimately heralded the British withdrawal.[5] Muriel went on a lecture tour of the United States in the winter of 1920, during which she was presented with the key to the city of New York by Mayor John Hyland in a ceremony in the City Hall. The *New York Times* noted:

> *Mrs MacSwiney has been adopted into New York's municipal family with all the privileges extended to the many prominent persons who have preceded her. The 'key' consists of a handsomely engrossed certificate granting her all the rights and immunities, which was presented to her tied with a broad green ribbon and encased in a green leather case.*[6]

Like in most jurisdictions, the American 'key to the city' is purely a symbolic honour but it is used widely – and sometimes controversially – by the bigger cities. For example, the key to the city of Detroit was awarded in 1980 to the Iraqi President (formally called the Chairman of the Revolutionary Command Council of Iraq) Saddam Hussein for donating a significant sum of money to a local church.[7] Sporting achievements figure prominently in the awards by American cities. In 2008 and 2012, the players, coaches and owners of the New York Giants received keys to the city in recognition of Super Bowl victories. Staying with American football, the Buffalo Bills player, Terrell Owens, was presented with the key to the city of Buffalo in May 2009 but it was conditional on him catching a minimum of ten touchdown passes and leading his team into the National Football League playoffs (neither target was reached and Owens left the Buffalo Bills at the end of the season).[8]

In the United Kingdom there is a distinction drawn between a military award of freedom of the city (which permits martial organisations to march into the city) and a non-military or civilian award. The latter, not surprisingly, is used more commonly and, for example, the civilian freedom of the city of Liverpool was awarded to the four members of The Beatles – George Harrison, John Lennon, Paul McCartney and Ringo Starr – in March 1984.

The noteworthy feature of this ceremony was that the award to Lennon was posthumous following his death in 1980. Liverpool also has the distinction of awarding its freedom honour to the entire city of New York in 2003 to mark the second anniversary of the September 11 terror attacks. Linking back to The Beatles, the presentation ceremony took place in Strawberry Fields in Central Park.

London, of course, has had many prestigious recipients of the freedom including Florence

The freeman of London, Stephen Fry, walks a sheep over London Bridge in April 2013

Bono and The Edge let two lambs run freely around St Stephen's Green in March 2000

Nightingale, Charles Lindbergh, Winston Churchill, Princess Diana, Nelson Mandela and Luciano Pavarotti. In London, as in many cities, the rights or privileges apocryphally associated with freemen are merely symbolic, such as the right to drive sheep and cattle over London Bridge, the right to a silken rope if being hanged or the right to carry a naked sword in the city. The English actor and author Stephen Fry received the freedom of London in 2011 and exercised his historical right to drive sheep over London Bridge in April 2013.

In an Irish context, the freedom of Dublin confers the right to pasture sheep on St Stephen's Green and defend the city with a longbow and arrow.[9] U2 band members, Bono and The Edge, chose the sheep grazing option after receiving the freedom of Dublin in 2000.[10]

In Tokyo, the equivalent award to the freedom of the city is the 'key to the Metropolis of Tokyo' and noted recipients include Helen Keller and John Glenn. In sports-mad Sydney, the Australian Olympic teams of 2000, 2004, 2008 and 2012 (as well as the Paralympic teams of 2008 and 2012) have all been recognised as was the Sydney Swans Australian Rules football team after they won the Premiership in 2005. Amongst the recipients was their Irish team member Tadhg Kennelly.

In Paris, the honorary citizenship of the city (*citoyen d'honneur de Paris*) is awarded sparingly and has mainly been presented to international figures. Two recent recipients are the Franco-Colombian and Burmese politicians, Íngrid Betancourt and Aung San Suu Kyi respectively. In March 2013, through a unanimous decision of the Council of Paris, it was agreed that the South African anti-apartheid politician Nelson Mandela should receive honorary citizenship of the French capital.

Today, the practical reasons for obtaining the freedom of a city are effectively obsolete. Nevertheless, while the conferring of the privilege is now solely an honorary one, the accolade remains the highest honour a city can bestow upon a citizen or eminent guest.

HISTORICAL CONTEXT: BECOMING A FREEMAN IN IRELAND

Though the Local Government (Ireland) Act, 1898, is regularly cited as marking the beginning of modern local government in Ireland, the roots of the current system can be traced back much further. The 'Golden Age' of Anglo-Norman Ireland (1169–1300) 'represented a major turning point in Ireland's urban history'[11] and 'saw the first flowering of urban self-government in the country'.[12] Historian Matthew Potter explains that municipal self-government was attained when the king (or sometimes feudal lord or senior clergyman) granted a charter that was effectively a written local constitution.[13] Along with Dublin, Waterford, Limerick and Drogheda, Cork received its earliest charter from the king (through his son) in 1185. When Prince John, Lord of Ireland, granted Cork city its charter, Cork became a corporate town with powers of local government.[14]

The powerful people under this system of local government were the burgesses, also known as 'full citizens' or 'freemen'. In essence, there was a distinction made, and typically enshrined in the charters, between freemen and vassals of a feudal lord. The burgesses were granted narrow strips of land, called burgages, on which they could build their dwelling houses.[15] Local democracy, to the extent that it existed, was generally confined to the burgesses, a small elite group, predominantly male and propertied.

Therefore, the freedom of a borough was not necessarily an honorary distinction as it might be known today but rather an acknowledgement of status and a recognition that a person was entitled to join the 'politically active section of the community'.[16]

Potter notes that there were usually six paths available to be granted the freedom of a borough, pointing out that only the first three were considered to be traditional and legitimate:[17]

1. Being the son (or, in some cases, only the eldest son) of a freeman;
2. Marrying the daughter of a freeman;
3. Completing a seven-year apprenticeship with a freeman;
4. By vote of the common council;
5. In some cases, through direct appointment of the mayor;
6. By purchase.

LEGISLATIVE CONTEXT: THE AWARD OF FREEDOM

Irish borough corporations gained new civic traditions with the passing of the Municipal Privileges (Ireland) Act of 1876,[18] including the right to elect and admit individuals to the honorary freedom of the borough, the highest honour in the corporation's gift.[19] This legislation regulated the practice of conferring freedom and 'established honorary freedom on an entirely new plane'.[20] Thus, the post-1876 honorary freedom superseded the ancient concept of the freedom which Potter argues 'had become obsolete since 1840'.[21]

In that year (1840), the Municipal Corporations (Ireland) Act reformed municipal government in Ireland – a total of fifty-eight corporations were dissolved and only ten survived in Cork, Dublin, Limerick, Waterford, Belfast, Londonderry, Clonmel, Drogheda, Kilkenny and Sligo.[22] The significance of the 1840 act was that the franchise of the ten remaining municipal corporations was widened to include all ratepayers with a valuation of more than £10 annually. This meant a lifting of restrictions in allowing people to stand for membership of the corporation and thus the 1840 act was an important step in partly democratising local government. In Dublin, Daniel O'Connell became the first Lord Mayor of the city under the newly extended franchise.

The Municipal Privileges (Ireland) Act, 1876, continued the legislative reform of Irish local government and it offers a clear demarcation between honorary freemen and those who attained the status of freemen by birthright, servitude and marriage – not to mention those who bought their 'freedom' in order to take advantage of the opportunities and benefits associated with the title.

Section 11 of the Municipal Privileges (Ireland Act), 1876, stated:

> *It shall be lawful for the council of any borough in Ireland to elect and admit any person to be an honorary burgess of such borough, but no person so elected or admitted shall be entitled to vote at any election or to exercise any corporate privilege or hold any corporate office by reason of such election or admission; and no person, except the person himself who is so elected and admitted, shall be entitled to make any claims by reason thereof, or to have or enjoy any right or claim by descent, inheritance, or otherwise.*

Section 12 then expressly stated that no person who had been convicted of a felony would be capable of being elected as a freeman into the rank of honorary burgess. The conferring of the freedom following the 1876 act 'became a highly political action … and was used to demonstrate support for Home Rule'.[23]

The Municipal Privileges (Ireland) Act, 1876, was not repealed until the passing of the Local Government Act, 1991. Section 48 (1) (Part VII) of that legislation stated:

> *A local authority may confer a civic honour on a distinguished person in such manner as it may determine including the admission of the person to the honorary freedom of its functional area and may establish and maintain a roll in which to enter the names of persons so honoured.*

The interesting element of this section is that – by virtue of the reference to 'a local authority' – it extended the right to confer the freedom on counties, as well as cities. Section 48 (2) states that the decision to confer the civic honour is a reserved function for the elected members of a local authority and Section 48 (3), while repealing the 1876 legislation, expressly states that people who were conferred under Section 11 of that act remain freemen.

Currently, the award of freedom of a local authority jurisdiction is governed by the Local Government Act, 2001. For the most part, Section 74 of the 2001 act merely restates the provisions of the 1991 act. However, Section 74 (1) (b) provides that the Cathaoirleach (Chairperson) may propose a person for the civic honour. The decision to elect a new freeman, however, remains a reserved function for the full council.

It is worth noting that the legislation governing the freedom as a civic honour does not bestow any special privileges on the conferees, although some historical 'rights' survive.

LOCAL CONTEXT: FREEDOM OF CORK CITY

In Cork, the custom of awarding the freedom of the city whereby persons distinguished for public service become honorary burgesses of the city dates from the fourteenth century and was attained through any one of the six paths described earlier. Due to the destruction of municipal documents in a fire at the courthouse (where corporation meetings were held at the time) in 1891, records do not exist from this time period. The Cork City Council website claims that, following acquisitions by the City Library, a complete list of freemen from 1609 to 1841 is available. In addition, staff of the Cork City and County Archives have produced a useful alphabetical list of freemen from 31 October 1710 to 25 October 1841 (the last assembly of the old corporation before the Municipal Corporations Act, 1840, came into effect). There is also an article by M.V. Conlon from 1947 in the *Journal of the Cork Historical and Archaeological Society* with a list of freemen covering the period 1690 to 1946. Conlon claims that 'the effort to compile an exact and reliable list of freemen is difficult'[24] and he draws a distinction between **honorary freemen** (who were bestowed with the honour as they had distinguished themselves) and **ordinary freemen** who qualified by birthright, servitude, marriage, or payment. The term **freemen-at-large** is also used quite frequently in corporation minutes to denote honorary freemen.

One of the earliest surviving minute books of Cork Corporation dates to 1722 and the extract (facing page) is from the meeting of 8 July that year. The meeting was chaired by Mayor William Hawkins (the title of Lord Mayor was conferred by Queen Victoria in 1900; previously Cork's 'First Citizen' was known as Provost from 1199 to 1272 and as Mayor from 1273 to 1899) and the minutes show that the councillors 'ordered that the Rt. Honourable Lord Shannon, one of the Lords Justices of Ireland, be presented with his freedom in a gold box'.

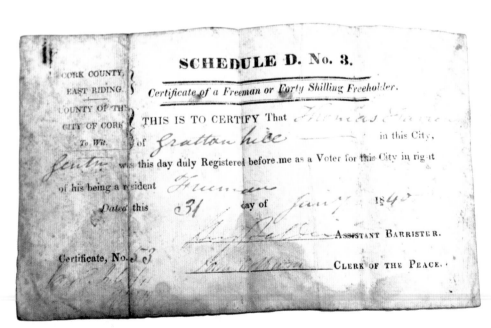

A freeman's certificate in the Cork Public Museum, Fitzgerald's Park, showing that Thomas Farren of Grattan Hill was a freeman of Cork in 1840.
PHOTOGRAPH BY TONY O'CONNELL

The compiling of a complete and reliable list of Cork freemen is further complicated by the fact that the corporation occasionally ordered the freedom to be granted if the person whom it was intended to honour visited the city.[25] For example, on 1 September 1769, it was decided to confer the freedom in a gold box on the eldest son of the Lord Lieutenant 'should he visit the city' but there is no further record on the matter.[26]

The context of the award of freedom changed significantly during the nineteenth century due to the legislation of 1840 and 1876 previously described. The composition of Cork Corporation in the early nineteenth century was confined to a minority of inhabitants but this changed dramatically after the extension of the franchise and the lifting of membership restrictions in 1840.

One of the earliest surviving minute books of Cork Corporation, which dates back to 1722.

In anticipation of the impending reforms Cork Corporation had begun electing a strong body of freemen in an effort to safeguard the positions of those elite few who ran the city. This attempt by the corporation to bolster its ranks in a relatively short period of time is reflected in the fact that 3,259 persons were enrolled as freemen of the city over the relatively short period of forty years since the turn of the century. The reforms were resisted by the existing corporation in Cork. Richard Dowden, a freeman of the city who became mayor in 1845, organised a series of anti-reform meetings in the early 1830s. One such meeting, in March 1831, was called 'The Poor Freemen of the City of Cork' and the freemen who attended the gathering argued that if the proposed reforms were carried into law 'the property and vested interests of our loyal and disinterested body will be grossly and outrageously violated'.[27]

Yet, the efforts of Dowden and the corporation were in vain. The Municipal Reform Act of 1840 brought the power of the existing elitist corporation to a shuddering halt and changed how elections would take place from that point onwards. The privileged of Cork realised that the power that had been reserved for the select few and had been exercised for over 200 years was now defunct.

As previously stated, up to the corporation's reform in 1840 there was a clearly defined charter of rights for freemen of the County Borough of Cork. The chief rights and privileges of citizenship were:

1. To engage in trade and commerce;
2. To have guilds;
3. To be exempt from certain tolls and dues;
4. To be exempt from the quartering of soldiers or the taking of lodging and entertainment against their will by officers or soldiers;
5. To be exempt from the office of sheriff, coroner, bailiff, etc.;
6. To marry, and to have their sons and daughters marry, without having to purchase the licence of the king or his lords and from whose custody the estates of their children during minority were also exempted;
7. To the demise and alienation of their lands (non-freemen could not alienate their lands except to freemen, natives and inhabitants without the license of the mayor);
8. To vote, and hold municipal offices;
9. To acquire corporate property and later to take shares in the pipe-water company;
10. To have a trial by jury, by the oath of twenty-four lawful men instead of by wager of battle.[28]

There are essentially four distinct periods covering the award of the honorary freemen in Cork city.

Period 1 (fourteenth century to 1875): Honorary Burgesses

The granting of the freedom of the borough from the fourteenth century was largely based on family status or purchase but there were also some distinguished honorary recipients.

Period 2 (1876 to 1921): Nationalist Heroes

The honour was more structured after a proper legislative framework was applied by the Municipal Privileges (Ireland) Act, 1876. The practice in the period from 1876 to 1921 was to honour activists in the nationalist movement.

Period 3 (1922 to 1989): Catholic Clergy and Statesmen

The period from 1922 to 1989 was a relatively conservative one (with some notable exceptions) regarding the award of freeman and the dominant category of recipients (55 per cent) in Cork during this time was Roman Catholic clergy.

Period 4 (1990 to present): High Achievers

From 1990 to the present time, the award of freedom of Cork has taken on a different complexion with recognition for outstanding individuals, locally, nationally and internationally.

The Cork City Council website commences its listing from 1887, giving us sixty freemen of Cork up to the end of June 2013 (an average of one recipient every two years). We might expect the council to commence its listing from 1876 (as is the case with Dublin City Council) with the passing of the Municipal Privileges Act. However, the explanation comes in the opening page of the Register of Honorary Burgesses which notes:

> *The roll of the honorary burgesses admitted prior to 1887 was destroyed in the burning of the courthouse (1891), and no record is forthcoming of the admission prior to that date of many notable men amongst others, the late Charles S. Parnell and the late William E. Gladstone. The subsequent roll was also destroyed in the burning of the municipal buildings (December 1920).*[29]

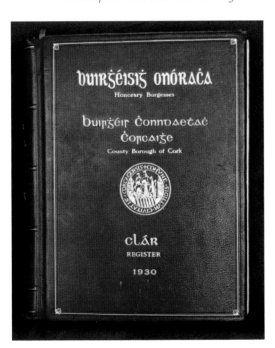

The register then begins its listing of freemen from 1887, starting with General Patrick Collins (United States Member of Congress) but between 1876 and 1887, there were some illustrious recipients of the freedom of Cork, including Isaac Butt, Charles Stewart Parnell, William Gladstone, Sir John Pope Hennessy and William O'Brien. The register also contains the signed enrolment forms of conferees and their full citations from 1930 onwards (the complete list, with citations, from 1930 to the present day is contained in Appendix 1).

The Register of Freemen from 1930 to the present is held in the Cork City and County Archive. PHOTOGRAPH BY TONY O'CONNELL

FREEDOM OF CORK RECIPIENTS FROM 1887 TO 2013

	RECIPIENT	DATE OF ELECTION	DATE OF CONFERRING
1	Patrick A. Collins	15 July 1887	
2	John Redmond	10 January 1902	4 April 1902
3	Cardinal Patrick Francis Moran	22 August 1902	29 August 1902
4	Andrew Carnegie	5 September 1902	21 October 1903
5	Cardinal Vincenzo Vanutelli	5 August 1904	5 August 1904
6	Jeremiah O'Donovan Rossa	24 November 1904	16 December 1904
7	Douglas Hyde	22 June 1906	1 August 1906
8	Cardinal Michael Logue	12 June 1908	
9	Matthew Cumming	21 May 1909	
10	Edward O'Meaghar Condon	17 September 1909	
11	Redmond Barry	20 October 1911	
12	Peadar Ó Laoghaire	10 May 1912	25 September 1912
13	Kuno Meyer*	10 May 1912	25 September 1912
14	Ignatius O'Brien	25 April 1913	18 July 1913
15	John Campbell	22 January 1915	3 February 1915
16	Fr Thomas Dowling	10 May 1918	
17	Woodrow Wilson	10 January 1919	
18	Monsignor Daniel Mannix	6 August 1920	28 October 1925
19	Archbishop Robert Spence	27 August 1920	24 November 1930
20	Archbishop William Barry	10 September 1920	
21	Fr Dominick	25 February 1922	
22	Sir Frank Benson	25 January 1930	22 January 1931
23	Fr Paschal Robinson	11 March 1930	16 July 1930
24	Archbishop Finbar Ryan	22 June 1937	5 October 1937
25	Seán T. O'Kelly	25 November 1947	8 September 1948
26	Cardinal John D'Alton	28 April 1953	16 June 1953
27	Archbishop Richard Cushing	12 August 1958	26 August 1958
28	Cardinal Michael Browne	31 July 1962	13 August 1962
29	John Fitzgerald Kennedy	11 June 1963	28 June 1963
30	Cardinal William Conway	25 May 1965	15 June 1965

* Kuno Meyer was elected as a freeman on 10 May 1912 and conferred on 25 September that year. However, he was expunged from Cork's freedom register on 8 January 1915 before being re-elected a freeman of the city on 14 May 1920.

	RECIPIENT	DATE OF ELECTION	DATE OF CONFERRING
31	**Éamon de Valera**	26 February 1973	31 March 1973
32	**Cardinal Timothy Manning**	12 November 1973	4 December 1973
33	**Professor Aloys G. Fleischmann**	16 January 1978	28 April 1978
34	**Bishop Cornelius Lucey**	4 November 1980	19 December 1980
35	**Jack Lynch**	4 November 1980	19 December 1980
36	**Thomas P. O'Neill Jr**	11 February 1985	16 March 1985
37	**Monsignor James Dean Bastible**	10 November 1986	24 January 1987
38	**Dr Seán Ó Faoláin**	13 June 1988	9 July 1988
39	**Mary Robinson**	17 December 1990	23 February 1991
40	**Fr Roch Bennett**	11 May 1992	13 June 1992
41	**Maurice Hickey**	11 May 1992	13 June 1992
42	**Maureen Curtis-Black**	26 April 1993	19 June 1993
43	**Br Jerome Kelly**	28 March 1994	21 May 1994
44	**Con Murphy**	27 March 1995	24 June 1995
45	**John Bermingham**	11 November 1996	24 May 1997
46	**George Mitchell**	14 September 1998	28 November 1998
47	**John Hume**	26 April 2004	8 May 2004
48	**Sonia O'Sullivan**	23 May 2005	14 June 2005
49	**Roy Keane**	23 May 2005	14 June 2005
50	**Mary McAleese**	8 May 2006	30 May 2006
51	**Michael Flatley**	10 April 2007	2 June 2007
52	**Albert Reynolds**	12 May 2008	20 June 2008
53	**Sir John Major**	12 May 2008	20 June 2008
54	**Dean Denis O'Connor**	9 March 2009	22 May 2009
55	**Sr Eucharia Buckley**	9 March 2009	22 May 2009
56	**Peter Barry**	26 April 2010	11 June 2010
57	**Seán Óg Ó hAilpín**	26 April 2011	27 May 2011
58	**Frank Duggan**	28 May 2013	17 June 2013
59	**Michael Twomey**	28 May 2013	17 June 2013
60	**Billa O'Connell**	28 May 2013	17 June 2013

NO 19.

DATE OF ENROLMENT
23RD February 1991.

NAME AND QUALIFICATION

MARY ROBINSON
Uachtarán na hÉireann,

The entry for Mary Robinson, the first female recipient of the freedom of Cork, in the Register of Freemen from 1930 to the present which is held in the Cork City and County Archive.

PHOTOGRAPH BY TONY O'CONNELL

A number of things stand out from this impressive list of recipients. One is gender imbalance with the award being made on only five occasions (out of sixty) to women, starting with Mary Robinson who was elected a freewoman in December 1990 and conferred in February 1991.

A second feature is that while the freedom conferring ceremonies are splendid events, it is the date of election which is more important as this is the occasion when the city council formally passes the motion to elect a new freeman or freewoman. In some cases from the above list of sixty recipients, conferring ceremonies did not take place at all. In other cases, there was a long gap between the election and the conferring – Archbishop Robert Spence was elected as a freeman of Cork in August 1920 but was conferred a decade later in November 1930. In the case of Cardinal Vincenzo Vanutelli, the election and conferring took place on the same day, 5 August 1904. The above list is nearly complete but there are gaps in some conferring dates, partly as a result of a missing minute book of Cork Corporation covering the period from 13 October 1906 to 12 December 1912.[30] Different venues have also been used for the conferring ceremonies in Cork, including the civic offices in Fitzgerald's Park, the courthouse on Washington Street, the old municipal City Hall building (burned to the ground by the Black and Tans in 1920) and the 'new' City Hall, opened by Éamon de Valera in 1936 (he subsequently received the freedom of Cork in 1973). The actor Frank Benson was conferred with his freedom on the stage of the Cork Opera House in 1931 while Most Reverend Paschal Robinson, the Papal Nuncio to Ireland, was conferred at a garden party in University College Cork in 1930.

The gaps in the list are a third notable element. For example, no person was elected as a freeman of the city between February 1922 and January 1930. There are a couple of probable reasons for this. It was, of course, a turbulent period after the War of Independence, then the foundation of the Free State and the subsequent Civil War; many prominent buildings had been destroyed in the 1920 burning of Cork and the city was in a weak financial state. One must also factor in the fact that Cork Corporation had been dissolved in 1924 (replaced by Commissioner Philip Monahan) and was not reinstated until 1929. There was also a ten-year gap from 1937 to 1947, encompassing the years of the Second World War. The table to the right demonstrates that after a few quiet decades, the freedom of Cork was given out freely from 1990 onwards. Over the twenty-four years from 1990 to 2013 inclusive, twenty-two people received the freedom of the city. This is more than the total number of recipients (seventeen) over the previous sixty years from 1930 to 1989.

A fourth feature from the list is the relative dominance of the Catholic clergy. This is especially apparent during Period 3 (1922 to 1989) but has continued right up to present times with the election of Dean Denis O'Connor and Sr Eucharia Buckley in March 2009.

A fifth element is the tendency over the past thirty years or so to elect and confer two people at the same time

DECADE	NUMBER OF ELECTED FREEMEN / FREEWOMEN
1900–1909	9
1910–1919	6
1920–1929	5
1930–1939	3
1940–1949	1
1950–1959	2
1960–1969	3
1970–1979	3
1980–1989	5
1990–1999	8
2000–2009	9
2010–2013	5

(although Canon Peadar Ó Laoghaire and Kuno Meyer were jointly conferred on 25 September 1912). This modern trend commenced with Bishop Cornelius Lucey and Jack Lynch in 1980 and has continued with Fr Roch Bennett and Maurice Hickey (1992), Sonia O'Sullivan and Roy Keane (2005), Albert Reynolds and Sir John Major (2008) and the aforementioned Dean Denis O'Connor and Sr Eucharia Buckley (2009). In all bar one of these examples, two people were individually elected and conferred with separate citations. The exceptions are Albert Reynolds and John Major who were conferred jointly, insofar as there is one single entry and citation in the freedom register recognising them 'for their combined contribution' to the Northern Ireland peace process. Dean Denis O'Connor and Sr Eucharia Buckley have separate citations in the freedom register but the same wording is used. In May 2013, Cork City Council took the unprecedented decision to confer the freedom of the city on three people – Frank Duggan, Michael Twomey and Billa O'Connell.

One thing which cannot be gleaned from the official list of freemen is an appreciation of the people who were proposed for the honour but who did not receive it. Cork Corporation minutes from the early 1920s show that James Larkin, the trade union leader and socialist activist, was discussed as a possible recipient of the freedom of Cork but the matter was not progressed.[31]

There is some confusion about Pope Pius XI possibly receiving the award. Most Rev. Dr Finbar Ryan was elected as a freeman on 22 June 1937 in recognition of his appointment by the Pope as the coadjutor Archbishop of the Port-of-Spain and Archbishop of Gubula. In including Archbishop

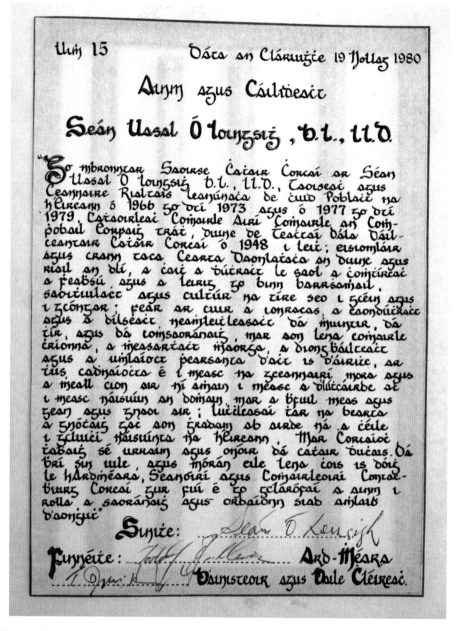

The entry for Jack Lynch in the Register of Freemen from 1930 to the present in the Cork City and County Archive.
PHOTOGRAPH BY TONY O'CONNELL

Ryan on his list of recipients, Conlon claims that Pope Pius was also elected a freeman of Cork on the same day but there is no evidence to support this in the minutes of Cork Corporation or elsewhere.

In January 1987, Councillors Kelleher and Lynch proposed a motion that the freedom be conferred upon Nelson Mandela, leader of the African National Congress (ANC) 'in recognition of his life-long struggle for justice in South Africa and in recognition of the seventy-fifth anniversary of the founding of the A.N.C.'.[32] The motion was defeated by eight votes to five and so Mandela was not elected a freeman of Cork. The organiser of Cork's Over-60s Talent Competition, Paddy

O'Brien, was considered for the honour in 1995, with the minutes of the Cork Corporation meeting of 27 March stating, 'Council agreed to discuss the nomination of Paddy O'Brien for the freedom of the city at a meeting of party whips.' Again, as with James Larkin, the matter was not progressed and no formal nomination went before council.

LOCAL CONTEXT: FREEDOM OF CORK CASKETS

The custom of presenting the freedom of the borough in silver or sometimes gold boxes dates to around 1670. The first record of a silver box accompanying the presentation of a freedom parchment was in 1666 and the practice was restricted for a period of time from 1738 after Dean Jonathan Swift returned his box to Cork Corporation (see next chapter).

In the records of the borough of Cork, frequent mention is made of the commissioning of an appropriate silver or gold box that held the parchment bearing the freedom of the borough for the distinguished recipient.[33] Freedom boxes were particularly popular in the late eighteenth and early nineteenth centuries. The boxes, which initially held the recipient's freedom parchment conferring the freedom of a city or town on an important visitor, were usually finely engraved and of a size and shape that rendered them serviceable as snuff or tobacco boxes.[34] It is also the case though that Cork Corporation occasionally marked special occasions by presenting people with tobacco boxes and caskets without conferring the freedom of the city. This adds to the aforementioned difficulty of compiling a complete and accurate list of freedom recipients in Cork. For example, the box pictured below from the Cork Public Museum looks like a freedom box but it is merely a tobacco box presented to Andrew Sullivan in 1839.

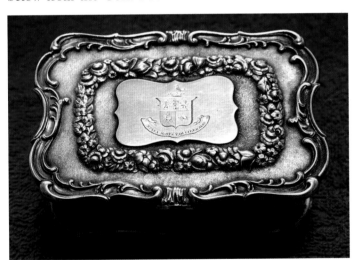

An example of a silver tobacco box on display in the Cork Public Museum, Fitzgerald's Park. PHOTOGRAPH BY TONY O'CONNELL

The earliest presentation of a freedom box on record for Cork is 10 September 1666 when 'the most Hon'ble James Duke of Ormond' was conferred with the freedom of Cork 'ex gratia'. In addition, the Duke was also made a present of the presage (customs duty) on wine imported through Cork. The legal document relinquishing this revenue to Ormond was presented in a silver box, engraved with the city arms and was presented by the mayor of the time. This began the tradition of incorporated towns and cities in Ireland, and later in Britain, of making presentations in precious metal boxes, later to become known as caskets.[35]

Gold freedom box with parchment from 1782 by William Reynolds.

An example of a silver freedom box which is on display in the Cork Public Museum, Fitzgerald's Park. This box was presented to the Rt. Hon. Standish O'Grady on 14 September 1803 in recognition of the 'ability, moderation and firmness' with which he conducted the trial of United Irishman, Robert Emmet. PHOTOGRAPH BY TONY O'CONNELL

Silver Cork freedom box by Carden Terry and Jane Williams.

A number of these freedom boxes from the late eighteenth and early nineteenth centuries have reappeared in recent years, with examples in the National Museum of Ireland,[36] the Museum of Fine Arts, Boston, and the National Museum of Women in the Arts, Washington DC. Indeed, a gold freedom box crafted in Cork around 1795 by Carden Terry and Jane Williams was sold at auction for almost €30,000 by Christie's of London in 2009.[37]

There is some dispute as to the number of freedom boxes presented by Cork Corporation in the period up to the Municipal Corporations (Ireland) Act, 1840. Historian Richard Caulfield, in his research on the freedom of the city of Cork, states that there were 34 gold boxes and 293 silver boxes presented.[38] However, in *Cork Silver and Gold*, John R. Bowen asserts that there were at least 41 gold and 371 silver boxes presented by Cork. Regardless, it is clear from records that Cork city, up to the abolition of the old corporation in 1841, exceeds by far the number presented by any other body in Ireland.[39] One possible explanation for this 'generosity' is that Cork was an important victualing port. Many fleets of His Majesty's ships destined or returning from the other side of the Atlantic called on the port for provision. It became customary, therefore, to present freedom boxes to 'Admirals or Commanders of Men of War' and 'Governors of the Foreign Plantations that may be of some use to the trades of this City' as noted in the Register of Freeman of Cork.[40] One notable presentation was made on 9 January 1778 to the captain of the HMS *Wasp*, Captain William Bligh,[41] later to become captain of the HMS *Bounty*, infamous for the mutiny which took place in 1789.

The history of the craft of making freedom boxes is also interesting. Initially, the freedom boxes were made in Cork by craftsmen and women such as George Hodder,[42] Robert Goble, Jonathan Buck, William Reynolds and Carden Terry – who was later joined in the business by his daughter, Jane Williams, the first female silversmith in Cork. The silver trade fell into decline in the nineteenth century due to the imposition of a high rate of duty, the advent of railways and ease of transportation which led to an influx of cheaper imported silver from Britain. By the mid-1850s it is believed that no silversmith remained in the trade in Cork city.[43] This led to the corporation ordering freedom boxes from Britain – though this had occurred while the Cork silversmiths were still crafting also, as recorded in the minute books of Cork Corporation.

It was not until 1910 and the re-establishment of the firm William Egan and Sons Ltd that quality handwrought silver was once again made in the city of Cork. This materialised as a result of a request by Sir Bertram Windle, the President of University College Cork. Windle commissioned William Egan and Sons to make a ceremonial silver mace for the college to reflect the recently acquired status of constituent college of the National University of Ireland. The one stipulation Windle insisted upon was that the piece be made entirely in Cork. Due to the absence of skilled craftsmen, Egan brought silversmiths from Dublin to fulfil the commission. As part of the arrangement, Egan hired a number of local boys from the North Monastery School to act as apprentices to the seconded silversmiths, thereby passing skills on to the local citizens and regenerating the craft of the silversmith in Cork. The range and quality of work produced by Egans in the twentieth century make many of their pieces much sought-after,[44] with some of these items being freedom caskets of the city of Cork.

William Egan and Sons retained the commission to produce the freedom caskets until the firm's closure in 1986 (though Egan and Sons had been taken over in 1979 by a business consortium that created a separate company that traded as both Cork Silver and William Egan and Sons simultaneously). Quite often, bespoke pieces crafted in the Egan's workshop would carry the Cork Silver hallmark punch, C.S. Ltd. It was not uncommon, however, for some customers to insist upon the Egan hallmark on commissioned work in preference to the newly created Cork Silver hallmark, which lacked the historical prestige the Egan's hallmark carried.[45]

In recent years, the freedom caskets have been hand raised and planished by Seán Carroll and Sons. The firm, founded in February 1985 by Seán Carroll, a former silversmith with William Egan and Sons, is today operated by his son Chris Carroll. Many of the modern freedom caskets that are crafted in the workshop of Carroll and Sons are made using the same tools and equipment from the workshop of William Egan and Sons. This is due to the fact that Seán Carroll took possession of most of the equipment from the Egan and Sons workshop (in lieu of a redundancy payment) when the firm closed. Carroll and Sons are also the only silversmiths where three generations of one family have worked on freedom caskets for the city of Cork.

Chris Carroll at work on a piece of silver in his workshop at Granary Hall, Rutland Street, Cork.
PHOTOGRAPH BY TONY O'CONNELL

While he manufactured a number of freedom caskets under the hallmark of his own firm, Seán Carroll – during his employment with William Egan and Sons – also fashioned the silver Cork coat of arms that adorns the lid of the freedom casket presented to US President John F. Kennedy in 1963. Seán's grandson, Andrew, created the casket for John Major which was presented in 2008, and Chris Carroll – the current proprietor of Seán Carroll and Sons – has raised and planished the majority of freedom caskets commissioned since the early 1990s.[46] Chris, who also crafted a personalised commission for Queen Elizabeth II on her visit to Cork in 2011, likened the task of creating a Cork freedom casket to being the pinnacle of a Cork silversmith's career and a task highly prized in the industry.[47]

In relation to the actual creation of the freedom casket itself, the first thing the silversmith must do is ascertain the exact dimensions of the freedom scroll that will be awarded to the new honorary freeman or woman of the city. This is a vital step in the creation of the freedom casket, as the freedom scroll should fit perfectly into the cylindrical scroll holder of the casket, with no room for movement of the scroll. This is both to ensure a professional finish to the completed casket while simultaneously protecting the scroll parchment itself from damage.[48]

Above: The freedom casket of John Bermingham who was elected freeman on 11 November 1996 and conferred on 24 May 1997. The casket was donated to Cork City Council by the Bermingham family and is on display in the Lord Mayor's offices. PHOTOGRAPH BY TONY O'CONNELL

Right: 'Presidential Package', a close-up of Mary Robinson's casket. COURTESY *IRISH EXAMINER*

HONORARY BURGESSES – 1609 TO 1841

The recipients of the freedom of Cork covered in this chapter are:

JONATHAN SWIFT	FRANCIS ANDREWS
CAPTAIN RICHARD ROBERTS	CHARLES LENNOX
JOHN BRINKLEY	JOHN MILNER BARRY
ADMIRAL ADAM DUNCAN	BISHOP FRANCIS MOYLAN
ADMIRAL AMELIUS BEAUCLERK	CHARLES FITZWILLIAM

As noted previously, the freedom of the borough of Cork from the fourteenth century to the passing of the Municipal Privileges Act, 1876, was not necessarily an honorary distinction as it is today but rather was largely based on family status or, indeed, the purchase of the title. That is not to say, however, that there were not some eminent recipients during this period as will be seen below. The period can more accurately be condensed to 1609 to 1841. The reason for this is that the official (surviving) records of Cork Corporation with regard to the admission of freemen commences in 1609 with a complete record from 1710. The appropriate ending point for the period is 25 October 1841, the last day of the 'old' corporation as constituted previous to the coming into operation of the Municipal Corporations (Ireland) Act, 1840, which produced local democratic elections. The power of admitting freemen only by birth or right also ceased in 1841 and the honour was not revived until the legislative framework was put in place by the Municipal Privileges Act, 1876.[1]

Left and following page: The old Registry of Freemen from the Cork Public Museum, Fitzgerald's Park. The register has the dates 1656 to 1741 on its cover but it starts with 1710. PHOTOGRAPHS BY TONY O'CONNELL

One notable freeman admitted in this period was Dublin-born writer, clergyman, and political activist **Jonathan Swift (1667–1745)**, regarded as the foremost English language satirist of his time. While principally known for his books such as *Gulliver's Travels* and *A Tale of a Tub*, he became Dean of St Patrick's Cathedral in Dublin (hence he is often referred to as Dean Swift) and was also politically involved during his long life (Swift was seventy-seven when he died, which would have been considered a remarkable age at the time). Swift's alma mater was Trinity College Dublin where he started studying history and poetry in 1682 at the tender age of fifteen. He received his Bachelor of Arts degree in 1686 *speciali gratia* ('by special dispensation'), 'implying academic weakness'.[2] He then went to England where he graduated with a Masters in Arts at Hart Hall, Oxford, before returning to Dublin to be ordained a priest three years later.[3] He was then awarded a Doctor of Divinity from Trinity in 1702.

Portrait of Jonathan Swift from the National Portrait Collection in the National Gallery. He also featured on the old Irish £10 note.

In 1707, 'the Archbishop of Dublin, William King, approached Swift on the question of taxes levied on the church by the crown, asking him to go to London and petition the Whig Party directly for the removal of these taxes'.[4] Swift failed to convince the Whigs but McMinn records that 'this entry into the world of parliament and court was to transform his life and work dramatically'.[5] He spent the following years, until 1713, working as the Tories' chief protagonist and promoting their policies at home and abroad.[6]

Swift's circumstances changed dramatically when he was made Dean of St Patrick's Cathedral in 1713, a position he held until his death in 1745.[7] Initially, Swift was not overjoyed to receive the deanship of St Patrick's as he had hoped for 'a prominent English clerical position'.[8] Having refused all payment for his services to the Tories, Swift trusted that they would 'secure him a senior clerical appointment in England, such as a bishopric'[9] but Queen Anne did not reward him as he had expected.

Overcoming his initial disappointment, Swift spent the next two decades combining his work as Dean with political campaigning (he fought hard against what he regarded as unjust impositions on the Irish people) and with writing, culminating in the publication of *Gulliver's Travels* in 1726 which became an immediate success, 'going through three editions before the end of the year, and soon translated throughout Europe'.[10]

One of his successful political campaigns revolved around his writings using the name M.B. Drapier (*The Drapier's Letters* were a series of seven pamphlets) which helped prevent a debased currency from being imposed by the British government on the Irish people.[11] His contribution to this cause was one of the main factors in Swift being presented with the freedom of Dublin city by Dublin Corporation in 1730. It may also have been a reason behind receiving the honour in Cork but there is no specific information about how this came about. The date of Swift's admission to the roll of freemen is entered in Cork Corporation's records as 20 January 1736 with the note that 'the celebrated Dean Swift' was sent a silver box.[12]

Swift sent a remarkable letter in reply dated 15 August 1737 from Deanery House in Dublin to the Mayor of Cork and the Common Council of the City of Cork. In the letter, the text of which is reproduced below, Swift expresses surprise at having received the freedom of Cork and states that he is returning the silver casket because 'there is not so much as my name upon it, nor any one syllable to show it was a present from your city'.[13]

Deanery House, Dublin, August 15, 1737.

Gentlemen,

I received from you, some weeks ago, the honour of my freedom, in a silver box, by the hands of Mr. Stannard; but it was not delivered to me in as many weeks more; because, I suppose, he was too full of more important business. Since that time, I have been wholly confined by sickness, so that I was not able to return you my acknowledgment; and it is with much difficulty I do it now, my head continuing in great disorder. Mr. Faulkner will be the bearer of my letter, who sets out this morning for Cork.

I could have wished, as I am a private man, that, in the instrument of my freedom, you had pleased to assign your reasons for making choice of me. I know it is a usual compliment to bestow the freedom of the city on an archbishop, or lord-chancellor, and other persons of great titles, merely on account of their stations or power: but a private man, and a perfect stranger, without power or grandeur, may justly expect to find the motives assigned in the instrument of his freedom, on what account he is thus distinguished. And yet I cannot discover, in the whole parchment scrip, any one reason offered. Next, as to the silver box, there is not so much as my name upon it, nor any one syllable to show it was a present from your city. Therefore I have, by the advice of friends, agreeable with my opinion, sent back the box and instrument of freedom by Mr. Faulkner, to be returned to you; leaving to your choice whether to insert the reasons for which you were pleased to give me my freedom, or bestow the box upon some more worthy person whom you may have an intention to honour, because it will equally fit everybody.

I am, with true esteem and gratitude,

Gentlemen, Your most obedient and obliged servant, Jon. Swift.

Letter from Jonathan Swift addressed to the Right Worshipful the Mayor, Aldermen, Sheriffs, and Common Council of the City of Cork

There is no indication of the response from Cork Corporation but it is presumed that the silver casket was appropriately engraved and returned to Swift. Jonathan Swift's later life was diminished by ill-health. He was troubled by imbalance and noises in his ears and suffered a stroke in 1742. That same year he was pronounced to be of unsound mind and memory (but not insane) and his affairs were managed by a group of trustees.[14] Swift died on 19 October 1745 and he was laid to rest in St Patrick's Cathedral under a now famous epitaph which he wrote himself. It reads:[15]

Here lies the body of Jonathan Swift, Doctor of Sacred Theology, Dean of this Cathedral, where savage indignation can no longer tear at his heart. Pass on, traveller, and, if you can, emulate his tireless efforts in defence of liberty. He died on the 19th. day of the month of October, 1745, in the 78th year of his age.

Ninety years after his death, Jonathan Swift's body was exhumed and examined by one of Dublin's most prominent physicians, Sir William Wilde (father of Oscar Wilde). He discovered that Swift had a loose bone in his inner ear and that 'Ménière's disease' was the root cause of many of his problems.[16]

Captain Richard Roberts (1803–1841), born in Passage West, County Cork, received the freedom of Cork in recognition of his role as captain of the ship *Sirius*, the first vessel to cross the Atlantic entirely under the power of steam. *Sirius* was built in Leith, Edinburgh in Scotland before coming to Cork in 1837, having been purchased by the St George Steam Packet Company.[17] According to T. Sheppard, *Sirius* was an impressive vessel with a gross tonnage of 703.[18] She was 178 feet 4 inches long from stem to stern with a depth of 18 feet 3 inches.[19] Her stern was square and a dog figurehead decorated her bow – this was a fine work of art with the dog holding a star in its paws, a theme also used in the ship's saloon.[20]

The *Sirius* made a few journeys between Cork and London before being chartered by the British and American Steam Navigation Company to voyage to New York in 1938.[21] With forty passengers and thirty-eight crew members on board, she set sail from London on 28 March, calling to Cork on 4 April (two days later than intended) to voyage from Leeside to New York. The ship was commanded by Captain Richard Roberts who wrote the following in his log:[22]

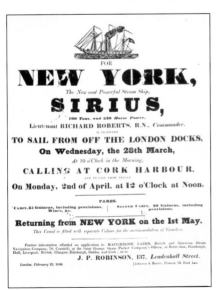

An advertisement for the famous Atlantic crossing of the *Sirius*. COURTESY OF THE CORK PUBLIC MUSEUM, FITZGERALD'S PARK

On leaving Passage, about 7 miles below Cork, we were loudly cheered by the inhabitants, together with the most respectable families in Cork, who had assembled with warm hearts and handsome faces (the ladies, I mean) to witness our departure and wish us success on our passage to our transatlantic brethren. Most of the gentlemen interested in our vessel proceeded with us as far as the Cove (Cobh) of Cork, where we stopped to let Ocean come alongside to take the above gentlemen out, which having been done, with three hearty cheers and many heartier wishes, we gallantly bent our way for New York.

Despite encountering bad weather, the *Sirius* arrived in New York on 22 April 1838 under the expert guidance of Roberts. The voyage created quite a stir in America, as can be garnered from the following account:[23]

She arrived in New York on the 22nd of April amidst a scene of the greatest excitement, the whole city being thrown into a state of commotion. She was decorated with sixty flags of all nations, and the river was crowded with vessels of all descriptions which sailed round her.

In the *Dictionary of Irish Biography*, David Murphy states that 'Roberts and his crew became instant celebrities'[24] and were received in New York by the Mayor and aldermen. Roberts commenced his journey home on 1 May, 'thousands turning out to see the *Sirius* off'[25] and set sail after a seventeen-gun salute.

This model of the *Sirius* is the Lord Mayor's office in City Hall, Cork. It was made by Seán Carroll and Sons, and was presented to the city of Cork by Irish Distillers for the Cork 800 celebrations in 1985. PHOTOGRAPH BY TONY O'CONNELL

Captain Roberts received various awards on his return including the freedom of Cork and the freedom of London as well as being presented with a silver salver by the people of his home town in Passage.[26] His entry into the honorary roll of freemen in Cork is dated as 10 June 1838 and it is noted that he received a silver box in recognition for his skill in command of the *Sirius* 'on the first voyage ever made by a steamer from Europe to America'.[27]

Unfortunately, both Roberts and the *Sirius* had sad endings. Roberts and his entire crew were lost when the SS *President* went down on a return voyage from New York in 1841.[28] It was later concluded that the *President* had sunk in the mid-Atlantic during a storm.[29]

The *Sirius* was lost in 1847 in a voyage from Glasgow to Cork via Dublin when, in dense fog, she went ashore and was shipwrecked at Ballycotton Bay.[30] For fifty-one years the *Sirius* lay at the bottom of the sea before being salvaged – her metal was purchased by Messrs. Mason Limited of Birmingham.[31] The firm made souvenirs from the metal in the form of paper weights, one of which was sent to the King of England.[32] Another was presented to the American Ambassador to England who promised to send it to the President of the United States.[33]

The departure of the *Sirius* from Cork on 4 April 1838 was re-enacted in 1988 to mark the 150th anniversary of the famous sailing. Amongst those who attended the re-enactment were the US Ambassador Margaret M. O'Shaughnessy Heckler and the Minister for the Marine Brendan Daly.

The renowned astronomer and mathematician **John Brinkley (c.1766–1835)** received the freedom of Cork late in his life when he was the Bishop of Cloyne. There is some confusion about when Brinkley was born. According to his memorial at Trinity College Dublin he entered the world in 1765 but the *Biographical Encyclopaedia of Astronomers* claims he was born in 1767. Biographer Linde Lunney asserts that Brinkley was probably born in 1766 but notes that the only thing about which there is certainty is that he was baptised in Suffolk, England, on 31 January 1767.[34]

He was the illegitimate son of Sarah Brinkley, a butcher's daughter from Woodbridge in Suffolk, and was educated in a school in Benhall before going to Caius College, Cambridge.[35] He graduated from Cambridge with a Bachelor of Arts degree in 1788 and a Masters of Arts in 1791.[36] While a fellow at Cambridge he took holy orders and was ordained in 1791. His distinguished career at Cambridge 'attracted the attention of the board of Trinity College Dublin'[37] and, in 1792, he was appointed Professor of Astronomy and director of the Dunsink Observatory.[38] These appointments were controversial 'as some at Trinity would have preferred an Irish candidate'.[39]

Later that same year he was given the title Astronomer Royal of Ireland. It is recorded that he had to wait until 1808 for a proper telescope to be constructed in Dunsink, 'during which time he established himself as an accomplished mathematician'.[40] Armed with his new telescope (an 8-foot meridian circle) from 1808, Brinkley turned his attention once again to astronomy and made a major

Portrait of John Brinkley from the Dibner Library of the History of Science and Technology (Smithsonian Libraries' Catalogue).

discovery of the parallax of fixed stars in 1814.[41] His research results were disputed by the Astronomer Royal, John Pond, but nonetheless Brinkley was awarded the prestigious Royal Society's Copley Medal in 1824 for his work on stellar parallax.[42] His textbook, *Elements of Astronomy*, first published in 1813, went through numerous editions to become a standard reference work.[43] Brinkley's work 'was known internationally, greatly increasing the status of Dunsink Observatory'.[44]

In 1826, John Brinkley was appointed Bishop of Cloyne and for the remaining years of his life he devoted his attention to religion and moved away from the worlds of science, astronomy and mathematics. Lunney notes that 'increased ecclesiastical duties curtailed astronomical activity; indeed, it is said he refused to allow a telescope into the episcopal palace at Cloyne, lest he be distracted from his religious responsibilities'.[45]

He died on 14 September 1835 and was buried in the vaults of Trinity College Dublin, survived by his wife Esther and two sons, John and Matthew.[46] On his death, Cloyne became united with the sees of Cork and Ross.[47]

Admiral Adam Duncan (1731–1804) was admitted to the list of honorary freemen in Cork in November 1797, the month after he led a Royal Navy fleet to victory over a Dutch Navy fleet in the Battle of Camperdown, considered one of the most significant actions in naval history. Born at Lundie, Angus, in Scotland on 1 July 1731, Duncan entered the navy at the age of fifteen and, over the next fifty years, earned a reputation for great bravery and for performing several brilliant exploits including one during a conflict which took place off the Straits of Gibraltar in October 1782.[48] He was rewarded in 1795 when he was appointed commander-in-chief in the North Seas and hoisted his flag on board the *Venerable*, a significant ship which boasted seventy-four guns.[49]

His crowning glory came in October 1797 when he obtained a decisive victory over a Dutch fleet off the village of Camperdown during the French Revolutionary Wars. Earlier, Duncan had blockaded the Dutch at the Texel with only the *Venerable*, the *Adamant* and three small vessels while ninety-five enemy ships lay inside the port.[50] In a 'triumph of audacity and courage'[51] Duncan confused signals and changed flags to make the Dutch Admiral, De Winter, believe that a great fleet was in the distance. On the morning of 11 October, Duncan attacked De Winter's Dutch line of battle and broke through. The Dutch ships were forced to surrender and they either sank, fled or were claimed by Duncan, thus ending their hopes of invading England. Duncan triumphantly arrived back to Yarmouth on 18 October 'to a hero's welcome'.[52]

In honour of his great victory, Duncan was given a massive pension of £2,000 per annum by the British government, he was awarded the Large Naval Gold Medal, and the titles Viscount Duncan of Camperdown and Baron Duncan of Lundie were created for him. Additionally, he was given the freedom of several cities including London (where he was presented with a sword worth 200 guineas),[53] Liverpool, Portsmouth, Dundee and, of course, Cork. For the Cork honour, he received a gold box (this was something of a rarity as silver boxes were normally presented) 'for his great merit and exertions in so gloriously defeating the Dutch fleet on the 11th of October last in the Battle of Camperdown'.[54] With his pension, Duncan built the 'imposing neo-classical Camperdown House beside his home town of Dundee'[55] which is contained within what is now Camperdown Country Park. Admiral Adam Duncan, 1st Viscount of Camperdown, died on 4 August 1804 at the age of seventy-three, with an intact reputation 'for coolness, courage, and daring'.[56]

This portrait of Admiral Adam Duncan hangs in the Historic Scotland Collection in Edinburgh.[57]

Another person who received the freedom of Cork based on his naval exploits was **Admiral Amelius Beauclerk (1771–1846)**. In Beauclerk's case there was at least a local link as the honour was bestowed on him for his victory over the French frigate *Proserpine* off Cape Clear in June 1796. He was admitted to the roll of freemen in Cork the following month and was sent a silver box 'in testimony of his services in protection of trade and support of the British flag'.[58] Beauclerk had a distinguished career in the British Navy and served on some famous ships including *Nemesis*, *Juno*, *Fortunée*, *Majestic*, *Saturn* and *Royal Oak*.

In 1796 he held the rank of captain when he led the *Dryad* into battle with the *Proserpine* and achieved a brilliant victory despite being significantly outmanned. Laughton states that the *Dryad* had 44 guns and 251 men compared to the *Proserpine* with 42 guns and 348 men.[59] Beauclerk lost two men and had seven wounded, compared to the French casualties of thirty deaths with forty-five wounded.[60]

While this triumph brought Beauclerk to the attention of Cork Corporation, it was by no means the peak of his naval career and he went on to serve with distinction until 1839. Beauclerk was made Rear-Admiral in 1811, before being promoted to Vice-Admiral in 1819 and finally to the level of Admiral in 1830.[61] He then served as Commander-in-Chief at Portsmouth from 1836 to 1839.[62] He died, unmarried, at Winchfield House in Hampshire on 10 December 1846.[63]

The portrait of Admiral Amelius Beauclerk which hangs in the British Maritime Museum.[64]

Derry born **Francis Andrews (1718–1774)** was Provost of Trinity College Dublin when he was issued with a silver box and admitted to the roll of freemen in Cork in August 1761. Andrews had been appointed as Provost in 1758 and it was an historical appointment as he was the first layman since 1626 to hold the post.[65] The following year he was elected to parliament and there was a Cork connection in that his stated constituency was Midleton. In 1761, Andrews was appointed to the Irish Privy Council of Ireland, an advisory body to the Dublin Castle administration.

Andrews was a reforming Provost in Trinity. He built Provost House and he initiated a new system of public entrance examinations which led to an education exchange between Dublin schools and the college.[66] Andrews is described as 'a fashionable and energetic figure who liked to be in the public eye'[67] and he ruled Trinity with 'an easy rein'.[68] Lunney portrays him as 'the very model of an Augustan gentleman, fond of society and elegantly accomplished, as well as a noted *bon viveur*'.[69]

Upon his death at the age of fifty-six in 1774, Francis Andrews bequeathed money to Trinity College to build, and in part endow, an astronomical observatory.[70] He was buried in the vaults of the chapel in Trinity and his portrait hangs in the college.[71] He also left money to Dunsink Observatory which provides a link to another recipient of the freedom of Cork, John Brinkley.

Following his death, there was a dispute involving Trinity, his executors and his heirs about 'whether all or some of Andrews's dealings with college landed property had been strictly legal'.[72] The establishment of the Andrews Professorship of Astronomy was therefore delayed until 1785, 'after a parliamentary committee in 1780 had examined the evidence'.[73] Andrews was survived by his mother and her adopted daughter; he never married despite being 'noted for his gallantries'.[74]

The portrait of Francis Andrews by Anton von Maron in Trinity College Dublin.[75]

The portrait of a young Charles Lennox which hangs in the English Heritage Collection at Battle Abbey.[82]

Charles Lennox (1764–1819), the fourth Duke of Richmond and future Lord Lieutenant of Ireland, was made a freeman of Cork in September 1800 largely as a result of a famous duel he fought with Frederick Augustus, the Duke of York and second son of King George III. Lennox joined the British army at a young age and was promoted quickly through the ranks, due in no small measure to the friendship between his uncle and the Prime Minister, William Pitt.[76] When young Lennox obtained a captaincy in the Coldstream Foot Guards in 1789 the Duke of York was indignant and made disparaging remarks about the courage of the Lennox family.[77] Charles Lennox challenged the Duke of York to a duel and the encounter took place on 26 May on Wimbledon Common. Given that Lennox's opponent was the son of the king, the duel attracted much attention but it turned out to be something of an anti-climax. Lennox fired his weapon but his ball merely 'grazed his Highness's curls'.[78] The duke chose not to fire at Lennox in return but rather fired into the air, declaring that he bore his opponent no animosity.[79]

In 1790 Lennox was elected to his father's seat of Sussex in the House of Commons and was re-elected in 1796, 1802 and 1806 (the same year he succeeded to the Dukedom of Richmond and Lennox on the death of his uncle). The following year he was appointed Lord Lieutenant of Ireland and enjoyed an untroubled time there despite his rigid political and religious views.[80] It is reported that, in June 1812, he wrote to the Colonial Secretary, Lord Bathurst, stating that he was happy to remain in Ireland 'as long as nothing is done for the Catholics'.[81] In the event, his appointment ended in 1813 and his next big job came in 1818 when he was made Governor-in-Chief of British North America. He died the following year in bizarre circumstances when, during a tour of upper and lower Canada, he was bitten by a fox and contracted rabies.

John Milner Barry (1768–1822) has the distinction of being a Cork-born recipient of the freedom honour – somewhat rare during this period. Barry was born in Kilgobbin, near Bandon, and he was educated at Bandon and at the University of Edinburgh, where he was awarded an MD degree in 1792 for a thesis on ascites.[83] Following his studies in Edinburgh, Barry returned to Cork to practice medicine. Writing in the *Oxford Dictionary of National Biography*, Laurence M. Geary states that Barry's professional life was 'marked by energy, enterprise, and innovation'.[84] In particular he was a great supporter of Edward Jenner and saw the potential importance of the smallpox vaccination. He obtained the vaccine by post from a colleague in Dublin and used it in Cork from 6 June 1800, making him the first to vaccinate in Ireland outside of Dublin.[85] The following year he published *A Report on the Infectious Diseases of the City of Cork* in which he called for the establishment of a fever hospital. Money was raised and the Cork House of Recovery and Fever Hospital was opened on 8 November 1802, with Barry and Charles Daly (who was also made a freeman of Cork) as its first physicians.[86] It was primarily for his work in establishing the hospital that Barry was made a freeman of Cork.

During his career in medicine, Barry was outspoken on two issues in particular. He was a passionate advocate of female education and he rallied against drunkenness and the abuse of alcohol. He did not do so from a moral standpoint but 'he regarded it as one of the primary agents in the propagation of disease'.[87] Dr John Milner Barry died from apoplexy at his home on Patrick's Hill in Cork on 16 May 1822. He was buried at Ballinaltig Cemetery near Watergrasshill and in 1824 a cenotaph was erected in his remembrance on the grounds of the fever hospital. The inscription claims that the institution had been 'the means of preventing the pernicious contagion of typhus fever from diffusing itself widely in the populous city of Cork'.[88]

A portrait of Bishop Moylan, courtesy of the Diocese of Cork and Ross.

While members of the Roman Catholic Church enjoy a dominant place in the roll of freemen of Cork in later periods, probably the first Catholic clergyman to receive the honour was **Bishop Francis Moylan (1735–1815)**[89] on 30 December 1796. Indeed, during Period 1 up to 1876, the only two Catholic clergymen admitted were Moylan and Bishop John Murphy (1846). Francis Moylan was born into a wealthy Cork family and he was educated in Paris as the penal laws made it impossible for him to receive a suitable education at home.[90] He pursued a religious way of life and he was ordained a priest in 1761 after graduating as a Doctor of Theology at the University of Toulouse.[91] He subsequently worked in Paris for a number of years before returning to Cork as a pastor in St Finbarr's. He remained there until 1775 when he became Bishop of Kerry but came back, once again, to Cork as bishop in 1787.

As a bishop his efforts were unwavering 'to obtain the removal of restraints on Catholics'[92] and 'this brought him into the vortex of contemporary politics'.[93] In the *Oxford Dictionary of National Biography*, Angela Bolster notes that the 'views and the positions he took were close to Edmund Burke, with whom he corresponded'.[94]

In December 1796 Bishop Moylan publicly urged his flock to resist the French during the failed invasion attempt at Bantry Bay under General Hoche. It was for this reason that he was admitted to the roll of freemen of Cork. He was presented with a silver box 'to perpetuate our grateful approbation of his pious exertions in promoting the peace and order of this country at the moment of the menaced invasion'.[95] During Moylan's time as Bishop of Cork, the Christian Brothers were introduced and also the Ursuline and Presentation Nuns; he was known as a trusted friend and adviser of Nano Nagle.[96] Bishop Moylan oversaw the completion of the Cathedral in Cork as well as the building of a seminary and he helped establish Maynooth University, of which he became a trustee.[97] Moylan devoted much of his life to the education and welfare of the poor and Bolster concludes that he was 'a dedicated pastor whose solicitude for those entrusted to his care was second to no other commitment or involvement'.[98]

Correspondence from Bishop Moylan from 1775 to his death in 1815 is contained in the Cork City and County Archives.[99] His was the first public funeral accorded to a Catholic bishop since the Protestant reformation.[100]

One of the stranger entries in the *List of Freemen of Cork City 1710–1841* is that of **Charles FitzWilliam, later Viscount Milton (1786–1857)**. He seems to have been admitted as a freeman of Cork on 24 January 1795 before he reached the age of nine and he is listed as the Principal Secretary to Earl FitzWilliam, his father. A note against his name in the list suggests that there was 'perhaps some error in this admission'[101] and that 'it appears rather strange that he would have been Principal Secretary or admitted a freeman during his minority'.[102]

The purpose behind this chapter has been to provide colour and context to some of the men who received the freedom of Cork between 1710 and 1841. It has to be stated again, however, that admission to the roll of freemen during this period did not necessarily constitute an honorary distinction as we understand it today. Rather, in many cases, it was an acknowledgement of status and an entry into the elitist world of local politics. The majority of recipients in the *List of Freemen of Cork City 1710–1841* (produced by Cork City and County Archives) come with the remark 'Gentleman', 'Esquire' or 'Merchant'. In other cases it is stated that the person was made a freeman based on the payment of either £5 or £10. There are exceptions in terms of men who were admitted due to exceptional acts of distinction and some of these have been captured in this chapter, from Jonathan Swift to John Brinkley to John Milner Barry.

PERIOD 2
NATIONALIST HEROES – 1876 TO 1921

As stated previously, the year 1876 and the enactment of the Municipal Privileges (Ireland) Act, 1876, provides a clear demarcation in the story of the freedom honour. Prior to 1876, as described in the last chapter, the status of honorary burgess was attained by birthright, status, marriage or purchase. The Municipal Privileges legislation of 1876 made it lawful for any borough council in Ireland to elect and admit any person to be an honorary burgess. Thus the award of freedom attained the honorary distinction we have today.

The new powers afforded to borough councils under the 1876 act were immediately used in Cork city when Isaac Butt was honoured in the same year. Other celebrated recipients in the following years included Charles Stewart Parnell, Sir John Pope Hennessy, William Gladstone and William O'Brien although the official records relating to these were lost in the courthouse fire of 1891. It is for this reason that the 'modern' list of freemen starts in 1887 with General Patrick Collins, United States Member of Congress.

Period 2, as it has been categorised in this book, lasted until 1921 and there was a clear policy over these years to elect heroes of the nationalist struggle. This chapter profiles ten recipients of the freedom of Cork during Period 2, commencing with Isaac Butt.

The recipients of the freedom of Cork covered in this chapter are:

ISAAC BUTT	DOUGLAS HYDE
CHARLES STEWART PARNELL	KUNO MEYER
WILLIAM GLADSTONE	CANON PEADAR Ó LAOGHAIRE
ANDREW CARNEGIE	WOODROW WILSON
JEREMIAH O'DONOVAN ROSSA	MONSIGNOR DANIEL MANNIX

ISACC BUTT

(1813–1879)

Elected as Freeman of Cork on 2 October 1876

'*That the honorary freedom of the city of Cork be conferred on Isaac Butt, Esq. QC, MP, pursuant to the provisions of the Municipal Privileges (Ireland) Act, 1876, which extends to certain municipal corporations in Ireland certain privileges heretofore exercised by the municipalities of England, and which act became law owing to Mr. Butt's exertions.*'

BIOGRAPHY

As alluded to in the citation above, Isaac Butt was an immediate beneficiary of the new powers afforded to Irish borough councils under Section 11 of the Municipal Privileges (Ireland) Act, 1876, to elect and admit people to the roll of honorary burgesses. In Butt's case this was entirely appropriate as he had been a leading figure behind the legislation.

Isaac Butt was born at Glenfin, County Donegal, on 6 September 1813, the only son of Robert Butt (rector of Stranorlar) and his wife, Berkeley.[1] Most of Butt's childhood was spent in Donegal but he also spent time with his grandfather in Adare, Limerick, and with his uncle in Cloyne, Cork, where he attended Midleton College.[2] At the age of fifteen he took first place in the entrance examination to Trinity College Dublin, where he excelled as a scholar.[3] He graduated with a BA in 1835, was awarded an LL B in 1836, and then received an MA and LL D in 1840.[4]

During his time in Trinity College, Butt was 'unequivocally Tory and a staunch defender of Protestant ascendancy'.[5] As a junior barrister in 1840 he had been selected to plead the case of Dublin Corporation against the Municipal Reform Bill in the House of Lords.[6] As founder of the *Dublin University Magazine* in Trinity, Butt demonstrated the qualities of a rising Protestant Tory politician while also expressing views 'not generally associated with Toryism'.[7] These views included questioning the Irish property settlement, criticising aristocratic privilege and expressing sympathy for the plight of Irish peasants.[8]

Butt's core belief was that 'the union and Protestant ascendancy were essential attributes of the identity of the Irish nation, and guarantees of Ireland's position, not as a colony, but as a partner with Britain in its great imperial venture'.[9] However, the Great Famine of 1845–1849 represented a turning point in Butt's thinking about nationalism and led him in the direction of advocating Home Rule for Ireland.

He was elected to parliament as a Conservative at the Harwich by-election in May 1852 but 'had barely taken his seat when parliament was dissolved'.[10] In the subsequent election of July 1852 he won a seat (by two votes) as a Conservative representative in the borough of Youghal. He was returned unopposed to parliament, as a Liberal, in 1857 and triumphed again electorally in 1859.[11] He lost his seat in 1865 and his political record in the House of Commons is described as 'nondescript'.[12] He used his speaking time in parliament demanding tenant rights in Ireland, urging state sponsorship of Irish railway construction and defending Catholic interests.[13]

Butt lost his seat 'just as a sea change was taking place in Irish politics'[14] and he devoted the following years to defending Young Ireland and Fenian prisoners who were being arrested as conspirators. Though usually unable to save the Fenians from a prison sentence, Butt 'won their respect for his understanding of the well-springs from which their actions derived'.[15] Butt had sympathy for the injustices Ireland suffered and – through his legal efforts on behalf of Fenian prisoners – he 'was transmuted into a nationalist icon'.[16]

Butt was keen to return to the world of politics, especially since William Gladstone had secured a Liberal victory in the general election of 1868 on a platform of remedying Irish disaffection.[17] Butt won a seat in Limerick city in September 1871 and the next two years was a period in which the support for Home Rule grew. During this time, 'Home Rule's fortunes rode heavily on Butt's shoulders'.[18] David Thornley claims that, by 1874, Isaac Butt was 'the unquestioned leader of the Irish people'.[19] However, by 1878, Butt was regarded as 'an anachronistic survival [and] a barrier to the development of the national movement'.[20] This 'collapse of starting swiftness'[21] was due to a number of factors – Butt's declining morale and personal financial problems as well as the rise to prominence of Charles Stewart Parnell. Butt and Parnell 'routinely locked horns over parliamentary business'[22] with Butt's gentlemanly approach being usurped by younger and more radical members of the nationalist movement who sought 'to make the floor of the Commons a battlefield on which the cause of Ireland could be fought out'.[23] The likes of Parnell, Joseph Biggar and John O'Connor Power pursued a policy of parliamentary 'obstruction' that did not sit well with Butt.

With his political position and health declining, Butt did not appear in the House of Commons after 1878. He died in Dublin on 5 May 1879 from the effects of a stroke. Philip Bull, writing in the *Dictionary of Irish Biography*, contends that 'mounting political opposition from his colleagues, aggravated by financial difficulties and bad health, almost certainly contributed to his death'.[24] The tragedy of Isaac Butt's final years is that he essentially advocated the same position as Parnell – only their methods differed. Unlike Parnell, Butt 'was unable to exploit revolution … he did not approve of revolution'.[25] Thornley sums up Butt's position very well:

Home Rule was not for him a tight-rope between English obstinacy and Irish nationalism, a compromise to be won by waving the green flag of separation in the face of John Bull; it was the best and most honourable arrangement between the two islands.[26]

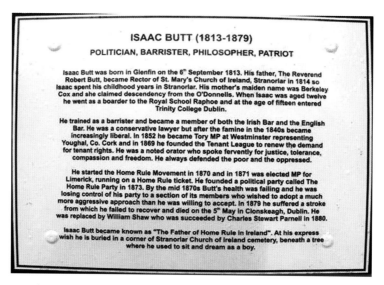

The commemorative plaque to Isaac Butt at 'The Pound', Stranorlar Historical Park, County Donegal.

Isaac Butt was buried in Stranorlar Cemetery, County Donegal, on 10 May 1879 and was survived by his wife, Elizabeth (Swanzy), with whom he had eight children. These were not his only children however 'and the attempt to take responsibility for children born out of wedlock contributed to his abiding financial problems'.[27]

FREEDOM OF CORK

As highlighted above, Isaac Butt was at the peak of his powers when he was conferred with the freedom of Cork on 2 October 1876 (even though his subsequent decline was swift). Alderman Dwyer formally moved the motion 'that the honorary freedom of the city of Cork be conferred on Isaac Butt, Esq. QC, MP, pursuant to the provisions of the Municipal Privileges (Ireland) Act, 1876, which extends to certain municipal corporations in Ireland certain privileges heretofore exercised by the municipalities of England, and which act became law owing to Mr. Butt's exertions'.[28] He added that Butt was a man who had made many sacrifices for his country. Alderman Dwyer contended that Butt had given up an honourable and lucrative profession and had applied himself to benefitting the country in every way he could.[29]

Alderman Nagle seconded the motion and added that the Town Clerk should forward a copy of the resolution to Isaac Butt engrossed on parchment. The resolution was unanimously passed. There is no record of any conferring ceremony taking place.

CHARLES STEWART PARNELL

(1846–1891)

Elected as Freeman of Cork on 8 April 1880

Conferred as Freeman of Cork on 15 April 1880

by Pádraig Mac Consaidín

BIOGRAPHY

Born on 27 June 1846 in Avondale, County Wicklow, into a family of Anglo-Irish Protestant land owners, Charles Stewart Parnell was the second son and seventh child of twelve born to John Henry Parnell and Delia Tudor Stewart.[1] Parnell is at once one of the best-known and one of the least-known Irish leaders of the nineteenth century. While his outward persona as a political leader and his much publicised relationship with Katherine O'Shea may be well known, the private person Parnell remains an elusive, even enigmatic figure.[2]

During his formative years Parnell's interests were scientific rather than literary; he was not known to be particularly well-read or possess a talent for writing, which contrasts with the interests of many of his political peers.[3] Indeed, Parnell had 'no special love for his books'[4] which could account for the lack of rhetorical skills and fear of public speaking that never left him.[5] However, despite his educational bias, Parnell attended Cambridge University, though he did not complete his degree with various reasons cited for this.[6]

Little is known of Parnell's entry into politics as 'for a young man anxious to stand up to the Englishman, Ireland in the mid-1870s did not offer many opportunities'.[7] Then, approaching his twenty-eighth birthday Parnell offered himself to Isaac Butt and the cause of Home Rule.[8] On 22 April 1875 Parnell was elected to parliament, returned as MP for Meath as a member of Butt's Home Rule League.

In 1877 Parnell began a policy of obstruction in parliament, a move opposed by Butt. This process involved an extension of the Joseph Biggar technique, whereby opposition members consumed as much parliamentary time as possible in order to prevent ministers the opportunity to legislate on matters to which the opposition objected.[9] In 1879, with Butt out of the picture, Parnell was elected President of the Irish Land League.

Parnell began 1880 with a tour of America where he fundraised for the Irish cause and also addressed the US House of Representatives. Returning from America he contested the general election where he was returned for Cork, Mayo and Meath – he chose to sit for Cork. This was also the year that he met Katherine 'Kitty' O'Shea with whom he was to have three children and later marry.

This drawing appeared in the *Illustrated London News* in 1890 and shows Parnell addressing his constituents from the window of the Victoria Hotel in Cork. COURTESY OF THE CORK PUBLIC MUSEUM, FITZGERALD'S PARK, CORK

During the elections of 1880 Parnell had supported the Liberal William Gladstone, however, when Gladstone's Land Act of 1881 failed to meet expectations, Parnell joined the opposition. Encouraging boycott in order to influence the landlords and land agents led to Parnell's arrest and subsequent imprisonment. He was released from Kilmainham Prison in 1882 following negotiations on an alliance with the Liberal Party, which became known as the 'Kilmainham Treaty'.[10]

Not long after his release in 1882, the fatal stabbings of Lord Frederick Cavendish (the newly appointed Chief Secretary for Ireland) and Thomas Burke (as Permanent Undersecretary, he was the most senior Irish civil servant) took place in Dublin's Phoenix Park (the Phoenix Park Murders).[11] Parnell immediately signed a manifesto to the Irish people denouncing the murders, and repeated the condemnation the next day in the House of Commons. His strong condemnation of the murders increased his already strong popularity in Ireland and Britain. In April 1887, the *Times* published a letter, allegedly bearing Parnell's signature that apparently claimed sympathy with the Phoenix Park murderers of 1882. This letter was later proved to be a forgery and Parnell was vindicated. On his next appearance in the House of Commons he received a standing ovation – to many this was the peak of his political career.

Politically, Parnell faced a difficult period after the defeat of Prime Minister Gladstone's Government of Ireland Bill, 1886 (commonly referred to as the First Home Rule Bill), to which Parnell gave a guarded welcome. His challenge was 'to maintain the momentum of Irish nationalism without alienating Liberal sympathy and moderate opinion in Britain'.[12] He was also accused by opponents during this period of neglecting his political responsibilities and his lengthy absences from the House of Commons were noted. As described by Frank Callanan, writing in the *Dictionary of Irish Biography*, there were three main reasons for these absences – Parnell's fragile health, his desire to maintain a low profile and his increasingly complicated personal relationship with Katherine O'Shea.

In 1889, William O'Shea, a once loyal Parnell supporter, filed for divorce from his wife Katherine on the grounds of adultery, naming Parnell as a co-respondent.[13] At this stage, Parnell had three daughters with Katherine – Claude Sophie was born in 1882 and died after two months, Clare (1883–1909) and Katie (1884–1947).[14] This scandal provoked a political split and Parnell was replaced as party leader. This effectively ended his political career. Parnell died in Brighton on 6 October 1891 at the age of forty-five, just three months after finally marrying Katherine O'Shea in a registry office ceremony. Ireland lamented the loss of its 'uncrowned King' and 'Chief', and Parnell was laid to rest in Glasnevin Cemetery, Dublin.

Charles Stewart Parnell's reputation lives to this day and Callanan claims that he 'embodied in a way that no Irish leader had, before him or since, a sense of Irish statehood'.[15] In his book *Great Contemporaries*, Winston Churchill wrote of Parnell as 'a being who seemed to exercise unconsciously an indefinable sense of power in repose – of command awaiting the hour'.[16] There is no doubt that Parnell, following on from the work of Isaac Butt, 'brought about a transformation of the relationship of Ireland to Britain, and to the world'.[17]

FREEDOM OF CORK

At two o'clock on 15 April 1880 Charles Stewart Parnell MP was conferred a freeman of the city of Cork at the City Courthouse, having been formally elected the previous week. The honour was bestowed upon Parnell following a resolution of the corporation at its previous meeting, where it was unanimously voted that the honour be conferred.

On the ceremony itself, the *Cork Examiner* reported that 'a very small number of the members council were present, and the great majority of the people in attendance belonged to what might be called the "advanced party" in local politics'.[18] *The Irish Times* preferred to refer to those who filled the council chamber as 'idlers'.[19] Many solicitors who were engaged in nearby court sittings also attended, though out of curiosity rather than genuine interest it seems.

The Mayor, Councillor Patrick Kennedy, in his robes accompanied Parnell into the chamber where they were greeted by a burst of applause. Having taken his place on the bench 'on which were placed the maces and the other insignia of office',[20] proceedings commenced. During a lengthy address, the Mayor delivered a glowing tribute to Parnell which outlined that Irish people always want to offer reward to the great men of their country, and in this instance the Mayor said he spoke for the people of Cork. The Mayor went on to note Parnell's tireless work on behalf of the people of Ireland. The selflessness in travelling to the United States to labour for the Irish, at Parnell's own expense of time and money, was also noted. He then advised that the freedom of the city of Cork was the greatest honour the city could bestow upon a non-resident and presented Parnell with a parchment, sealed with the city arms and welcomed the new freeman as a citizen of Cork.

In reply, Parnell thanked the Mayor and his fellow citizens for the honour conferred upon him. He went on to say that despite receiving many such honours in the United States, he felt 'more pride and pleasure'[21] in receiving this particular freedom above all others. He also alluded to the fact that advances in the cause for Irish freedom were made by the 'restoration of ancient privileges rather than anything of an advance beyond the ancient lines'.[22] Parnell proceeded to speak of his experiences in America, where any man from any class could aspire to be Mayor, and that this was his hope for all Irish men one day and what he would work towards. Following further contributions from Aldermen Dwyer and Nagle the proceedings ended, with Charles Stewart Parnell enrolled on the ancient list of freemen of the city of Cork.

Parnell left Cork that evening on the ten past ten train, having been accompanied from the Victoria Hotel by a fife and drum band and a crowd carrying tar-barrels. The *Cork Examiner* reported that there was 'an ugly rush' at the railway station as Parnell approached and that the platform was crowded 'to a dangerous extent'.[23] The new freeman of Cork addressed the crowd from the window of his train carriage and thanked everyone once again for his warm welcome on Leeside.

WILLIAM GLADSTONE

(1809–1898)

Elected as Freeman of Cork in August 1886

Conferred as Freeman of Cork on 5 October 1886

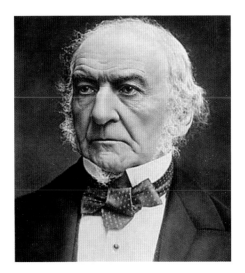

BIOGRAPHY

The four-times Liberal Prime Minister of the United Kingdom, William Ewart Gladstone, was born on 29 December 1809 at 62 Rodney Street in Liverpool.[1] The son of a Scottish merchant, Gladstone was born into an evangelical family. Henry Colin Gray Matthew, writing in the *Oxford Dictionary of National Biography*, records that Gladstone's mother and his sister Anne (who was also his godmother) combined 'prolonged illnesses with intense evangelical pietism'.[2] The Gladstones were a rich family, 'their fortune based on transatlantic corn and tobacco trade and on the slave-labour sugar plantations they owned in the West Indies'.[3] Young William initially went to school in Bootle, near Liverpool, before attending Eton College from 1821 to 1827. On the completion of his second-level studies in Eton, Gladstone went to Christ Church, Oxford, for the period of 1828 to 1831. At Christ Church he studied classics and mathematics and received a Double First in both subjects. While at university, Gladstone 'was active in the newly formed Oxford Union Society, of which he was President in 1830'.[4] By the end of his time at Christ Church, Gladstone was already 'a rising star of British public life'.[5]

In February 1832, accompanied by his brother John, Gladstone went on a grand tour of Europe, visiting Belgium, France and Italy.[6] According to Matthew, 'the chief import of the tour was his first extended experience of Roman Catholicism, which both attracted and repelled him'.[7] It was during his continental tour that Gladstone received an invitation from the Duke of Newcastle to stand for election. Gladstone accepted the invitation and was elected as a Conservative MP for Newark-on-Trent, taking his seat on 29 January 1833.[8]

His maiden speech was delivered on 3 June 1833 in a debate on the abolition of slavery in the British empire during which he defended his father against allegations of maltreating his slaves in the West Indies.[9] That year, 1833, also marked Gladstone's entry to Lincoln's Inn to study to become a barrister but by 1839 he had requested that his name be removed from the list as he no longer had an interest in a legal career.[10]

Gladstone enjoyed re-election to parliament in both 1835 and 1841 but during this period of six years he was in opposition. In 1838, he published his first book, *The State in its Relations with the Church*, and, the following year, he married Catherine Glynne, the daughter of Sir Stephen Glynne of Hawarden Castle.[11] In 1840, Gladstone started his work of rescuing and rehabilitating London prostitutes, a charitable cause that he supported throughout his life.[12]

With Robert Peel forming a government after the general election of 1841, Gladstone was appointed as Vice-President of the Board of Trade. By 1843 he had been appointed as President of the Board of Trade with a seat at cabinet. The upward curve of Gladstone's political career was temporarily stalled in 1845 when he resigned in strange circumstances. In his 1838 book, Gladstone had defended Anglican exclusivity in Ireland and heavily criticised the annual grant of £9,000 that was given to the Maynooth Seminary in Ireland. Gladstone's argument was that 'giving money for the training of Roman Catholic priests was inappropriate for a Protestant nation and would lead to mortal danger'.[13] However, his position softened over the coming years and he came not only to see a value in the annual grant but he also pursued a policy of conciliation in Ireland. Nonetheless, in February 1845, when Peel proposed an increase in the Maynooth grant from £9,000 to £30,000, Gladstone resigned on principle as he had publicly opposed the grant in his book. The setback proved a temporary one and Gladstone was back in the cabinet, as Secretary of State for War and the Colonies, by December of the same year after Peel reshuffled his government.

The fluctuating fortunes of a political life were evident over the next six years (1846 to 1852) during which Gladstone again spent time on the opposition benches. The Conservative Party was in disarray during these years and Gladstone split from the mainstream Conservatives to form the Peelites (he became leader of this group in 1850 following the death of Peel). In 1852, with Lord Aberdeen as Prime Minister of a Whig-Peelite coalition government, Gladstone returned to the political centre stage as Chancellor of the Exchequer. With the exception of the period in opposition from 1855 to 1859, Gladstone served as Chancellor of the Exchequer until 1866. In the intervening period, Gladstone was one of the founding members of the Liberal Party in 1859.

In December 1868, Gladstone was appointed as Prime Minister for the first time and he announced that his 'mission was to pacify Ireland'.[14] In total, remarkably, he had four different spells as Prime Minister – from 1868 to 1874, 1880–1885, 1886–1886 and 1892–1894. During his first term as Prime Minister Gladstone enjoyed a keen political rivalry with the leader of the Tory Party, Benjamin Disraeli. One of his major reform efforts during that first term was the disestablishment of the Church of Ireland which meant that farmers no longer had to pay tithes to the Church. Gladstone followed this up by pushing through the first Irish Land Act whereby any farmer who had been evicted but who had made improvements to his land could claim compensation.

The second ministry 'was taken up mainly with Irish affairs'[15] and a second Irish Land Act introduced the concept of the three Fs – fixity of tenure, fair rents and free sale of land. Even though the legislation gave tenants greater rights, Charles Stewart Parnell, the Irish nationalist political leader, argued strongly that it did not go far enough and he was jailed under Gladstone's Coercion Act, 1881. Under this act, people suspected of committing an offence could be detained without trial; it was a rather crude attempt to establish law and order in Ireland (Parnell spent six months in prison and later formed an alliance with Gladstone in promoting Irish Home Rule).

Gladstone's third administration in 1886 was brief and lasted only a handful of months. In April of that year he introduced the first Irish Home Rule Bill containing a proposal to establish an Irish legislature. Matthew describes Gladstone's plan as 'bold and broad'.[16] Ireland was to have a legislative body of two houses in Dublin; there would be a financial settlement (as negotiated with Charles Stewart Parnell) and Irish MPs would no longer sit at Westminster.[17] For Gladstone, 'the proposed settlement was the best way to conserve a degree of union; he wished to impose responsibility on the Irish, who since 1800 had had representation with no prospect of power'.[18] Despite delivering a stirring speech in June in favour of the Home Rule Bill, Gladstone's proposal was defeated in the House of Commons by 341 votes to 311, with a number of his own Liberal Party colleagues voting against.[19] Gladstone felt that the issue should be brought before the people; parliament was dissolved and an election, which he lost, was called for July 1886.

Gladstone's political career was not ended by the general election defeat of 1886 and he made an astonishing comeback as Prime Minster (for the fourth time) in 1892 at the tender age of eighty-two. It is hardly surprising that he remains 'the only person in British history to begin a premiership over the age of 80'.[20] Despite working with a minority government, Gladstone introduced a second Home Rule Bill for Ireland which passed through the House of Commons but was defeated in the House of Lords. With his health failing, especially his eyesight, Gladstone chaired the last of his 556 cabinet meetings on 1 March 1894.[21] Due to the many tears of his colleagues, this meeting famously became known as the 'blubbering cabinet'.[22] His last speech in the House of Commons, on the same day, was an attack on the Lords and he resigned two days later on 3 March.[23] Gladstone had always had a difficult relationship with the queen and he declined a peerage after his resignation (as he had done in 1874 and 1885) and his wife also declined one, on his advice.[24]

Gladstone was diagnosed with cancer during his retirement and he died at Hawarden on 19 May 1898. He was given a state funeral and after his body had lain in rest for three days in Westminster Hall, he was buried in the statesman's corner of Westminster Abbey on 28 May.[25]

For Matthew, the legacy of William Gladstone was threefold.[26] First were his financial policies as Chancellor of the Exchequer and Prime Minister in the areas of free trade, retrenchment and taxation. He was responsible for many innovative financial reforms including the modern budget.[27] Secondly, Gladstone is remembered for his efforts to introduce Home Rule to Ireland. In his book *Gladstone and the Irish Nation*, John Lawrence Hammond states that Gladstone 'wanted to see Ireland a free vigorous society'[28] and that what distinguished him was that 'from first to last he thought of the Irish as a people, and he held that the ultimate test of a policy was whether or not it helped this people to satisfy its self-respect and to find its dignity and happiness in its self-governing life'.[29] Thirdly, Gladstone left a legacy in terms of his idea of a political party being progressive, reforming, broadly-based and capable of accommodating and conciliating varying interests.[30] Matthew expresses it very well as follows:

The Gladstonian Liberal Party was fractious, argumentative, and sometimes self-destructive, but it had a comprehensive role unique among its European contemporaries; even when, late in Gladstone's career, labourist groups began to appear, they did so as developments from the Liberal Party, not as enemies of it.[31]

Of course, Gladstone is also remembered for his big policy ideas, his powerful speeches at public meetings and his longevity and resilience given that he finally resigned as Prime Minister and as a member of parliament aged eighty-four. Hammond described him as 'the largest-minded man of his age'[32] while Lord Acton wrote in 1880 that Gladstone was one of the three greatest Liberals (along with Edmund Burke and Lord Macaulay).[33] Winston Churchill hailed Gladstone as one of his greatest inspirations.[34]

Gladstone was a keen diarist so a full personal record of his life and times exists. He was survived by his wife Catherine (who was buried in a double grave with her husband in 1900) and by six children – Agnes, Stephen Edward, Mary, Helen, Henry Neville and Herbert John. Two other children died before him, Catherine Jessy (in 1850, aged five) and William Henry (in 1891, aged fifty-one).[35]

FREEDOM OF CORK

William Gladstone was conferred with the freedoms of Cork, Limerick, Waterford and Clonmel in a joint ceremony on 5 October 1886 at his estate, Hawarden Castle in Flintshire, Wales. Gladstone was seventy-six years old at this point and had lost the July 1886 general election, thus ending his third (brief) premiership. Cork Corporation had formally elected Gladstone as a freeman in August and invited him to a conferring ceremony. He responded by letter, thanking the corporation for the honour and the invitation to the city but stating he had no intention of visiting Ireland at that time.[36] Accordingly, an alternative arrangement was made for a joint conferring ceremony at Hawarden Castle.

At the commencement of the proceedings, the caskets from the four Irish local authorities were placed on a table near where Gladstone was standing. A deputation from the 'Ladies of Dublin' was also present and the Lord Mayor of Dublin was first to speak. He introduced the Lady Mayoress, Kate Sullivan, who presented Gladstone with a document 'bearing the signatures of some hundreds of thousands of Irish women, expressing their heartfelt thanks for the noble endeavour you have made to promote the peace and welfare of Ireland'.[37]

The Mayor of Cork, Councillor Paul Madden, then rose to speak and explained to Gladstone that he had been delegated to speak by Cork Corporation 'to convey to you, in suitable form, the highest honour which it is in their power to confer on anyone outside their own body'.[38] The Mayor continued by listing some of the men who had received the freedom of Cork after the passing of the

Municipal Privileges Act of 1876, including Isaac Butt, Charles Stewart Parnell and Sir John Pope Hennessy. Next, he praised Gladstone for his 'entrancing eloquence', his 'mighty power over the minds of men' and his 'heroic self-sacrifice'.[39] In concluding, the Mayor said:

> *You will on the day of victory which is at hand be a sharer in the joy and the glory which will yet be ours in the dear old land that has given us birth, and which will gladly welcome you to her bosom as the greatest of her benefactors.*[40]

Mayor Madden then called on the Town Clerk of Cork Corporation to present Gladstone with an illuminated copy of the resolution conferring him with the freedom of Cork. He also received a casket of Irish oak, adorned with local and national emblems.

The conferring process was repeated by the mayors of Limerick, Waterford and Clonmel before Gladstone stood to deliver a customary lengthy speech. In thanking the representatives of the local authorities conferring him with the freedom honour, he stated:

> *I rejoice to receive you within the walls of a humble private residence because I feel that here we are little exposed to the dangers of that excitement which in great public meetings may sometimes carry away even the wisest of us.*[41]

Gladstone then spoke extensively about the position of Ireland in relation to Britain and claimed that it was the prospect of playing a part in the settlement of Ireland that was keeping him from retiring from public and political life. He asserted:

> *In the North of England, the majority are with you. In London, unhappily, the majority are against you. Well, I have the greatest respect for the people of London but the people of London have one great and terrible misfortune, and that is that they know nothing of local self-government.*[42]

At the end of his speech, the new honorary citizen of Cork signed the freedom rolls of the four boroughs. A celebratory lunch followed during which Gladstone proposed the toast 'Success to the Irish cause, which is also the cause of England and the Empire'.[43]

ANDREW CARNEGIE

(1835–1919)

Elected as Freeman of Cork on 5 September 1902

Conferred as Freeman of Cork on 21 October 1903

'In recognition of the philanthropic spirit which has animated Mr Andrew Carnegie in his gift to various cities and towns of large sums of money for the benefit of people who had no special claim on him, and, in particular as an acknowledgement of the munificent donation of £10,000 to Cork for the erection of a Free Library.'

BIOGRAPHY

The son of a handloom weaver, Andrew Carnegie was born in Dunfermline, Scotland, on 25 November 1835. Owing to difficult economic conditions in Scotland, the Carnegie family emigrated to the United States of America in 1848. The Carnegies joined a Scottish colony in Allegheny, near Pittsburgh, and when he was twelve years old Andrew began working in a local cotton factory while attending night school. Andrew's determination to succeed in America is evidenced in a letter he wrote as a sixteen year-old to his Uncle Lauder in May 1852. Andrew concluded a lengthy correspondence by stating:

> *Although I sometimes think I would like to be back in Dunfermline, I am sure it is far better for me that I came here. If I had been in Dunfermline working at the loom it is very likely I would have been a poor weaver all my days, but here I can surely do something better than that, if I don't it will be my own fault, for anyone can get along in this country. I intend going to night school this fall to learn something more.[1]*

At this stage, young Andrew was working as a secretary to Thomas A. Scott, the superintendent of the western division of the Pennsylvania Railroad. When the Civil War broke out, Scott was appointed Assistant Secretary of War and Carnegie accompanied him to Washington where, amongst other things, his work included organising the military telegraph system.[2]

When the war ended, Carnegie succeeded Scott as superintendent of the western division of the Pennsylvania Railroad and he invested his money in a series of small mills and factories as well as the Keystone Bridge Company.[3] During this period he travelled to Britain a lot and was very impressed by the converter invented by Henry Bessemer. The Bessemer method converted molten pig iron into steel and transformed engineering processes. Carnegie returned to America convinced by this new approach and aware that for the production of heavy goods, steel was going to replace iron. Carnegie's biographer, Burton J. Hendrick, vividly captures this period in the Scot's life by noting: 'A mind that had lived in apparent darkness was illuminated by a sudden flash of light. In this instance the statement is more than a figurative one, for it was the dazzling brilliance of a Bessemer converter that, in the twinkling of an eye, transformed Andrew Carnegie into a new man.'[4]

Using the ideas of Bessemer, Carnegie erected his first blast furnace in 1870 and, four years later, established his steel furnace at Braddock.[5] One of his partners in this venture was Henry Frick who would later become chairman of the Carnegie Company and would have a bitter falling out with Andrew Carnegie. By 1892, having taken control of other mills and furnaces in Pittsburgh, the Carnegie Steel Company was valued at $25 million and was the largest steel company in the world. Further expansion followed and in 1899, having fallen out with Frick, Carnegie bought out his partner for $15 million. A mere two years later, Frick joined forces with John Pierpont Morgan and bought the Carnegie Steel Company for an estimated $480 million, establishing the US Steel Corporation. Carnegie's share from the sale amounted to $225 million and he now had a significant personal fortune at his disposal.

One of the first things he did after the sale of his company was to donate over $5 million for the construction of sixty-five branch libraries in New York.[6] Carnegie was being true to the philosophy he had espoused in an 1889 article he wrote entitled 'Gospel of Wealth' in which he asserted that it was the duty of rich men and women to use their wealth to benefit the welfare of the community. He concluded the article by stating that 'a man who dies rich dies disgraced'.[7]

Carnegie now devoted himself to philanthropy and set up a trust fund 'for the improvement of mankind'[8] and Ireland was one of the countries that benefitted. By early 1905 he had pledged $39,325,240 for 1,200 libraries in English-speaking countries and, of this, $598,000 was for Ireland.[9] While the money given to Ireland was small in proportion to his total expenditure, 'it greatly helped the library movement in Ireland'.[10] One such library was the Carnegie Free Library which was opened on Anglesea Street in Cork on 12 September 1905 (the library was destroyed during the burning of Cork in 1920 and the site now houses Cork City Council's civic offices adjoining City Hall). By 1919, 81 per cent of the towns in Ireland which had rate-supported libraries received contributions from Carnegie.[11]

It is estimated that by the time Andrew Carnegie died in August 1919, he had given away $350 million with a further $125 million placed with the Carnegie Corporation to continue his works.[12]

While Carnegie is legitimately associated with libraries, he also established the Carnegie Institute of Pittsburgh, the Carnegie Institute of Technology and the Carnegie Institution of Washington to further research into science. In addition, he was a prolific writer and contributed articles and books on a range of social and political issues.

FREEDOM OF CORK

Andrew Carnegie was proposed for the award of freedom of Cork at a meeting of Cork Corporation on Friday 5 September 1902. In nominating the world-famous philanthropist, Alderman Henry Dale stated that the freedom was the greatest compliment conferred on any individual and was offered only 'in special cases for special services rendered or for special distinction attained by the recipient of the honour'.[13] The Lord Mayor declared the motion unanimously carried and expressed the hope that Carnegie would accept his honorary award in person.

This came to pass more than a year later on Wednesday 21 October 1903 at what the *Cork Examiner* described in its headline as 'an interesting corporate function'.[14] Carnegie had received the freedom of Waterford on Monday and the freedom of Limerick on Tuesday. Accordingly, the millionaire came to Cork from Limerick on a train that arrived more than half an hour late. Carnegie was received at the train station by the Lord Mayor, Sir Edward Fitzgerald, the Town Clerk, F.W. McCarthy, and many members of the corporation. A large body of citizens also gathered at the platform to greet the famous visitor and musical entertainment was provided by the Butter Exchange and Father Mathew Temperance Association bands. The Lord Mayor accompanied Carnegie and his private secretary, James Bertram, by carriage to the Imperial Hotel led by the Father Mathew Band with the Butter Exchange Band bringing up the rear.

The freedom ceremony began at twenty minutes past twelve o'clock in the Municipal Buildings which the *Cork Examiner* described as being 'lavishly decorated with bunting'.[15] After the Town Clerk conducted a roll call and read the minutes from 5 September 1902, the Lord Mayor stood to speak. He described Carnegie as 'a distinguished stranger' and praised him not only for his indomitable energy, enterprise and industry which had enabled him to amass a colossal fortune but for his large-heartedness and noble generosity which drove him to share his wealth 'without distinction of nationality, of creed or of class'.[16] The Lord Mayor thanked him for his 'splendid gift to the people of Cork', adding that Corkonians had long enjoyed the reputation of being distinguished for their love of literature and the pursuit of intellectual pleasures. Carnegie was then invited to sign the honorary burgess roll and did so amidst great applause. Next he was presented with the certificate of his enrolment, laminated and enclosed in a casket of Irish oak, carved and mounted in silver.

The casket presented to Andrew Carnegie was designed by M.J. McNamara with the assistance of pupils in the wood-carving class at the School of Art. The silver work was done by Egan and Sons. The lid of the casket is surmounted by the Arms of the City; on the centre of the lid is a carved representation of the new Free Library, funded by Carnegie, surrounded by carved panels adapted from the Book of Kells. There are also views of Blackrock Castle and Blarney Castle in embossed silver, as well as of Shandon Church (opposite side).

When Andrew Carnegie rose to speak he had to wait a few minutes for sustained applause and cheering to die down. In a lengthy address, he spoke first of the political context of the time and predicted 'there will be an end of Ireland's wrongs and Ireland's woes when she becomes a Sovereign State … she will get all the Home Rule that is good for her'.[17] He then moved on to talk of his delight that Ireland was awakening to the importance of Free Libraries and added, 'To no country do I respond with deeper satisfaction than to applications from Ireland.'[18] He ended by saying:

Your youngest burgess knows very well that he has not deserved the honour conferred upon him by the ancient city of Cork, but he knows also very well that it would bring indelible disgrace upon your latest fellow citizen were he ever to discredit it.

After the conferring ceremony, Carnegie and the members of the corporation went to the new library building which was in the course of construction in the Cornmarket, adjoining the Municipal Buildings. Carnegie was presented with an engraved silver trowel adorned with an ivory handle, with which he placed a piece of mortar on the bed intended for the memorial stone's resting place. The stone was then lowered into place and Carnegie said:

My Lord Mayor, I pronounce this stone well and truly laid, and I do this firm in the faith that in the days to come it will prove as a fountain from which only healing waters can flow for the good of the people of Cork.[19]

The Lord Mayor then hosted a luncheon in the Municipal Buildings with a menu of clear soup, fillets of sole, mutton cutlets with peas, roast turkey, boiled turkey, roast beef, roast chicken, ham, cauliflower peas and potatoes. Following the luncheon, Carnegie was received in the Lord Mayor's pavilion, after which the party moved to the Concert Hall where Herr Kandt and his band performed. There followed a visit to the water-chute and to the Western Gardens before Carnegie was driven to the Glanmire Terminus from where he departed for Queenstown (Cobh). He stayed one night with the Bishop of Cloyne before leaving for New York on board the Cedric.

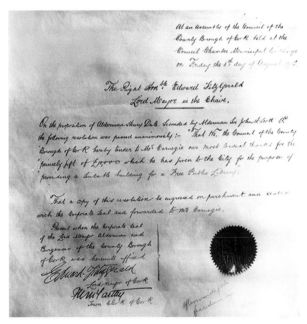

A letter from the Lord Mayor, thanking Andrew Carnegie for his donation of £10,000 for a Free Library in Cork.

JEREMIAH O'DONOVAN ROSSA

(1831–1915)

Elected as Freeman of Cork on 24 November 1904

Conferred as Freeman of Cork on 16 December 1904

> 'That the freedom of the city of Cork be conferred on Jeremiah O'Donovan Rossa,
> as a tribute to his sterling qualities as an Irish nationalist, and as one who has
> suffered a long term of penal servitude for this devotion to the cause of Ireland.'

BIOGRAPHY

The Fenian leader, Jeremiah O'Donovan Rossa, was seventy-three years of age when he received the freedom of Cork. A native of Rosscarbery, County Cork, he was born Jeremiah O'Donovan in 1831 – 'according to tradition, the family had come as displaced persons from Rosscarbery to Rossmore, hence "Rossa"'.[1] Jeremiah witnessed at first hand the potato crop failure and subsequent famine of 1845–1852. The O'Donovan family suffered badly during the famine and Jeremiah's book, *Rossa's Recollections, 1838–1898* (published in New York in 1898), 'gives a searing account of the repeated failure of their potato crops, the sale of their wheat to pay the rent, and the strain placed on family ties by the struggle for self-preservation'.[2]

Young Jeremiah's family was, in fact, ripped apart during the famine. In March 1847 his father died after contracting a fever and the following year his mother and siblings emigrated to America with the aid of a paternal uncle. Jeremiah, who was working in the hardware store of a relative in Skibbereen, was left behind to fend for himself.[3] During this period, Jeremiah's belief that the British should be removed from Ireland was fostered and he supported the view of nationalist and journalist John Mitchel that the famine was genocide.[4]

Rossa's political activism commenced in earnest in 1856 when he co-founded the Phoenix National and Literary Society. The aim of this group was the liberation of Ireland by whatever means necessary, including by force of arms.[5] In 1858 the Phoenix Society effectively became a front organisation for the Irish Republican Brotherhood (IRB), 'a small, secret, revolutionary body (known as the Fenian movement in the 1850s and 1860s) committed to the use of force to establish an independent Irish republic.[6] Rossa and other activists of the Phoenix Society/IRB were arrested in December 1858 following a demonstration. Rossa served eight months in Cork Gaol before being released. Not long after his release Rossa's wife Nora Eager (they married in 1853) died. Rossa was married again in 1861 – to Eileán Ní Bhuachalla – but she died just two years later, aged nineteen.[7]

Rossa moved to Dublin in July 1863 as manager of the Fenian newspaper *Irish People*[8] and the next year he married his third wife, Mary Jane Irwin, a poet who wrote for the newspaper. Rossa was arrested in 1865 when the offices of the *Irish People* were raided and he was accused of plotting a Fenian rising. Despite conducting his own robust defence, Rossa was sentenced to penal servitude for life. He served time in a variety of English prisons such as Pentonville, Portland, Millbank and Chatham. While there 'he suffered inhumane and cruel treatment at the hands of the prison authorities'.[9] At one period he spent thirty-four consecutive days with his hands cuffed behind his back, which was an illegal punishment.[10] While in prison, Rossa was elected to parliament for Tipperary but the election was declared void due to his incarceration.

In 1870 Rossa and other Fenian prisoners were released under a general amnesty from the British government (under pressure from the US government). Rossa's treatment in prison 'left him with a permanent spinal injury, which forced him to spend several hours a day in a reclining position'.[11] A commission under Lord Devon in 1870 'sensationally confirmed the truth of his account of his treatment and the conditions under which Fenian prisoners were kept'.[12]

A condition of Rossa's release from prison was that he would remain outside of the United Kingdom until the expiry of his sentence. Hence, he set sail for New York where he narrowly failed to win election to the New York State Senate and made a number of unsuccessful forays into the business world, including starting a passage ticket agency, a weekly newspaper (the *Era*) and two hotels. A more successful venture came in 1876 when he founded the *United Irishman* newspaper which lasted until the early twentieth century.[13] Rossa, unsurprisingly, became an active member of the American Fenian movement and he helped to establish the 'skirmishing fund' to be used to fund a bombing campaign in British cities.[14] The campaign lasted throughout the 1880s and Rossa became a hate figure for the British public. In 1885 he was shot outside his office near Broadway by an Englishwoman, Yseult Dudley, but his wounds were not life-threatening.[15]

By 1891, Rossa's original term of imprisonment had expired which left him free to visit the United Kingdom and he undertook a lecture tour of Ireland in 1894. For the remainder of his life, Rossa 'appeared at speaking engagements all over the country relating his prison experiences, performing readings of his books and giving accounts of his involvement in the Fenian Brotherhood and his fight against the British'.[16] On one such visit to Ireland in 1904 he received the freedom of Cork and in September 1905 he was appointed to a clerkship in the office of the Secretary of Cork County Council at a salary of £150 per annum, a position that also provided him with a cottage in Blackrock.[17] However, the appointment to Cork County Council lasted only one year and Rossa returned to New York where he took up a position as an inspector of street openings in Brooklyn.[18]

Rossa's final years were dogged by ill health and he died in St Vincent's Hospital, New Brighton, Staten Island on 29 June 1915. He was brought back to Ireland for burial at Glasnevin Cemetery in Dublin on 1 August. Rossa's graveside oration was delivered by Pádraig Pearse (subsequently martyred in the 1916 Easter Rising) who concluded with the famous lines:

This photograph shows a uniformed Pádraig Pearse in front of the officiating priest replacing a paper in his tunic pocket at the funeral of O'Donovan Rossa in Glasnevin, Dublin. Footage of Rossa's funeral and Pearse's oration have become YouTube classics.

They think they have pacified Ireland. They think they have purchased half of us and intimidated the other half. They think that they have foreseen everything, think that they have provided against everything but the fools, the fools, the fools! They have left us our Fenian dead, and while Ireland holds these graves, Ireland unfree shall never be at peace.

Many tributes have been paid to Jeremiah O'Donovan Rossa over the years since his death. For example, Richmond Bridge over the Liffey was renamed after Rossa in 1923 and a monument to him by Seamus Murphy was erected in St Stephen's Green in Dublin in 1954.[19] There is a Rossa Park in Skibbereen and several GAA clubs (including one in Skibbereen) bear his name. In 1981, a new stamp was issued to commemorate the 150th anniversary of Rossa's birth. The 15p stamp featured a drawing of Rossa based on a photograph by A.H. Poole which is in the National Library of Ireland.[20] His books include *O'Donovan Rossa's Prison Life: Six Years in English Prisons* (New York, 1874) and *Rossa's Recollections, 1838–1898* (New York, 1898). From his three marriages, Rossa had eighteen children and his youngest daughter, Margaret O'Donovan Rossa, wrote an affectionate memoir in 1939, *My Father and Mother were Irish*, in which Rossa is presented as a kindly and absent-minded parent.[21]

FREEDOM OF CORK

A special meeting of Cork Corporation was convened on 24 November 1904 to consider the motion – 'That the Freedom of the City of Cork be conferred on Jeremiah O'Donovan Rossa, as a tribute to his sterling qualities as an Irish nationalist, and as one who has suffered a long term of penal servitude for this devotion to the cause of Ireland.' The motion was formally proposed by Councillor Richard Cronin who declared that he thought he did not need to do anything more than simply move the motion.[22] The proposal was seconded by Alderman Jeremiah Kelleher who noted that the corporation had, from time to time, paid tribute to many exalted men but none had done more in the cause of his country than O'Donovan Rossa.[23] There was unanimous agreement in the corporation chamber and a letter was sent to Rossa who replied by way of letter (printed in the *Cork Examiner* on 28 November) that he was honoured to accept the award.

The conferring ceremony took place on 16 December and was a relatively low-key affair. After the Town Clerk had read the resolution of the corporation conferring the freedom of the city on Rossa, the Lord Mayor of Cork, Councillor Augustine Roche, stood to address the meeting. He claimed that all classes of their fellow citizens and their countrymen recognised the great part Rossa had played in the past with regard to political movements in Ireland. He asserted that Rossa had 'fearlessly resigned his life and liberty to serve the best interests of his country'[24] and that it gave him great pleasure to ask him to sign the burgess roll of honorary freemen.

Rossa then asked whether he should sign the roll in Irish or English to which the Lord Mayor replied 'sign it in Irish or English, whichever you like'.[25] There were several cries of 'sign it in both' and this is what Rossa did amidst great applause. When he stood to address the corporation he was afforded an enthusiastic standing ovation. The new freeman of Cork told the audience how sincerely he valued the honour and that he was accepting it 'as representing the cause for which I have suffered and the cause which I value still'.[26]

Rossa ended his short speech by declaring, 'I pride in the freedom of Cork, but there is a greater freedom than that – the freedom of Ireland – and I promise you while I have life I will be with you in any effort you may make to obtain the freedom of Ireland'.[27]

The low-key nature of Rossa's conferring ceremony – in comparison to the ceremonies of other recipients – is reflected in the fact that the Lord Mayor departed the council chamber after Rossa's speech to attend another meeting (Councillor Daniel Horgan took the chair) and the councillors moved on to discuss the Cork Junction Railways Bill.

DOUGLAS HYDE

(1860–1949)

Elected as Freeman of Cork on 22 June 1906

Conferred as Freeman of Cork on 1 August 1906

'That in recognition of his invaluable services towards the revival of the Irish language, Dr Douglas Hyde be and is herby admitted and enrolled an honorary burgess of the City and County Borough of Cork in accordance with the provisions of the Municipal Privileges (Ireland) Act, 1876; and that a copy of this resolution suitably engrossed and mounted, and sealed with our Common Seal, be presented to Dr Hyde in due form, on a day to be appointed for the purpose.'

BIOGRAPHY

Dr Douglas Hyde is one of the major figures in Irish history. He was a founding member and then President of the Gaelic League and became the first President of Ireland in 1938 following the Constitution of 1937. He was born on 17 January 1860 in Castlerea, County Roscommon, into a family steeped in the Protestant religion.[1] Hyde's ancestors had moved from Castle Hyde, Cork, where they lived since they were planted there in the sixteenth century under Queen Elizabeth I.[2] Though his family were not especially wealthy they 'moved in circles occupied by a relatively leisured, educated, privileged class'.[3] It is therefore ironic that young Douglas received no formal education, apart from what is described as 'a brief and unhappy experience at school in Kingstown (Dún Laoghaire) in 1873'.[4] Rather, he was educated at home by his father, Rev. Arthur Hyde, with whom he had a fractious relationship. In the *Dictionary of Irish Biography*, Philip Maume notes that 'relations with his father (who was brilliant but erratic and given to drinking-bouts) were tense; this encouraged identification with the Irish-speaking peasantry'.[5]

Hyde developed 'an extraordinary talent for languages and, in addition to Greek, Latin and English, he was able to communicate in German, French and Hebrew'.[6] His passion though was for Irish, a language he largely picked up from his father's servants and from local peasants. Later in life (as a twenty-year-old studying in Trinity College Dublin), Hyde claimed that Irish was the language he knew best, adding, 'I dream in Irish.'[7] As well as learning Irish from local people, Hyde developed a keen interest in politics and his views were strongly pro-nationalist and anti-British.[8] This is clear from a poem he wrote as a teenager that contains the lines:

I hate your law, I hate your rule,

I hate your people and your weak queen,

I hate your merchants who have riches and property,

Great is their arrogance – little their worth.

I hate your Parliament, half of them are boors

Wrangling together without manners or grace,

The men who govern the kingdom, false, insincere,

Skilled only in trickery and deceit.[9]

In 1880, Hyde entered Trinity College as a divinity student, 'partly under pressure from his father, partly because Irish was studied in the Faculty of Divinity'.[10] He graduated with first class honours in 1884 and, rather than returning home and pursuing a career in the Church of Ireland as his father wished, he stayed in Trinity studying Law, receiving an LL B in 1887 and an LL D in 1888. Hyde was involved in many student societies including the Contemporary Club and the Pan-Celtic Society. The Contemporary Club gave him the opportunity to discuss topics of the day with the likes of William Butler Yeats, Maud Gonne, John O'Leary and Michael Davitt.[11]

After completing his studies in Trinity, Hyde taught English at the University of New Brunswick for a short period of time before returning to Ireland where he published 'numerous bilingual collections of Connacht folk tales and folk poetry'.[12] In 1892 he became President of the National Literary Society and – in his inaugural address – explained his belief that Ireland as a nation and as a people had lost its dignity and self respect and the Irish language was the best way to restore lost pride.[13] This long-held belief drove Hyde on to co-found the Gaelic League in July 1893 and he became its first President. The aim of the Gaelic League was to get people speaking Irish again and it 'succeeded beyond all hopes and expectations of its original founders'[14] partly because the movement was not overly political. In an article on the Gaelic League, Arthur A. Clery claims that, by the turn of the century, the Gaelic League had over 600 branches and in excess of 20,000 members.[15] In Declan Kiberd's view, 'a civil rights agitation was mounted' by the movement.[16]

Three months after founding the Gaelic League, Douglas Hyde married Lucy Cometina Kurtz in Liverpool – she was a wealthy Englishwoman of remote German descent.[17] They had two daughters, Nuala and Una, but the marriage suffered due to Lucy's belief that the Gaelic League was exploiting her husband – 'she came to detest the League, the language, and the Roscommon countryside where they lived'.[18] Lucy was plagued by ill health and Hyde 'devoted considerable effort to caring for her'.[19] This may have been one of the reasons he declined the offer in 1904 by John Redmond, leader of the Irish Parliamentary Party, of a seat in parliament at Westminster.[20]

In the first decade of the twentieth century, Hyde continued to lead the Gaelic League skilfully and kept it 'from being torn apart by rival political and linguistic factions'.[21] In 1909 he became Professor of Irish at University College Dublin, a post he held until 1932. In 1915, the Árd Fheis of the Gaelic League voted to make it a specifically nationalist organisation. This led Hyde to resign his presidency of the League as he believed that it should have remained open to 'well-disposed unionists in the name of national reconciliation'.[22]

Hyde now devoted most of his time to University College Dublin (UCD) where he lectured 'with infectious enthusiasm'[23] and published, mainly on folklore. He was co-opted to the Free State Senate in 1925 but lost his seat in the election of the following year.[24] After his retirement from UCD in 1932, Hyde spent his days caring for his sick wife, shooting, and socialising with locals of all classes.[25]

Douglas Hyde had a momentous year in 1938, for many reasons. On 25 June he was inaugurated as the first President of Ireland in a ceremony lasting just fifteen minutes in Dublin Castle.[26] As a seventy-eight-year-old Protestant man who had been in retirement for the previous six years, Hyde might have been regarded as an unusual choice but Fianna Fáil and Fine Gael had agreed to select a unified candidate. Their logic was that it would be 'damaging to the new office if the first president was elected along party political lines'.[27] Hyde was elected unopposed and, in his first speech, he vowed to be a president for 'all creeds and classes'.[28]

On 13 November of the same year, the new President, along with Éamon de Valera (An Taoiseach), Oscar Traynor (Minister for Posts and Telegraphs), Paddy Lynch (Attorney General), and Alfie Byrne (Lord Mayor of Dublin) attended an international soccer match in Dalymount Park in Dublin between Ireland and Poland.[29] The match had attracted huge interest and broke the previous attendance record at a soccer match in Ireland.[30] Both Hyde and de Valera received standing ovations on their arrival and departure and the day proved a successful one with Ireland winning by three goals to two.[31] However, Hyde's attendance at the match had enormous and controversial ramifications as the Gaelic Athletic Association (GAA) removed him as a patron for breaking the principle of the 'ban on foreign games'. Hyde chose not to make an issue of the GAA's decision (which garnered much interest nationally and internationally)[32] to remove him as patron, partly because his primary concern was for the failing health of his wife Lucy, who passed away the following month. In his book on Hyde's removal as GAA patron, Cormac Moore, however, notes that the decision of the GAA was an extraordinary one as it was not only 'against the Head of State but it was against a man seen by most as the embodiment of the Irish-Ireland movement, a movement that had the GAA at its forefront'.[33]

In April 1940, Douglas Hyde suffered a stroke that confined him to a wheelchair. Nonetheless, he continued to perform his presidential duties with distinction and set 'important precedents by referring controversial legislation to the Supreme Court for rulings on its constitutionality, and insisting on taking advice from his staff before granting a Dáil dissolution to de Valera in 1944'.[34] Hyde finished his presidential term in 1945 (he declined a second term) but stayed in the Phoenix Park in a small residence that was made available to him.[35] He died there on 12 July 1949, aged eighty-nine.

Douglas Hyde's legacy to Ireland is a significant one. *The Irish Times* called him 'cultured, strenuous and far-seeing, his ideals were constructive. Intensely sociable, companionable and magnetic, his name will remain an inspiration.'[36] Political tributes were led by An Taoiseach, John A. Costello, and the leader of the opposition, Éamon de Valera, who both referred to the founding of the Gaelic League. The GAA sent a message of sympathy saying 'great was his prowess for country and language'.[37] When the GAA celebrated its centenary in 1984, a special memorial plaque was placed at Hyde's graveside; Moore describes this action as 'a small gesture acknowledging that the GAA had made a mistake and was, in some way, seeking atonement for the humiliating treatment of a true Irish-Irelander'.[38]

FREEDOM OF CORK

Douglas Hyde was elected as a freeman of Cork city on 22 June 1906, a full thirty-two years before he became the first President of Ireland. He was proposed for the honour by Councillor Richard Cronin who moved the resolution 'that in recognition of his invaluable services towards the revival of the Irish language, Dr Douglas Hyde be and is herby admitted and enrolled an honorary burgess of the City and County Borough of Cork in accordance with the provisions of the Municipal Privileges (Ireland) Act, 1876; and that a copy of this resolution suitably engrossed and mounted, and sealed with our Common Seal, be presented to Dr Hyde in due form, on a day to be appointed for the purpose'.[39] Councillor Cronin praised Hyde for devoting his life and learning to the cause of reviving the Irish language and described him as 'a brilliant scholar of European reputation'.[40] He also claimed that Hyde had made a major impact in the United States and had been received the previous November by American President Roosevelt who demonstrated a keen interest in the work of the Gaelic League. Other councillors followed Cronin in praising Hyde, especially for the fact that the Irish language 'was spreading like wildfire throughout the length and breadth of the land'.[41] Led by Lord Mayor, Councillor Joseph Barrett, the resolution admitting Douglas Hyde to the Register of the Freedom of Cork was agreed unanimously.

The freedom conferring ceremony was held on 1 August 1906. Hyde arrived in Cork by train and was met at the station 'by several prominent representatives of the Gaelic League in the city'.[42] The special meeting of Cork Corporation commenced shortly after three o'clock and was chaired by the Lord Mayor, Councillor Joseph Barrett. The Lord Mayor stated that the roll of freemen of Cork contained many great and illustrious names and that the addition of Douglas Hyde would add to its importance. He concluded his speech by addressing Hyde directly and saying, 'Allow me to hail you as a fellow-citizen, and to hope you may be long spared to carry on the crusade in favour of an Irish Ireland.'[43]

Having signed the roll of freemen, Hyde stood to speak and 'was received by loud and prolonged applause'.[44] He said that he accepted the great honour in the names of the workers of the Gaelic League, 'the men and women who are working in every county of Ireland and are doing much harder work than I am but get none of the honours'.[45] In helping to revive the Irish language, Hyde claimed that the Gaelic League was also 'increasing and planting amongst the people a sense of self-respect'.[46] He expressed pride in the fact that the Gaelic League 'brought together upon the same platform representatives of every creed, class, party and religious belief in Ireland'[47] (as described above, Hyde resigned as President of the Gaelic League in 1915 when members voted to make it a specifically nationalist organisation). In describing hatred as a negative thing, Hyde made the point that the Gaelic League was not founded upon hatred of England but upon love of Ireland. Hyde concluded his speech by re-stating that while the Gaelic League 'stood firm on the bedrock principles of nationality'[48] it was not a party or a faction and it had no cliques. Rather, it had members who were landlords and tenants, Protestants and Catholics, priests and parsons, Fenians and Sinn Féin men, and parliamentarians.

KUNO MEYER

(1858–1919)

Elected as Freeman of Cork on 10 May 1912

Conferred as Freeman of Cork on 25 September 1912

Expunged from Freedom Register on 8 January 1915

Re-elected as Freeman (posthumously) on 14 May 1920

BIOGRAPHY

German-born Kuno Meyer has the distinction of twice being elected a freeman of the city of Cork. He was initially granted the honour on 25 September 1912 (along with Canon Peadar Ó Laoghaire) but his name was expunged from the Freedom Register in January 1915 as a result of anti-German sentiment during the First World War. In May 1920, seven months after his death, Kuno Meyer was restored to the register.

Kuno Meyer was born in Hamburg on 20 December 1858 and, as a boy, he attended the Siemsenschen Privatschule and then the Johanneum (where his father, a noted historian, taught) to study classics.[1] After leaving school at the age of fifteen, Meyer lived in Edinburgh for the best part of three years, during which time he acquired a knowledge of English.[2] A visit to the Isle of Arran during this period also helped him to gain an understanding of Scots Gaelic.

Meyer returned to Germany in 1879 to study Germanic languages and comparative philology in Leipzig University and followed this up with a year's service as a military volunteer before returning to university and completing his doctoral thesis in 1884.[3]

During this hectic period in his young life, Meyer contracted rheumatic fever which later developed into rheumatoid arthritis – 'remarkably, this did not otherwise detract from his affable personality or from his prolific scholarly output'.[4]

The same year that he completed his doctorate, 1884, Meyer took up a position as lecturer in German in Liverpool University, where he stayed for the next twenty-seven years. This environment suited Meyer's character, as explained by Seán Ó Lúing, 'Liverpool was a new university, untrammelled by conservative traditions, liberally endowed by the city's great industrialists, with freedom to develop its own capacities'.[5] Meyer flourished in Liverpool and 'he established through his classes in Irish and Welsh an interest in Celtic studies there'.[6] Irish became an abiding passion for Meyer, as he had envisaged in a letter in June 1882 to his friend Whitley Stokes, when he wrote, 'I hope to be able to take up the study of the Irish language and literature as the principal object of my life's work'.[7]

While continuing to work in Liverpool, Meyer, together with John Strachan, founded the School of Irish Studies (sometimes referred to as the School of Irish Learning) in Dublin in 1903 'to train a new generation of native Irish scholars, the lack of which Meyer felt so keenly'.[8] The following year, under Meyer's guidance, the school began its own journal, called *Ériu*. In the *Dictionary of Irish Biography*, Aidan Breen contends that 'the existence of the School and its publications established the international importance of Dublin as a centre of Celtic studies'.[9]

Meyer was a frequent visitor to Ireland and he was 'a close associate of the Gaelic League founder and later President of Ireland, Douglas Hyde'.[10] Meyer's 'sensitive and beautiful translations from old Irish poetry and saga inspired W.B. Yeats and other figures of the revival in their literary work'[11] and Meyer created huge international interest in Irish literature.

Meyer entered a new phase of his life in 1911 when he obtained the chair of Celtic studies in Berlin University.[12] The following year he received the freedom of both Cork and Dublin but was stripped of both honours in 1915 after engaging in 'pro-German wartime propaganda'.[13] He was also removed from his posts as director of the School of Irish Studies and as editor-in-chief of *Ériu*.[14] Ó Lúing records 'for all that he espoused the cause of Fatherland with full heart and name, the sundering of friendships that this entailed must have been painful to Meyer'.[15] One of his friendships to suffer was that with George Moore. Meyer had written a warm letter to his friend in December 1914 but received a hostile reply in January 1915 which ended with the words, 'It is hardly necessary for me to add that I am taking leave of you forever, but not because of the German that is in you, but because of the man that is in you.'[16]

Meyer spent much of the war period in the United States of America where he lectured at the universities of Harvard and Illinois.[17] His lecture tour was dramatically interrupted on 9 September 1915 'when he was severely injured in a railroad collision between Corti Madera and Alto in California'.[18] He spent more than five weeks in the San Rafael Cottage Hospital before being moved to the German Hospital in San Francisco to continue his recuperation. In San Rafael, Meyer had been 'nursed back to health by Florence Lewis'[19] and, after a swift romance, married her on 10 December 1915 in California.[20] At the time of the wedding, Florence was a twenty-seven-year-old divorcée with a young daughter (aged nine) and Meyer was thirty years senior to his wife. The couple travelled back to Europe in 1916 and promptly separated.[21] It seems that Florence went to Berlin to work for the Red Cross while Meyer continued writing, researching and delivering lectures across Europe and the United States. Ó Lúing describes the couple's time together as 'incongruously short' but claims that the decision to separate was mutually agreed.[22]

Meyer died suddenly in a Leipzig nursing home on 11 October 1919, aged sixty with 'his death hastened, no doubt, by the grief he felt at Germany's defeat and its humiliation after the war'.[23] Unfortunately, he did not live to see the honour of the freedoms of Cork and Dublin restored to him in 1920.

FREEDOM OF CORK

On 25 September 1912, Kuno Meyer was conferred with the freedom of Cork along with his friend and fellow Irish writer, Canon Peadar Ó Laoghaire. Appropriately, it was the feast of St Finbarr, the patron of Cork, and – having been met at the railway station by the Lord Mayor, Councillor Henry O'Shea, and city dignitaries – Meyer and Ó Laoghaire were 'escorted amid cheering thousands to the City Hall'.[24] The *Cork Examiner* reported the 'enormous attendance' that was present and stated that the reception afforded to both recipients would 'be remembered in the annals of the city'.[25] After the Town Clerk called the roll, the resolution of the corporation was read aloud and both men signed the freedom register. The Lord Mayor then spoke, referring to the two great Irish scholars who had done so much in the cause of reviving the Gaelic language. Having presented each of them with a freedom casket, they were invited to speak.

Canon Ó Laoghaire made a brief speech in Irish and then 'Meyer addressed the audience in a speech which was widely reported because of its allusions to contemporary politics'.[26] He started by saying that the pleasure the corporation had given him by honouring him in this way was all the greater because of the association with 'his friend and fellow worker, Canon Peter O'Leary'.[27]

He then asserted that Irish people desired unity and added:

I believe that even in Ulster this feeling exists, and is so very widespread and strong that if the people there had been left to themselves better counsels would have prevailed. They would have chosen to cast in their lot with the rest of the motherland and to stand or fall with it.[28]

Meyer concluded his speech, which was widely quoted in the English newspapers, by saying:

There might be some who would think ill of him, a foreigner, to interfere in national politics, but the action of the corporation had made him half an Irishman, and thus he might be allowed to give expression to feelings and convictions which he shared with all patriotic Irishmen.[29]

As proud as Kuno Meyer must have felt in Cork's City Hall in September 1912, his heart sank on 8 January 1915 when his name was expunged from the roll of honorary freemen due to his pro-German speeches in America. In moving the motion, Councillor Hart 'pointed out that Germany had since the outbreak of war struck from her list of honours every writer, leader, statesman, soldier and scholar of every country in Europe with which she is at present engaged'.[30] With thousands of Irishmen offering up their lives in the war, Councillor Hart argued that they could not permit on their roll of freemen 'a man who attacked Ireland and glorified the people with whom she was at war'.[31] Even though a direct negative to the motion was tabled, Councillor Hart's motion was passed by twenty-four votes to three and the name of Kuno Meyer was removed from the freedom roll.

It was at a meeting of Cork Corporation on 14 May 1920 (seven months after his death) that the name of Meyer was restored to the roll. There was one dissenting voice, in the form of Councillor Byrne, who argued that he had gone out to fight the Germans and Kuno Meyer was a German whose kinsmen had murdered thousands of Irishmen.[32] The decision to restore Meyer's honour was reported in *The New York Times* on 16 May 1920 and received generally favourable commentary in the national and international press. However, Meyer's reputation remained tainted, leading Lieutenant-Colonel J.P. Duggan, a keen historian of Irish-German relations, to write an *Irish Times* article in 1990 calling on Ireland 'to heal the gratuitous wound inflicted on the great Irish scholar'.[33]

CANON PEADAR Ó LAOGHAIRE

(1839–1920)

Elected as Freeman of Cork on 10 May 1912

Conferred as Freeman of Cork on 25 September 1912

BIOGRAPHY

Douglas Hyde wrote an article in June 1920 in which he claimed Canon Peadar Ó Laoghaire (Peter O'Leary) and Kuno Meyer as two men who, in their own way, 'did work for Irish nationalism through the medium of Irish literature, which nobody else did, or in my opinion, could have done'.[1] The stories of Ó Laoghaire and Meyer are indeed interwoven and they both received the freedoms of Cork and Dublin together.

Ó Laoghaire was born on 30 April 1839 at 'Lios Carragáin, in an Irish speaking district some miles west of Macroom, county Cork'.[2] He was one of six children born to Diarmuid Ó Laoghaire, a small farmer, and Siobhán Ní Laoghaire, a teacher.[3] He was educated bilingually, initially at home and then in schools in Macroom and, later, at St Colman's College in Fermoy at a time when Dr Thomas Croke was its President.[4] From there he went on to study for the priesthood in Maynooth and he was ordained in 1867.[5] All his missionary life was spent in the Diocese of Cloyne, with more than twenty years as parish priest in Castlelyons.

Historian John A. Murphy claims that Ó Laoghaire's considerable reading and writing skills 'were probably acquired during his Maynooth days'.[6] This may well be the case but, remarkably, Ó Laoghaire did not take up a writing career until he was in his fifties. Despite his late start, one catalogue of his work lists almost 500 items.[7] It was the Gaelic League, famously founded by Douglas Hyde in 1893, which stimulated him to put pen to paper, 'thereby responding to a new demand by enthusiastic revivalists for reading materials in Irish'.[8] Over a twenty-five-year period from his fifties to his death at the age of eighty, Ó Laoghaire 'poured out a prolific stream of publications from his parochial house in the north Cork countryside'.[9]

According to Hyde:

Canon O'Leary's great merit – at least in my opinion – is that he utterly turned his back upon everything that was bookish and old and unclear, and turned his face resolutely towards the folk speech of his native county of Cork, which he wrote with a crystal clearness which has never been surpassed.[10]

One of his best-known works is *Scéal Séadna* (1904) which Murphy describes as 'a quasi-Faustian folk-tale and the first extensive literary composition in modern Irish'.[11] Hyde claimed that *Séadna* was *sui generis* in European literature and would stand the test of time.[12] Ó Laoghaire is also well remembered for *Mo Scéal Féin* (1915), 'the first modern Irish-language experiment in autobiography'.[13] In his autobiography, Ó Laoghaire contrasted the temperament of an Irish child before and after the Great Famine – 'the former was alert, humorous and quick to respond, while the latter was hesitant, surly and furtive'.[14] Ó Laoghaire attributed this change to the schooling under the English system and also the toll on self-confidence taken by the famine.[15]

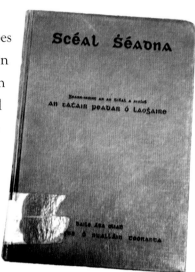

The cover of Canon Ó Laoghaire's *Scéal Séadna*, which is held in Cork Public Museum, Fitzgerald's Park.
PHOTOGRAPH BY TONY O'CONNELL

In *Mo Scéal Féin* Ó Laoghaire also makes it clear that he was vehemently opposed to the politicisation of the Gaelic League after 1915. He shared this conviction with Douglas Hyde who resigned his presidency of the League that year after members voted to make it a specifically nationalist organisation. Murphy contends that Ó Laoghaire 'reflected a prudish Gaelic League mentality'[16] in his dismissal of the 'racy work of Pádraic Ó Conaire as obscene'.[17]

As well as producing his own original work, Ó Laoghaire translated, modernised and retold 'some of the great stories of Ireland'.[18] In addition he translated into his local Cork dialect versions of *Don Quixote* and *Aesop's Fables*.

He died on 21 March 1920 at Castlelyons and 'his significance to the Irish revival movement cannot be overstated'.[19] Murphy records, 'There is general agreement among Irish scholars that he brought the language of the people into modern literature with superb clarity, precision, and style.'[20] Douglas Hyde paid Ó Laoghaire a fitting personal tribute three months after his death when he wrote:

Canon O'Leary had no enemies, so that his life may be pronounced to have been eminently peaceful, useful, and happy. We all loved him – I treasure the most delightful letters from him – and I never met anyone who knew him intimately who was not enthusiastic about him as a humorist, a conversationalist, and a companion.

As well as being made a freeman of Dublin and Cork in 1912, Canon Peadar Ó Laoghaire received an honorary LL D degree from the National University of Ireland in 1919.[21]

FREEDOM OF CORK

Canon Peadar Ó Laoghaire received the freedom of the city of Cork on 25 September 1912 in a joint ceremony with Kuno Meyer which has previously been recounted. Ó Laoghaire dedicates the final pages of *Mo Scéal Féin* to describing the ceremonies in Dublin and Cork, and his pride and joy at receiving the honours shines through the writing. The Dublin ceremony came first, which led Ó Laoghaire to note:

> *When the authorities in Cork heard what Dublin had done, they felt they ought to do something similar and they decided to give the freedom of Cork city to Dr Kuno Meyer and to myself. They appointed a day for it, and, by the luck of the world, wasn't it St Finbarr's Day, the saint of Gougane, who is the patron of the city.*[22]

Even though Ó Laoghaire had been impressed by the reception he and Meyer received in Dublin, there is greater excitement in his writing about the Cork honour:

> *I never expected the sight I saw that day! When myself and Kuno Meyer came out of the train in Cork, there was a great throng of children there to welcome us. They sang us a song in Gaelic, which Osborn Bergin had composed for them. The Mayor and his carriage were there to bring us to the City Hall. Out before and behind us on each side, we had an escort, armed and accoutred as in the time of Cuchulainn.*[23]

Ó Laoghaire continued the account of his special day in Cork as follows:

> *We proceeded through the city, over the main bridge, west to that great, wide street where the 'Yellow Horse' used to be long ago, east again and over across the other bridge to the City Hall. All along the way, the people, young and old, were crushed together on each side of us, cheering and clapping their hands as they welcomed us. When we entered the great hall, it was full of people, so full that it wasn't possible for any more to come in.*[24]

Having signed the roll of freemen, Ó Laoghaire addressed the large crowd in Irish. His speech was brief and focussed on the 'great deal of work that had been done for the Irish language in Cork and Munster during the past twenty years'.[25] He believed that they had worked 'against the spirit of indifference and of opposition'[26] and had brought the Irish language to a permanent and lasting position in the history of Ireland.

While Meyer was honoured for his work on Old Irish, Ó Laoghaire was recognised by Cork Corporation for his efforts in keeping living Irish vibrant. It is therefore fitting that he concluded his autobiography, *Mo Scéal Féin*, by expressing his 'heart-felt wonder'[27] at how well the young boys spoke Irish to him in Cork's City Hall.

WOODROW WILSON

(1856–1924)

Elected as Freeman of Cork on 10 January 1919

by Pádraig Mac Consaidín

'That the freedom of the City of Cork be conferred upon Dr Woodrow Wilson, President of the United States of America, as a mark of appreciation of the highest principles laid down by him for the settlement of the peace of the world, of justice between nations, and the rights of the peoples.'

BIOGRAPHY

Thomas Woodrow Wilson, son of a Presbyterian minister and the twenty-eighth President of the United States of America was unanimously elected freeman of the city of Cork by Cork Corporation on 10 January 1919.

Born to Reverend Joseph Ruggles and Janet Wilson on 28 December 1856, Thomas Woodrow was the second youngest of the four Wilson children. He was raised in the American South, initially in Georgia and later in South Carolina, where his father served as chaplain in the Confederate Army during the American Civil War.[1] Wilson attended Princeton University, graduating in the class of 1879 with a Bachelor of Arts degree, majoring in history and government.[2] Later he went on to study at the University of Virginia Law School, graduating in 1881 following which he was to be admitted to the bar a year later. Wilson's formal education concluded in Johns Hopkins University, where in 1886 he was to receive a Ph.D. in political science for his doctoral thesis 'Congressional Government, a Study in American Politics'.[3]

Academia was where Wilson's immediate future lay. Having already taught history and politics in Bryn Mawr College Pennsylvania, he moved to Wesleyan University Connecticut where he would teach until 1890. That year, Wilson was appointed Professor of Jurisprudence and Political Economy at Princeton University; he was later made President of the university and is distinguished in the fact that he was the first US President who had also been President of a major university.

On 15 September 1910 Wilson received the Democratic nomination as candidate for Governor of New Jersey. Having been elected, Wilson remained Governor until his election as President of the United States and inauguration in March 1913. In just 2 years and 170 days, Woodrow Wilson had moved from an ordinary citizen who never held public office to holding the most powerful office in the world, President of the United States of America.[4]

Wilson's presidency saw him introduce the Federal Reserve Act of 1913[5] domestically, a piece of legislation that to this day regulates US banks and money supply from the Federal Reserve. However, personal tragedy struck Wilson during his first term of office when Ellen Axson, his wife and mother of their three daughters, died in August of 1914. Wilson remarried in December 1915, taking Edith Bolling Galt, a Washington DC widow, as his second wife.[6]

In his second term of office, Wilson maintained the neutrality of the United States during the First World War until 1917. Indeed, one of Wilson's campaign slogans while running for re-election in 1916 was; 'He Kept Us Out Of War'.[7] This changed following the German policy of unrestricted submarine warfare, which Wilson saw as an attack on everyone, warring party or not.[8] This warfare had also included neutral US ships. On 2 April 1917 Wilson asked Congress for a declaration of war on Germany (see image below).[9]

Following victory by the Allies over Germany, Wilson sought to establish peace in Europe. He did so by setting out his 'Fourteen Point' policy which he believed was necessary for peace. Wilson participated in the drafting of the Treaty of Versailles; however, his efforts to ratify the treaty and secure support for the League of Nations in America proved futile[10] and almost fatal to Wilson himself. Against medical advice,[11] he embarked on a national tour to secure public support for the treaty but suffered a stroke and, just days later, a complete physical breakdown.[12] Despite his incapacity, Wilson refused to resign the Presidency and was nursed through his remaining years in office by his wife. In 1920, Wilson was awarded the Nobel Prize for Peace for undertaking to establish the League of Nations. Wilson left office in 1921, his health continuing to deteriorate until his death in 1924.

On 2 April 1917, President Woodrow Wilson asked Congress to declare war on Germany. The original image is in the Library of Congress.

Woodrow Wilson will probably be remembered as one of the most educated Presidents of the United States of America, a champion of peace, and as an academic of renown in the area of government.[13]

FREEDOM OF CORK

'I value the honour as evidence of the friendship of the people of Cork for the people of the United States, whom I have the honour at present to represent'[14]

– DR WOODROW WILSON

Dr Woodrow Wilson was elected as a freeman of the city of Cork at a special meeting of Cork Corporation at three o'clock on 10 January 1919. The honour was conferred on Wilson in recognition of his work for peace and equality amongst nations. The Lord Mayor presiding, Alderman Meade, moved the resolution awarding the freedom of the city to Wilson, which was passed unanimously. Interestingly, the resolution granting the honour to Wilson came following a formal invitation for the President to visit Cork, which was sent in December 1918 and subsequently declined by Wilson.[15]

Whether Cork Corporation was aware of the impending decline of the invitation or simply believed the invitation would not be accepted, the presiding Lord Mayor appointed a deputation to present the engrossment to Wilson.[16] The Town Clerk wrote to Wilson to advise of the honour and received a reply dated 13 February 1919 in which Wilson thanked the corporation for the honour, as quoted above. Wilson concluded the letter advising, 'It seems impossible at this time to say when I might receive a deputation from the city.'[17] This was an unfortunate development, as the delegation appointed to present Wilson with his award had only days before been granted their passports by the Petty Sessions Court.[18] Indeed, a plan had been made to set out for Paris once Wilson was in a position to receive the deputation, who were to be joined by Éamon de Valera.[19] The reasons Wilson could or would not commit to a date are unclear, however, it is possible the inclusion of de Valera in the Cork delegation was one of the reasons. Recently escaped from Lincoln Prison with the help of Philip Monahan[20] (future Cork City Manager), de Valera was one of three envoys appointed by the first Dáil to attend the peace conference in Versailles where they would petition Wilson, amongst others, on the issue of Ireland's freedom.

It is unclear if Wilson ever received his freedom of Cork casket. As stated earlier, failing health left the President incapacitated and it seems the deputation from Cork never met Wilson during his time in Paris.

MONSIGNOR DANIEL MANNIX

(1864–1963)

Elected as Freeman of Cork on 6 August 1920

Conferred as Freeman of Cork on 28 October 1925

by Pádraig Mac Consaidín

> *'That the freedom of the city of Cork be conferred on the Most Reverend
> Monsignor Mannix Archbishop of Melbourne, in recognition of his distinguished
> services in defence of the honour and liberty of our Country.'*

BIOGRAPHY

To write a biography, of any length, of the Most Reverend Monsignor Daniel Mannix DD, LL D, Archbishop of Melbourne, cannot be a biography in the typical sense of the word. This is due to the man himself. Mannix lived a personal life of austere discipline almost to the point of non-existence.[1] He is reputed to have burned personal documents, written letters sparingly and refused to keep diaries so that posterity could not 'analyse his soul'.[2]

A Cork native, Mannix was born in Deerpark, Charleville, County Cork, in 1864 to Timothy and Ellen Mannix. The eldest of five, Mannix was raised in a house where his father's Irish nationalism played a key role in his life but it was the determination of his mother that inspired him.[3] Mannix's education began with the Sisters of Mercy and continued with the Christian Brothers before he went on to St Colman's College in Fermoy, County Cork, for his second level teachings.

Mannix held his education through the Christian Brothers in high regard; soon after his arrival in Melbourne, Australia, many years later he was to comment, 'I am an old pupil of the Christian Brothers.' The high esteem in which Mannix held the Christian Brothers possibly reverts back to his education, where he honed his sense of Irish nationalism and Ireland as an independent nation, building on the nationalistic influences he experienced at home.[4] Mannix's education in St Colman's was to be the platform for his entry to St Patrick's College, Maynooth, due to the Cork institution's high standing in educational circles during the period. Mannix entered St Patrick's College in the autumn of 1883 and was to remain there for the next thirty years.[5] Initially as a student, later ordained a priest, Mannix became a lecturer of philosophy before being elevated to holding the chair of moral theology at Maynooth.[6]

Cardinal Mannix (left) accompanied by Queen Mary and the Archbishop of Dublin, William Joseph Walsh (right) on the grounds of St. Patrick's, Maynooth, in 1911.[7]

On Sunday 6 October 1912, in the college chapel of St Patrick's, Maynooth, Mannix was consecrated titular Bishop of Pharsalus and Coadjutor Archbishop of Melbourne. Mannix was the first bishop to be consecrated in the College chapel of Maynooth.[8] Though it saddened Mannix to be leaving his beloved Maynooth and Ireland, he accepted the appointment unquestioningly, such was his devotion to the church.

Mannix arrived in Australia on Easter Saturday 1913 and immediately questioned how he would endure the intense Australian heat. This apprehension was soon allayed by the enthusiastic reception he received the following day at St Patrick's Cathedral, Melbourne. Here, Mannix was hailed as a world class theologian and educationalist;[9] it seemed the appointment to Australia would be bearable for him after all.

While abroad, Mannix maintained a keen interest in the happenings of Ireland and her fight for freedom. The 1916 Rising is seen as another episode in his progressive radicalisation. He could not support the position of the Catholic hierarchy in Ireland, who he believed did not comprehend the true significance of the rebellion. This support for the rebellion led to his alienation from the Irish Catholic hierarchy.[10] This was to be evident in his later visit to Ireland where he was ostracised by the Irish Church.[11] In Australia, Mannix became known as a workers' hero, denouncing inequality, endorsing strikes and condemning conscription.[12]

Melbourne was now truly Mannix's home, where he participated in the St Patrick's Day parade every year until his death in 1963. Mannix was as reserved in death as in life; he left instructions that there was to be no procession through the streets and the funeral service was to be as simple as the liturgy would allow.[13] This should not have come as a surprise, however, as Mannix had refused to live in the bishop's 'palace' during his tenure as Archbishop of Melbourne. A statue of Mannix stands outside St Patrick's Cathedral as a testament to his legacy in the region.

FREEDOM OF CORK

At the Cork Corporation meeting of 6 August 1920, at which the Lord Mayor Terence MacSwiney presided, a motion conferring the freedom of the city of Cork on Mannix was passed unanimously. The intention was to present the honour to Archbishop Mannix when he visited Ireland during the coming weeks. This, however, did not come to pass. Due to his outspoken views on Irish nationalism, Mannix was, in the eyes of the British Government, a threat and was not allowed to visit Ireland.

These sentiments were raised in the House of Commons in July 1920 where Mannix was described as 'a dangerous revolutionary' and accused of delivering 'mischievous speeches'.[14] As a result, the Prime Minister, David Lloyd George, gave instructions that any ship carrying Mannix was not permitted to dock in Ireland. These instructions carried with them threats of military action.[15] The conferring of the freedom of Cork on Archbishop Mannix would have to wait.

Mannix was finally able to visit Ireland in 1925, staying with his sister in Charleville for the duration, only venturing from the sanctity of the residence to collect freedoms conferred upon him[16] around Ireland. One of the occasions that led to Mannix leaving the homestead was to collect – finally – the freedom of the city of Cork. The ceremony took place on 28 October 1925 in the County Council Chamber, Cork Courthouse. This ceremony would differ slightly from recent ceremonies, however; Cork Corporation had been dissolved with no guarantee of reinstatement,[17] with the Commissioner Philip Monahan holding power.

A large crowd filled the body of the County Council Chamber, in addition to the overcrowded public gallery, to witness the historic event. The Civic Guards were required to regulate the entry of further members of the public into the main Council Chamber as attendees from Cork County Council, Cork Harbour Board and the dissolved corporation filled the room. The Irish Volunteers' Pipe Band was on hand to provide the musical diversion for the event[18] and, as Mannix was accompanied into the chamber by the Lord Mayor Seán French, a rapturous welcome greeted the guest of honour. Though Cork Corporation had been dissolved, French maintained the title of Lord Mayor, unsalaried and in an honorary capacity during the commissionership of Monahan.[19]

The Lord Mayor opened the proceedings to a warm reception from the assembled guests, declaring; 'the freedom of the city they all loved so well was conferred on the Archbishop with all their hearts'.[20] Then, following the reading of the resolution, passed five years previously, the Lord Mayor thanked Mannix for his services to and for Ireland, before presenting His Grace with the silver casket which contained the parchment of the freedom of Cork. This again was greeted with great applause from the assembled audience. The Chairman of Cork County Council, D.L. O'Gorman then read an address to the Archbishop from the council, supporting his work for unity in Ireland, praising him for his patriotic work for Ireland abroad and commending his championing of truth and righteousness wherever he went.[21]

Mannix stood to acknowledge the honour bestowed upon him amid a cacophony of applause that lasted for several moments. He began by stating that he had received many such honours during his visit, in many towns 'south of the sectarian border drawn by the British Government' that had a corporation. Mannix went on to say:

> *But there would be something wanting if, having visited so many places in Ireland, and having received so much honour and distinction, [I] had failed to visit [my] own native county and city to receive at the hands of those who knew [me] best the highest honour in their gift.*[22]

Following this, His Grace stated that on his return to Australia he would hold no memory more fondly than that of the welcome he received upon his arrival in his native Cork. During his address, Mannix referred to a number of other issues including the partition of the island, the new found contentment of many Irish people and the blight of emigration on the country.

In concluding his speech, and the proceedings, Mannix reflected that on his next visit to Ireland, he hoped it would not be as merely a freeman of Cork, but as a freeman of a united, prosperous and contented Ireland. He hoped that Ireland would not be subject to covetous eyes on its territory or treasures, but a nation friendly with all its neighbours.[23]

Regretfully, Mannix was never to set foot in Ireland again. His alienation by the authorities in the Irish Catholic Church and the loss of a sense of belonging meant he accepted his exile and returned resolutely to Melbourne.[24] However, despite his rejection nationally, the Most Reverend Monsignor Mannix DD, LL D, Archbishop of Melbourne, would remain, until his death, a freeman of Cork.

PERIOD 3
CATHOLIC CLERGY AND STATESMEN – 1922 TO 1989

The recipients of the freedom of Cork covered in this chapter are:

FRANK BENSON

SEÁN T. O'KELLY

CARDINAL JOHN D'ALTON

JOHN FITZGERALD KENNEDY

ÉAMON DE VALERA

PROFESSOR ALOYS FLEISCHMANN

BISHOP CORNELIUS LUCEY

JACK LYNCH

THOMAS 'TIP' O'NEILL

SEÁN Ó FAOLÁIN

Cardinal John D'Alton signs the Roll of Freemen in Cork City Hall on Wednesday 16 June 1953. COURTESY *IRISH EXAMINER*

John F. Kennedy arrives at City Hall, Cork, ahead of the Freedom of Cork ceremony on 28 June 1963. COURTESY *IRISH EXAMINER*

SIR FRANK BENSON

(1858–1939)

Elected as Freeman of Cork on 25 January 1930

Conferred as Freeman of Cork on 22 January 1931

'To mark the farewell visit of the distinguished actor, and in appreciation of his great work on behalf of art and drama, and of his long association with the city of Cork.'

BIOGRAPHY

Sir Frank Benson was an actor and the theatre manager of a company which was the precursor to the Royal Shakespeare Company.[1] Born in Tunbridge Wells, Kent, on 4 November 1858, Benson had 'an idyllic rural childhood'.[2] After receiving his early primary education locally, he attended Darch's Preparatory School in Brighton from 1867 before going to Winchester College in 1871. At Winchester, he 'preferred sports to academics, but was attracted to Shakespeare and played female roles'.[3] In 1878, Benson continued his education in New College, Oxford, and his successful production of Aeschylus's *Agamemnon* in 1880 was a turning point in his life.[4] This was the first serious attempt to perform *Agamemnon* in the original Greek and Benson excelled in the role of Clytemnestra, wife of Agamemnon.[5] The production received much praise and, afterwards, Henry Irving and Ellen Terry showed interest in Benson's ability 'and it was probably because of their backing that he [Benson] decided that acting was to become his profession'.[6] Benson left Oxford in 1881 but not before he had again demonstrated his sporting prowess by winning the inter-varsity 3-mile race against Oxford in a time of fifteen minutes and five seconds.[7]

Benson's next venture was to present *Romeo and Juliet* (he played the role of Romeo himself) for a single performance at the Imperial Theatre in London in July 1881 but it was not a success.[8] In describing the production as 'amateurish and financially disastrous', John Peter Wearing comments, in the *Oxford Dictionary of National Biography*, 'indeed, this early effort epitomises Benson's whole career: his own limited acting and managerial capabilities, his abundant enthusiasm, and his ensuing financial woes, which resulted in someone else bailing him out'.[9]

Driven by his natural enthusiasm and 'an almost arrogant conviction he could improve conditions'[10] Benson undertook training in stage-fighting, dancing, boxing and elocution. Yet, his first professional engagement (playing Paris in *Romeo and Juliet* at the Lyceum Theatre) was disappointing and 'no further roles materialised'.[11] At this point, Benson was advised by his benefactors, Henry Irving and Ellen Terry, to work with a provincial touring company. This advice 'fundamentally dictated the remainder of his career'.[12]

Having joined Walter Bentley's touring company in 1883 Benson soon took it over when Bentley 'decamped for financial reasons'[13] and re-named it the F.R. Benson Company. Thus began a long career of provincial touring during which Benson became more prominent. His focus from the start was on performing Shakespeare and Benson's actors showed tremendous loyalty to him despite often difficult conditions and negligible salaries.[14] Nonetheless, the company was very popular and not only for acting reasons. A visit to a town nearly always consisted of Benson and his company playing local teams in a variety of sports such as cricket, soccer and water polo. Wearing notes that all sports 'were played with equal zest as occasion demanded'.[15] Benson continued to link theatre and sport when he toured Ireland. A profile of him in *The Irish Times* noted, 'rugby was another game in which the Bensonians shone, and they played many a good match against local clubs in Cork, Limerick, Waterford and other cities visited by them'.[16]

Based on his growing reputation in the provinces, Benson was asked in 1886 to direct a week-long spring festival in Stratford-upon-Avon, Shakespeare's birthplace. He accepted the job and began a life-long association with the town. Benson's company performed each year from 1889 to 1913 at the Stratford-upon-Avon festival, 'making him a prominent figure in its history and development, if only for his longevity'.[17]

According to Wearing, the provinces and Stratford were never enough for Benson 'and he always yearned to make his mark in London'.[18] He certainly did so during the winter of 1889/1890 when his production of *A Midsummer Night's Dream* ran for 110 performances, a record at the time.[19] Benson continued to work and tour extensively even though the critics were not always kind and he was 'the reciprocant of wildly contrasting reviews'.[20] Generally, the local press described his performances as excellent and inspired but the London and national newspapers were frequently harsh in their criticisms. Benson toured Canada and the United States in 1913 and 1914, with some success although 'he was mauled by the critics in Chicago'.[21] While in Montreal, however, he received an honorary doctorate from McGill University 'in recognition of his services to the theatre'.[22]

This honour was topped on 2 May 1916 when Frank Benson was knighted by King George V during the Shakespearian tercentenary performance of *Julius Caesar* at Drury Lane, 'the first actor to be so honoured within the walls of a theatre'.[23] Wearing described the occasion as follows: 'still in costume, he [Benson] was knighted in the royal box with a sword borrowed from a local armourer, the first instance of an actor being knighted in a theatre'.[24]

The knighthood represented a high point of Benson's life and his career went into decline after the First World War. His last appearance at Stratford took place in 1919 but his final performance on stage (after many 'farewell' tours) was as Dr Caius in *The Merry Wives of Windsor* at the Windsor Garden, Drury Lane, on 26 December 1932.[25] Three months later, in March 1933, he was knocked down by a cyclist in Bradford and hit his head on a lamp-post, after which he did not act again.[26] In retirement, Sir Frank Benson had little money but was awarded a civil-list pension of £100 in July

1933 in recognition of his services to dramatic art.[27] He died in London of broncho-pnuemonia and a kidney infection on 31 December 1939, not long after his eighty-first birthday.

Wearing sums up Benson's contribution to the world of acting and theatre:

> It is true he was never a great actor. His noble Roman appearance with his aquiline nose lent physical distinction to his roles but he could become easily bored by his own performances and was notorious for 'ponging' or extemporising blank verse (albeit expertly). His great talent was for nurturing actors, teaching them, affording them opportunities, and creating a theatrical nursery, and for bringing Shakespeare to countless provincial towns; perhaps his greatest contribution was laying a solid foundation for theatrical performances at Stratford.[28]

Benson was survived by his wife Constance who he had married in July 1886. The couple had two children, William (born in 1887) and Brynhild Lucy (born in 1888), but William died as a young man in 1916. Benson had an affair in 1921 with an actress, Geneviève Smeek, after which Constance left him.[29] At the time of Benson's death in 1939, the couple was separated but not divorced.

FREEDOM OF CORK

Frank Benson was a regular and popular visitor to Cork where 'he was like a personal friend to everybody'.[30] On Saturday 25 January 1930, after the concluding Cork performance as part of one of his infamous Irish 'farewell tours' (Benson had played Shylock in *The Merchant of Venice*), he was greeted on stage by the Lord Mayor of Cork, Frank J. Daly. The Lord Mayor, wearing his formal robes of office, announced that the members of Cork Corporation had decided to present him with the freedom of the city and that they were not going to accept his latest appearance as a farewell one.[31] Benson thanked the Lord Mayor and said he would be very proud to be made a citizen of the beautiful city of Cork.[32] He commented on the coat of arms of Cork – a safe harbour for ships – and stated that he enjoyed the wonderful spirit of generosity and hospitality in the city.[33]

The ceremony conferring the freedom of Cork city on Sir Frank Benson took place a full year later on Thursday 22 January 1931. With similarities to the awarding of his knighthood in 1916, the ceremony was conducted on the stage of the Cork Opera House at the conclusion of a matinee performance of *She Stoops to Conquer*. Dressed in his stage clothes, Benson was presented with a gold casket containing his freedom scroll.[34] He received the casket with a typically theatrical courtly bow. Alderman Daly, deputising for his namesake the Lord Mayor, thanked Benson 'for his work in the cause of true art'[35] and paid tribute to him for the manifest kindness he had shown to Cork since his first visit. This kindness included benefit performances on behalf of Corkonians rendered homeless by flooding in Blackpool in the closing years of the nineteenth century.

Frank Benson receives his Freedom of Cork casket on the stage of the Cork Opera House. COURTESY *IRISH EXAMINER*

The Irish Times reported that 'there was sadness in Sir Frank's voice as he rose to reply'.[36] He recalled a bright day in May, forty years ago, when, with his wife and company, they made their first acquaintance with Cork.[37] He said that his fondness for the city had grown over the years but now, on his last visit to end his career, he was filled with a sense of not having in any way achieved half of the things he had set out to achieve. Benson continued on this theme by noting:

> There are many things I have done which I should not have done, and many things I have left undone which I should have done. I think of them now as I bring my ships home to port, ships that are now sailing their final voyage. The presentation of the city's freedom is the culminating kindness of all the acts shown to me by Cork people.[38]

SEÁN T. O'KELLY

(1882–1966)

Elected as Freeman of Cork on 25 November 1947

Conferred as Freeman of Cork on 8 September 1948

by Pádraig Mac Consaidín

'That the freedom of the City of Cork be conferred on His Excellency, Seán T. O'Kelly, President of Ireland, on the occasion of his first official visit to Cork City.'

BIOGRAPHY

Seán T. O'Kelly was born on 26 June 1882 at 55 Wellington Street, near Mountjoy Street, Dublin. He was one of four children, though his twin sister died shortly before her fifth birthday leaving just Seán and his two brothers. A year or so after Seán's birth, his father left his job at Shorts shoe shop, and moved the family to Berkeley Road,[1] where he opened his own shop.[2] O'Kelly was educated by the Christian Brothers and then at O'Connell's School, North Richmond Street, Dublin. He did not learn the Irish language until he was preparing for his Intermediate Certificate examination; initially not enthusiastic about the language, he soon became proficient.[3]

On leaving school, O'Kelly was employed as a junior assistant in the National Library of Ireland. He remained there for four years until he tendered his resignation on ideological grounds, not wanting to take a salary from the British treasury. O'Kelly's less-than-understanding superior questioned where he (O'Kelly) expected to receive such a fine opportunity again.[4] O'Kelly proceeded to work for the *Evening Mail* newspaper and later the Irish language paper *Claiomh Solais* of which Pádraig Pearse was editor.[5]

O'Kelly joined the Gaelic League in 1889 and later became a member of the Irish Republican Brotherhood, the forerunner of the Irish Republican Army (IRA). In 1905, he was a founding member of Sinn Féin, also acting as manager for the organisation's self-titled newspaper. The British efforts to suppress the publication were futile; when one incarnation of the publication was shut down, another would replace it under a different masthead.[6]

O'Kelly stood in the municipal elections of 1906 and won a seat on Dublin Corporation; this position allowed him to obtain a broad knowledge on public matters. O'Kelly, still actively opposed to British rule of Ireland, travelled to New York in 1915 to advise Clann na nGaedheal of the impending Rising and to raise funds for the effort. During the Rising itself, O'Kelly, though assigned Staff Captain to Pádraig Pearse, spent most of Easter Monday 1916 taking orders from James Connolly. O'Kelly was, however, present at the General Post Office when Pearse read the Proclamation at the main entrance.[7] In the days that followed, O'Kelly was shot by a sniper but remained in the Mater Hospital only overnight, discharging himself against doctor's orders, desperate to rejoin the conflict. However, the leaders of the Rising had been taken as prisoners following the surrendering of the GPO. Later the same week O'Kelly was captured and jailed in England.[8]

Both personally and politically 1918 was a significant year for O'Kelly. Having returned home for the general election, he was made Director of Organisation for Sinn Féin, drafting their manifesto for the campaign.[9] O'Kelly also stood and was elected with a substantial majority in the College Green constituency of Dublin.[10] The successful Sinn Féin candidates, refusing to take their seats in Westminster and declaring Ireland an independent state, took the title Dáil Éireann for their new parliament.[11] O'Kelly became the first Ceann Comhairle (Speaker)[11] of the newly formed Dáil.[12] The same year O'Kelly married Mary Kate Ryan from Wexford.

Following the outbreak of hostilities in the Irish Civil War, O'Kelly joined de Valera on the anti-treaty side of the conflict. He travelled to America as an envoy for the Republican anti-treaty cause in 1924. When O'Kelly came home he joined a new political party, Fianna Fáil, which had been founded by de Valera. O'Kelly was returned to the Dáil throughout the 1920s and was held in high esteem as a debater of renown, known for his forthrightness.[13] With the success of Fianna Fáil in the 1932 general election, O'Kelly was appointed Minister for Local Government, a post he held until the outbreak of the Second World War. During his period in this ministerial position, O'Kelly advocated the 1932 Housing Act which was an incentive for local authorities to become more active in the area of housing.[14] This policy was embraced enthusiastically by the Cork City Manager, Philip Monahan, in providing housing schemes to the underprivileged of Cork. This policy initiative also echoed O'Kelly's previous work while an alderman on the Dublin Corporation.[15] In 1934 O'Kelly suffered a personal tragedy when his wife, Mary Kate, died.[16] Two years later he remarried Phyllis, the sister of his first wife.

In 1945, President Douglas Hyde retired from the office, paving the way for the first contested presidential election in the history of the state. Gerald Boland, Minister for Justice, confirmed that Fianna Fáil would be putting forward Seán T. O'Kelly as a candidate for the presidency.[17] O'Kelly, deputy leader of Fianna Fáil at the time, fought the campaign against two other candidates and was elected the second President of Ireland on the second count.[18] During his first term in office, O'Kelly had the honour of formally declaring Ireland a Republic and made a state visit to the Vatican where he met Pope Pius XII. In the aftermath of the visit O'Kelly received much publicity following a significant diplomatic faux pas. The President revealed to the press the Pope's private views on communism which led to strained relations between the Vatican and the Soviet Union.[19]

President O'Kelly arriving at Cork's City Hall, accompanied by the Lord Mayor, Councillor Michael Sheehan. COURTESY *IRISH EXAMINER*

O'Kelly was returned for a second term of office uncontested in 1952. Whilst the divide in Irish politics as a result of the Civil War remained, O'Kelly did not seem to harbour resentment. Though the presidency is to be 'above politics', in 1957 O'Kelly sponsored an attempt by Deputy Tony Barry of Cork and Senator James Crosbie to bring Fianna Fáil and Fine Gael together, banishing once and for all the scars of the Civil War.[20] O'Kelly maintained a busy schedule of state visits during his second term of office. On one such trip to America his purpose was to address a joint session of the US Congress – this took place on 18 March 1959 as part of an unofficial extension to the St Patrick's Day celebrations.[21] A hallmark of O'Kelly's presidency was his ability to transcend the political sphere in discharging his role as president.[22] He managed this despite his intimate involvement in the fight for Irish freedom, the Civil War and the foundation of the state. O'Kelly is remembered as a popular president, referred to at the time more commonly as 'Seán T.' rather than 'the President'.[23] He died on 23 November 1966.

FREEDOM OF CORK

Cork Corporation unanimously elected President Seán T. O'Kelly a freeman of the city of Cork on 25 November 1947. The matter arose following notification from Mrs T. Barry, Honorary Secretary of the Cork Branch of the Irish Red Cross Society, that the President had accepted an invitation to open the society's children's hospital in Montenotte, Cork. The Lord Mayor, Councillor Michael Sheehan, said that it would be the first visit of Mr O'Kelly to Cork as President of Ireland and it would be a nice gesture to confer upon him the freedom of the city.[24] It had been intended that the visit would take place in April or May of 1948, during which the corporation would hold the freedom conferring ceremony. However, due to unspecified delays, the visit did not take place until later in the year.

O'Kelly eventually travelled to Munster in September 1948, where he fulfilled a number of public engagements, including the opening of St Raphael's tuberculosis preventorium in Montenotte, Cork. O'Kelly also made a personal donation of £100 to the Irish Red Cross Society for the facility.[25]

On the day of the freedom of the city of Cork ceremony (8 September 1948), O'Kelly left his hotel shortly after noon destined for the City Hall, accompanied by his wife and aides-de-camp. An honour guard drawn from the 4th Battalion of the Army awaited his arrival at the Anglesea Street entrance to the municipal buildings, along with the No. 2 Army Band and a large crowd of well-wishers. The President alighted from his car to loud applause from the assembled gathering and, under the baton of Lieutenant R.E. Kelly, the band struck up the 'Presidential Salute'. O'Kelly proceeded to inspect the honour guard before making his way to the entrance of City Hall where he was received by the Lord Mayor. Both men then made their way to the mayoral chambers preceded by the mace-bearers where his Excellency was introduced to the members of the corporation, all bedecked in their civic robes for the occasion. Following a roll call, the Chief Officer read the formal minutes of the corporation meeting which elected to confer the freedom of Cork on the President.[26]

The Lord Mayor then rose, welcoming the President to Cork, and explaining the reasons behind awarding the President the freedom of the city. Referencing O'Kelly's work for the freedom of Ireland, his membership of movements long associated with the struggle for Irish independence and his achievements in the pursuit of liberty, the Lord Mayor likened his efforts to those of Lord Mayors MacCurtain and MacSwiney. President O'Kelly thanked the Lord Mayor and the corporation for the honour before being invited to sign the roll of freemen of Cork. This concluded the proceeding and the President and his party were again escorted from the chamber by the Lord Mayor to the civic luncheon which immediately followed.

The luncheon was attended by many local dignitaries including the Bishop of Cork, the Rt. Rev. Bishop of Cork, Cloyne and Ross, the President of University College Cork and the US Vice-Consul among others. A toast to the newly enrolled freeman of Cork was proposed by Monsignor Scannell, thanking O'Kelly for his work of Christian charity and philanthropy which he had conducted during his visit. The Monsignor expressed his hope that the President would live for many years and enjoy the affectionate regard of his fellow citizens of Cork.[27]

Replying in Irish, O'Kelly thanked the Lord Mayor and the corporation for bestowing upon him the greatest honour the city could confer, appreciating that it was in his capacity as President that he had been selected for the distinguished honour. O'Kelly went on to extol the virtues of the Munster capital and its citizens, saying they 'had earned a reputation for the strictest probity and keenness wherever they went, due to their intelligence, energy and application'.[28] O'Kelly further added, 'If ever compiled, Cork's roll of honour would be an impressive one. It should prove that where men of genius and distinction have been concerned, Cork is second to none.'

The President also thanked the people of Cork for their work with the Church, referring specifically to missionary activity abroad, which had spread the Cork brogue to many a distant shore. O'Kelly also spoke of Cork's proud history, the citizens who fought for independence, the courage they displayed, and his pride in having served alongside many of them. He remembered the fallen souls from the fight for Irish freedom, articulating that he would require more time than was at hand to remember all those from Cork who served Ireland devoutly. O'Kelly did single out a few figures, however, stating 'In all history, no race or country has produced a more heroic figure than Cork city gave to Ireland in the person of Terence MacSwiney.'

The President of Ireland continued to recount the role Cork played in the independence movement and battle, asking, 'When will the glory of Cork, its pride and inspiration to the people of Ireland, the account of the heroic struggle and gallantry against overwhelming odds and the true story of the burning of Cork be available for all to read?'

Finally, the President spoke of Cork's natural advantages, its harbour and river, which he hoped would play a part in industrial, commercial and cultural development of the city over the coming years. He again thanked the Lord Mayor and the corporation for the honour of making him a Corkman and concluded by saying, 'I have proved that it is to the advantage, not only of the people of Ireland, but of the world to have Cork people such as you and I to lead them. Where would they be without us?'

Shortly thereafter, President O'Kelly took his seat to rapturous applause and the formalities were completed.[29]

CARDINAL JOHN D'ALTON

(1882–1963)

Elected as Freeman of Cork on 28 April 1953

Conferred as Freeman of Cork on 16 June 1953

'In recognition of his outstanding services to the Church and to the nation and as a mark of appreciation of the great honour bestowed upon our country by his Holiness Pope Pius XII in elevating him to the Sacred College of Cardinals.'

BIOGRAPHY

John Francis D'Alton was born on 11 October 1882 in Claremorris, County Mayo. He received an extraordinarily extensive education, beginning in the local Sister of Mercy school before attending Blackrock College in Dublin from 1895 to 1900 where one of his fellow students was Éamon de Valera, future President of Ireland.[1] He enjoyed many scholastic triumphs while at Blackrock College and received scholarships, primarily as a result of his excellence in Latin, Greek, classics and maths.[2] He continued his education at Holy Cross College, Clonliffe, and University College Dublin before moving to the Irish College in Rome.[3] He excelled in Rome and received a Doctorate of Divinity *summa cum laude* (the highest award given by the institution) in 1908, the year he was ordained a priest. Similar awards followed for his continuing studies in the University of Oxford and the University of Cambridge.[4]

In 1910 he began teaching Ancient Classics, Latin and Greek in St Patrick's College in Maynooth (he held a teaching post there until 1942). D'Alton had a stellar career in Maynooth during which time he held the chairs of Ancient Classics (1912), Greek (1922) and the offices of Vice-President (1934) and President (1936). He was regarded as an innovative administrator and 'he was instrumental in expanding the size of the college campus and in implementing a less austere approach to study, allowing for more recreation time.'[5] He also produced some immense scholarly work, most notably 'Horace and His Age' (for which he received the degree of Doctor of Litt.) and 'Roman Literary Theory and Criticism'.[6]

D'Alton moved out of academia on 25 April 1942 when he was elected Titular Bishop of Binda and appointed coadjutor Bishop of Meath. He was consecrated on 29 June 1942 in Maynooth by Cardinal Joseph MacRory, Archbishop of Armagh and Primate of Ireland. He became the fully-fledged Bishop of Meath the following year and in 1946 succeeded MacRory as Archbishop of

Armagh and Primate of All Ireland, making him 'the first Connacht-born bishop to be appointed to the primatial see for 180 years'.[7]

His upward march through the Church hierarchy continued in January 1953 when he was named a Cardinal by Pope Pius XII and assigned the Titular Church of St Agatha, Rome.[8] The previous year, D'Alton 'became the first member of the Irish Catholic hierarchy to receive an honorary degree from Queen's University Belfast, when he was conferred with a D.Litt.'.[9]

He was a very active Cardinal and also an outspoken one at times, publicly condemning the use of violence by the IRA as a means for political expression.[10] He often denounced partition, stating on one occasion, 'as a lover of my country I naturally deplore the political partition of this island of ours which God intended to be one and individual'.[11]

In August 1956, he held a Plenary Council of the Irish Church (the first since 1927) in Maynooth and he participated in the conclave of 1958 which elected Pope John XXIII.[12] In 1961, he celebrated the Patrician Year to commemorate the fifteenth centenary of the death of St Patrick and in 1962, despite ill health, he attended the first session of the Second Vatican Council.

On 1 February 1963, Cardinal D'Alton died of a heart attack in Dublin and was laid to rest at St Patrick's Cathedral in Armagh. In addition to the many academic qualifications he received early in his life, D'Alton was conferred with a Doctorate in Literature by Queen's University Belfast, in 1952 (he was the first member of the Irish Church hierarchy to receive an honorary degree from Queen's). In 1958, the National University of Ireland conferred on him the honorary degree of Doctor of Laws.[13] His name is included on a marble tablet in the Portico of St Peter's Basilica, Rome, naming the bishops who attended the definition by Pope Pius XII on 1 November 1950 of the Dogma of the Assumption of the Blessed Virgin Mary into Heaven.

D'Alton's Episcopal motto following his elevation to the role of Bishop was *Judicium Sine Ira*, meaning 'judgement without anger'.[14]

FREEDOM OF CORK

The decision to confer the freedom of Cork on Cardinal D'Alton was approved unanimously by the members of Cork Corporation at a meeting on Tuesday 28 April 1953. Lord Mayor, Alderman Patrick McGrath, proposed D'Alton for his outstanding services to the Church and to the nation. It was clear that discussions had already taken place with Bishop Lucey of Cork about D'Alton's proposed visit to the city on 16 June and council members were presented with a detailed itinerary. This included the plan that members of the corporation, accompanied by Bishop Lucey, would greet the Cardinal at the city boundary and they would walk in procession to the Cathedral where a solemn liturgical reception would be afforded to His Eminence. This would then be followed by the freedom of the city conferring ceremony in the City Hall. Having presented the itinerary to the corporation members, the Lord Mayor concluded by saying he had no doubt that 'Cork would give a thoroughly Catholic welcome to the Cardinal'.[15]

Cardinal D'Alton enters Cork City Hall, accompanied by Lord Mayor Alderman Patrick McGrath. COURTESY *IRISH EXAMINER*

The careful planning over a number of months by the Church and civic authorities paid off as the Cardinal's visit to Cork on 16 June passed off smoothly. The *Cork Examiner* reported that the only contingency for which arrangements could not be made was the weather but, despite overcast skies, conditions were fine.[16] The *Examiner* described 'unrivalled scenes of pomp and pageantry, colour and spectacle, enthusiasm and acclamation and fervour';[17] *The Irish Times* report was more low-key, describing the reception afforded to Cardinal D'Alton as merely 'enthusiastic' but conceding that the local shops were closed earlier than usual and that 'the beflagged streets were thronged'.[18]

After the liturgical reception in the Cathedral, Cardinal D'Alton and other Church dignitaries left for City Hall, making their way though vast crowds. The Cardinal was driven in Bishop Lucey's car as far as St Patrick's Bridge where he was met by the Lord Mayor, Alderman Patrick McGrath, and the Chairman of the Cork Harbour Commissioners, John J. Horgan. The Cardinal changed into an open landau drawn by two dark horses and proceeded towards City Hall, led by the St Nicholas Pipe Band through streets that were 'thickly lined with cheering throngs'.[19]

A great burst of cheering broke out when the Cardinal descended from the carriage and passed between the members of Cork Corporation to enter City Hall; he paused briefly at the door to acknowledge the crowd and impart his blessing.[20]

Following a speech by the Lord Mayor in the council chamber, Cardinal D'Alton signed the roll of freemen.

He commenced his acceptance speech by stating, 'The scenes of welcome I witnessed tonight will remain indelibly imprinted in my memory. I have received many ovations but I think nothing has surpassed the welcome I received this evening.'[21] In thanking the members of Cork Corporation for the honour, Cardinal D'Alton noted that he felt it was not a tribute paid to him personally but rather 'an expression of gratitude to the Holy Father for giving Ireland a representative in the Sacred College of Cardinals'.[22]

He continued by paying tribute to what he called 'the unique charm and beauty of Cork city'[23] and said that Ireland owed Cork a large debt for the valiant role it had played in the fight for freedom. Declaring that Cork had always been renowned for its love of learning, the Cardinal paid a tribute to the President of University College Cork, Dr Alfred O'Rahilly, for his pioneering work in establishing extra-mural courses to help working people and rural areas.

Cardinal D'Alton concluded his speech with a blessing, 'I pray that Cork may enjoy continued and increased prosperity and that God may abundantly bless its citizens, their homes, and their families.'[24] The ceremony then ended with the Cardinal being presented with a silver casket, in the form of a replica of the City Hall, by the Lord Mayor.

JOHN FITZGERALD KENNEDY

(1917–1963)

Elected as Freeman of Cork on 11 June 1963

Conferred as Freeman of Cork 28 June 1963

by Aodh Quinlivan & Pádraig Mac Consaidín

'In token of our pride that this descendant of Irish emigrants should have been elected to such an exalted office, and of our appreciation of his action in coming to visit the country of his ancestors; as a tribute to his unceasing and fruitful work towards the attainment of prosperity and true peace by all the people of the world; and in recognition of the close ties that have always existed between our two countries.'

BIOGRAPHY

The most famous recipient of the freedom of Cork, John Fitzgerald Kennedy, was born on the afternoon of 29 May 1917 in Brookline, Massachusetts. The Kennedys were already one of America's most well-known families in 1917. His father, Joe, was 'ambitious and wealthy'[1] and his mother, Rose, was the daughter of John 'Honey Fitz' Fitzgerald, 'one of Boston's most colourful and mercurial characters',[2] the first Irish-American to be elected Mayor of Boston. Young John, known as Jack to his family and friends, had a privileged childhood and, having started his formal education at the local public school, Edward Devotion, he was sent, aged seven, to a local private school, Dexter, along with his older brother, Joe.[3] Jack later said of his childhood that 'it was an easy, prosperous life, supervised by maids and nurses, with more and more younger sisters to boss and to play with'.[4] In fact, Jack had eight siblings in total, three brothers (Joe, Robert and Edward) and five sisters (Rosemary, Kathleen, Eunice, Patricia and Jean). The main frustration of Jack's childhood was fragile physical health and he fell prey to the illnesses of bronchitis, chicken pox, German measles, measles, mumps, scarlet fever, and whooping cough.[5] When Jack was aged ten, the Kennedy family moved to New York and he studied at Canterbury School and later at Choate, 'an exclusive boarding school in Connecticut'.[6] He was 'an average student who was fascinated by history and English, but not remotely so by mathematics or the sciences'.[7] While at Canterbury (at the age of thirteen), Jack 'began to suffer from an undiagnosed illness that restricted his activities'.[8] Thus began many colon-related illnesses and he was later greatly restricted by back problems.

In his youth, Jack was constantly 'in the shadow of his irrepressible brother, Joe'[9] for whom his father had great ambitions and expectations. Jack followed his brother to Harvard, 'despite being

65th in a class of 110'[10] at Choate. He studied 'at his own pace'[11] and his 'greatest success in his first two years at Harvard was in winning friends and proving to be "a lady's man"'.[12] In the later years of his degree, Jack became more diligent as he increasingly focussed on the study of international relations. His 1940 thesis 'Appeasement in Munich' became a bestseller when he published it as a book entitled *Why England Slept* (mirroring Churchill's *While England Slept*).[13]

After graduating from Harvard with a degree in international relations, Kennedy had no specific career plans but he embarked on a tour of Latin America and Europe – 'his travels during this period would mold his understanding of world politics, such as the threat of Communism, which was spreading to developing countries'.[14] On his return he joined the navy in October 1941 after 'the board of medical examiners miraculously gave him a clean bill of health',[15] ignoring his chronic colon, stomach and back problems. Kennedy emerged from the Second World War as a national hero when 'he saved his crew members on a patrol boat, *PT-109*, which was rammed and sunk by a Japanese destroyer'.[16] For his heroics, Kennedy was presented with the Navy and Marine Corps Medal. Tragically, Kennedy's brother, Joe, did not survive the war after his plane exploded over southern England in 1944. Joe was being groomed for a political career by his father, Joe Sr, and attention now shifted to Jack. Joe Sr informed Jack that his brother was dead 'and that it was therefore his responsibility to run for Congress'.[17]

In the winter of 1944/1945, Kennedy was forced to leave the navy to recuperate from back surgery and he began to contemplate a political career. He was acutely aware of what he regarded as his family responsibilities and, later in life, as a US senator, he explained, 'Just as I went into politics because Joe died, if anything happens to me tomorrow, my brother Bobby would run for my seat in the Senate. And if Bobby died, Teddy would take over from him.'[18] Kennedy went on a European tour in the summer of 1945, which included a visit to Ireland, the country of his ancestors.

The following year, his political career commenced in earnest when he was elected as a Democrat to Congress (Massachusetts, 11th District) even though the elections 'produced a national and state-wide Republican tidal wave'.[19] Kennedy started work as a congressman in Washington in January 1947; nobody was in any doubt that this was little more than a first step. John Galvin, who was Kennedy's public relations director for the election, recalled that the Kennedys were 'always running for the next job'.[20] Kennedy could not be accused of lacking ambition and 'the possibility of becoming the first Catholic president intrigued him from the start of his political career'.[21] He served in Congress for six years before taking another step forward in 1952, by winning a seat in the Senate. The following year he married Jacqueline Lee Bouvier in 'a celebrity affair attended by the rich and famous and numerous members of the press, who described it as the social event of the year – the marriage of "Queen Deb" to America's most eligible bachelor'.[22]

Following his election to the Senate, Kennedy was effectively in campaign mode for the 1960 presidential election, eight years later. His already high profile received a further boost when he was awarded the Pulitzer Prize for his 1956 book, *Profiles in Courage*, recounting his war experiences.

Kennedy, however, continued to be plagued by health issues. He was frequently absent from the Senate as he recovered from serious spinal operations and his medical records from the time show that he had 'zero flexion and extension of his back, with difficulty reaching his left foot to pull up a sock, turn over in bed, or sit in a low chair.[23] Biographer Robert Dallek notes:

> *The treatments for his various ailments included oral and implanted cortisone for Addison's disease and massive doses of penicillin and other antibiotics to combat prostatitis and abscess. He also received anaesthetic injections of procaine at trigger points to relieve back pain, antispasmodics – principally, Lomotil and Trasentine – to control the colitis, testosterone to bulk him up or keep up his weight (which fell with each bout of colitis and diarrhoea), and Nembutal to help him sleep. He had terribly elevated cholesterol – apparently caused by the testosterone – which may also have heightened his libido and added to his stomach and prostate problems.[24]*

Nonetheless, despite all of these problems, 'on 8 November 1960, Kennedy beat Richard Nixon in one of the most closely fought Presidential elections of the 20th century'.[25] Out of 68 million votes cast, Kennedy received only 113,000 more votes than his opponent, 'which translated into a victory by a margin of 303 to 219 in the electoral college'.[26] One of the interesting dimensions of the 1960 presidential election campaign was that Kennedy and Nixon participated in the first televised presidential debate in history, ushering in 'a new era in which crafting a public image and taking advantage of media exposure became essential ingredients of a successful political campaign'.[27] The medium of television undoubtedly worked well for Kennedy who came across as believable, 'unlike Nixon, who never overcame a reputation for deceitfulness'.[28] Robert Dallek states, 'Kennedy's manner – his whole way of speaking, choice of words, inflection, and steady gaze – persuaded listeners to take him at his word. And the public loved it.'[29]

John F. Kennedy was sworn in as the thirty-fifth President of the United States on 20 January 1961. Aged forty-three, he was the youngest person ever elected American President and, of course, he was the first Catholic holder of the office. In his inaugural speech he spoke of the need for all Americans to be active citizens – 'Ask not what your country can do for you, ask what you can do for your country.' He also asked the nations of the world to join together to fight what he called the 'common enemies of man: tyranny, poverty, disease, and war itself'.[30] With his glamorous wife and two young children, Caroline (born in 1957) and John Jr (born in 1960) – Jackie gave birth to a stillborn baby girl in August 1956 whom the couple intended to name Arabella, and Patrick was born in August 1963 but died after two days – 'President Kennedy brought a new youthful, spirit to the White House'.[31]

Tragically, Kennedy's reign as President was short but dramatic, as evidenced from his position as a Cold War leader. Less than four months into his presidency, he oversaw the disastrous invasion of Cuba. The CIA-led Bay of Pigs invasion had the aim of instigating an uprising amongst Cuban people in the hopes of overthrowing Fidel Castro but it backfired badly with the majority of the US-trained invaders killed or captured.[32] The young President was then tested enormously during the Cuban Missile Crisis which was 'sparked by the discovery of Soviet nuclear missiles in Cuba on 18 October 1962, just 100 miles from American soil'.[33] In his 2010 book, *JFK in Ireland*, Ryan Tubridy records that 'the crisis lasted 13 days and brought the world to the brink of nuclear war before its eventual resolution'.[34] The resolution to the crisis showed off Kennedy's diplomatic skills at their best.

Domestically, Kennedy's presidency could not be classified as overly-successful, 'many of the Democratic Southern conservatives in Congress often joined the Republicans in opposing Kennedy's proposals for civil rights legislation, programmes for the aged, Medicare, and federal aid for education'.[35] However, President Kennedy did establish the Peace Corps and he 'was the first President to ask Congress to approve more than $22 billion for Project Apollo, which had the goal of landing an American man on the moon before the end of the decade'.[36] In addition to this, in January 1962, answering President Kennedy's call for an elite new force that would perform clandestine operations in a maritime environment, the US Navy established two teams, calling them Navy SEALs (forty-nine years later, it was a team, working under the original framework Kennedy envisaged, that eventually killed Osama Bin Laden, the mastermind behind the September 11, 2001 terrorist attacks on the United States).[37]

Ultimately, John F. Kennedy's vast potential to be a world-wide force for good as American President was never realised; he was assassinated in Dallas, Texas, on 22 November 1963 by Lee Harvey Oswald. Two days later, while in police custody, Oswald was shot dead by Jack Ruby. Kennedy's death – described by Dallek as 'a triumph of the worst in human relations over the promise of better times'[38] – shocked the world and he was deeply mourned in Ireland, where he had visited five months earlier.

Hundreds of thousands gathered in Washington for the President's funeral, with millions throughout the world watching on television.[39] He was laid to rest at Arlington National Cemetery in Virginia. At the request of his widow, Jackie, twenty-six Irish cadets participated in the military ceremony at the graveside.[40] Arabella and Patrick were re-buried alongside their father. The disinterment of the children's remains before their burial at Arlington National Cemetery was overseen by Cardinal Cushing, who was also a recipient of the freedom of Cork.

FREEDOM OF CORK

Initially, the visit of President Kennedy to Ireland did not include a trip to the southern capital but Kennedy asked for it to be included. His Press Secretary, Pierre Salinger, recalled how the President had called him into his office and told him that he must visit Cork. Salinger speculated that this was because Cork was a direct part of his family heritage as his ancestors on the Fitzgerald side came from the county.[41] Therefore, when the news broke publicly on Monday morning 20 May 1963 in the *Cork Examiner* that a visit to Cork had been included in the itinerary, a sense of anticipation began to grip the city. The Lord Mayor, Alderman Seán Casey, said he was delighted that the President would visit Cork, 'I know the corporation will be unanimous in extending every possible honour to him that the city can give. We look forward to his visit and he can be assured of a real Cork welcome'.[42] Expectation was heightened further when a front page story in the *Cork Examiner* on 27 May proclaimed 'Top Kennedy Men For Cork This Week'; the article went on to advise that President Kennedy's Secretary, Kenny O'Donnell, and White House Press Officer, Pierre Salinger, would be making a visit to discuss the President's upcoming visit and put in place plans for the Cork segment of the Irish tour.[43]

With the planning process for the President's visit to Cork now well underway, at a meeting of the Corporation on 26 May, and echoing the sentiments of the Lord Mayor that 'every possible honour' should be extended to the visiting dignitary, it was agreed that the freedom of Cork should be offered to President Kennedy. Though the procedural nomination and election of President Kennedy as a freeman of the city did not take place at the meeting, the responsibility of making the necessary arrangements was assigned to the Lord Mayor, Seán Casey, and the City Manager, Walter MacEvilly. In addition to the matter of conferring the freedom of the city on the President during his visit, the corporation also discussed a resolution whereby they would request all employers and public bodies to release their staff for a reasonable amount of time to give them the opportunity to welcome the President on his historic visit to the city. The motion was deferred, however, until the Manager and Lord Mayor had a chance to complete their arrangements.[44]

It was at a meeting of the Cork Corporation on 11 June that President John F. Kennedy was formally nominated and elected a freeman of the city of Cork, with the conferring ceremony to take place on the occasion of his visit to the city on 28 June 1963.

The arrangements were eventually finalised on 14 June when Pierre Salinger and the US Ambassador to Ireland, Matthew McCloskey, met with the Lord Mayor, a host of senior gardaí and military authorities and Hugh McCann, Secretary of the Department of External Affairs in City Hall, Cork.[45] The advance party took a driving tour of the proposed route the President's motorcade would follow, and on their return to City Hall to finalise the details, a change of location for the President's departure from Cork was agreed. Instead of returning to Collins' Barracks as originally intended, the President would instead depart from the playing fields at the junction of Monahan Road and Victoria Road, now called Kennedy Park. This was decided by aeronautical experts for safety reasons who were concerned that the fully loaded helicopters would only be able to take off from the elevated location at Collins' Barracks in almost perfect conditions.

The President's advance party was also advised by members of the Post Office who joined the meeting that sixty telephone lines were being installed in City Hall for the occasion along with specialist wired photograph facilities.[46] They were also informed that 900 gardaí would be on duty in Cork for the President's visit.[47] Furthermore, it was confirmed that the President would speak at

A large crowd gathers on St Patrick's Street, Cork, to greet John F. Kennedy as he travels to City Hall to collect his Freedom of Cork award.
COURTESY
IRISH EXAMINER

City Hall after the freedom of the city was conferred upon him. The meetings concluded before noon and the party returned to Cork Airport to depart in three US Army helicopters that struck an impressive sight on the runway in front of the terminal.[48]

As the momentous day approached, Cork Corporation began to release information pertaining to President Kennedy's Cork itinerary. At a press conference held in City Hall on Thursday 21 June, the Lord Mayor, City Manager and Chief Officer of the Corporation gave details of the President's visit. The Lord Mayor issued an appeal to employers to provide an opportunity for their employees and staff to welcome President Kennedy, while also requesting that businesses and households decorate their buildings for the great occasion, especially those that would line the President's route from Collins' Barracks to the City Hall. It was confirmed that the President would travel by jet helicopter to Cork where he would meet his motorcade for the journey to City Hall. The Lord Mayor also advised the press and public what they could expect when the Presidential motorcade rolled through the streets of Cork. The cavalcade would be comprised of fourteen vehicles, in order; a television truck, garda car, an open-top car bearing the President and Lord Mayor, a Secret Service car, a car to carry the US Ambassador along with a government minister, a vehicle for senior army and garda officers, a US Embassy vehicle, two cars for Irish and US staff, two additional 'pool' cars and three buses for the members of the world press. The President would be conveyed through the streets of Cork in his motorcade before arriving at City Hall to be conferred with the freedom of the city. Besides the large crowds expected to line the streets, the Lord Mayor also confirmed that approximately 1,000 invitations were extended to special guests for the ceremony in City Hall.[49] The plans had been laid, the public were buoyed by a sense of excitement and anticipation, all that remained was for the leader of the free world to touch down in Cork within the week.

On the morning of 28 June President Kennedy arrived by helicopter on Leeside to Collins' Barracks accompanied by his sisters and sister-in-law. *Marine One* landed five minutes ahead of schedule and the President was welcomed by the Lord Mayor of Cork, Alderman Seán Casey, and by the City Manager, Walter MacEvilly. However, the *Cork Examiner* reported on an incident that took place before President Kennedy took a standing position in his well-known blue car for the drive to the City Hall:

As the President strode towards his car everything was going with smiling military precision. Then, suddenly, with a boyish grin, America's chief citizen slipped out from the midst of security men and VIPs. In a window of the reception room he had spotted some nurses and with his escort trailing him he went across to shake hands and chat.[50]

The journey, which started with troops lining Military Hill and saluting the President, was a chaotic one with an estimated 100,000 on the streets to welcome the legendary US President. *The Irish Times* reported that 'rose petals, confetti, streamers and ticker tape'[51] were strewn along the streets and added:

> *Crowds surged forward yelling their goodwill and endeavouring to shake his hand, or clap his back. There were a few anxious minutes when the crowd broke through the strong police protection at Parnell Bridge, and a number of women and children received first-aid after the crushing that took place there.*[52]

In the context of his assassination in Dallas a few months later it is worth pointing out that President Kennedy was completely exposed to the crowd as the motorcade made its slow journey to the City Hall. Despite the erection of crash barriers, 'a seething mass of wildly-excited people'[53] streamed forward continuously while 'worried security men'[54] looked on.

At every corner a band, some pipes and drums, some brass and reed, some just a conglomeration of fiddles and melodeons, played for sheer joy at the presence of John Fitzgerald Kennedy, who frequently leaned from his car and brushed his hands against the outspread fingers of those nearest the motorcade.[55]

The bells of Shandon pealed out across the city for the President,[56] while flags and banners adorned the buildings along the route of Military Road, Summer Hill North, MacCurtain Street, St Patrick's Street, Grand Parade and South Mall, with one banner on Grand Parade reading, 'Don't worry Jack, the Iron Curtain will rust in peace'.[57] When the motorcade eventually reached City Hall, Kennedy was greeted by the city's councillors, dressed in their long, crimson robes, and by the US Ambassador to Ireland, Matthew McCloskey.

Included in the welcoming party on the steps of City Hall 'were four men who bore a startling resemblance to the esteemed guest, all of them Fitzgeralds from Skibbereen, who had been invited to say hello to their kinsman'.[58]

Inside the City Hall, the formal proceedings began in front of 2,000 assembled guests, which included heads of the religious orders, high ranking members of public organisations and the military, Congressmen from the US and staff of the corporation including the cleaning staff who had prepared the concert hall to a scene of colourful spectacular brilliance.[59] There were 'elaborate floral tributes on display, including some spelling out words of welcome and a large one in front of the lectern that reproduced the American flag in red, white and blue flowers'.[60] After the traditional roll call and prayer, the Town Clerk, Patrick Clayton, read the resolution conferring the freedom of Cork on Kennedy and then the Lord Mayor, Alderman Seán Casey, rose to speak. He stated that President Kennedy stood for the weak against the strong and for right against might and added:

Throughout its long history, Cork has received many famous visitors from many parts of the world but I can confidently say that no man has ever come within our walls who is more welcome than John Fitzgerald Kennedy, 35th President of the great republic of the west, leader of the powerful nation to whom we all owe so much.[61]

Tubridy describes the Lord Mayor's speech as 'articulate if lengthy'[62] but there is no doubt it came from the heart. Casey concluded by proclaiming:

You, sir, in our eyes, represent all that is best, all that is honourable, all that is valiant in our people. We remember proudly your stirring words in your inauguration address and your call to your fellow-Americans to work for their country, to live for their country and not to ask what America could do for them. To us in Ireland these were the words of a man in the best tradition of Wolfe Tone, of Pádraig Pearse, of James Connolly. These, to us, were the words we expected of a great Irishman, and that, Mr President, in our heart of hearts, is what we regard you to be.[63]

President Kennedy listened intently throughout the Lord Mayor's speech, although he did squirm in his seat and grimace on a couple of occasions – either out of concern at the length of the speech or because of pain from his well-documented bad back. When it was his turn to speak, he took a moment to look around the room before remarking, wearing his famous cheeky grin and tightly grasping his freedom casket in both hands, that 'the Irish have not lost their ability to speak'. The freedom casket itself was made of solid silver, gilted in fine gold, mounted on a plinth of Connemara marble and engraved with shamrock, Celtic design and the Kennedy and Cork coats of arms and US eagle crest. President Kennedy spoke for eight minutes, describing Ireland's unique history of immigration and explaining the necessity for strong, cooperative international relations in an increasingly global climate.

He said that he was delivering a welcome to Corkonians from the people of Galway, New York; Dublin, New Hampshire; Killarney, West Virginia; Kilkenny, Minnesota; Limerick, Maine; and Shamrock, Texas, noting, 'most countries send out oil or iron, steel or gold to somewhere else, but Ireland only has one export – its people'.[64]

Changing his tone, President Kennedy continued by stating that the world was in the most difficult and dangerous struggle it had ever seen and that weapons now existed 'which could annihilate the human race in a few hours'.[65] Tubridy comments that this statement was an extraordinary one 'that was at odds with the jollity of the occasion'.[66]

Right at the end of his address, Kennedy paused, lowered his voice, turned to the Lord Mayor and said, with some hint of emotion in his voice, 'When I am retired from public life, I will take the

John F. Kennedy speaking in City Hall, Cork, on 28 June 1963. COURTESY *IRISH EXAMINER*

greatest pride and satisfaction from not only having been President of my own country but a freeman of this city.'

After the ceremony, President Kennedy had to return to Dublin (he was in Cork for less than two hours) but, before leaving, he had to battle once again with the large, enthusiastic crowds. *The Irish Times* recorded:

When the President emerged from the building, his grin was as broad as ever, as he leaned to right and left giving the brush of the fingers. But this gesture was his undoing. A hand clasped his wrist, he pulled, the hand relaxed and he slipped down with a bump on the seat of the car while a security guard who had tried a blocking tackle went head first into the back seat. And through it all, the President smiled. [67]

President Kennedy departed from Cork in a helicopter, which was waiting in a local field along with a crowd of approximately 5,000 people. With spectators standing too close to the aircraft, a space had to be cleared to facilitate the take-off. One member of the White House Press Corps noted:

> *Gee, that was the most dangerous take-off I've ever seen in many years of covering American Presidents. Cork outdoes anything I've ever seen before. I thought the mobbing in Berlin was bad, but now I know better. My message home will be of this one helluva hooley we had in Cork.*[68]

Cork, it should be remembered, was the one part of the Irish trip the President specifically requested be added to the itinerary. Kennedy was no stranger to mentioning Cork in his speeches. In 1956 at the Irish Fellowship Club in Chicago and in 1957 at the Irish Institute in New York City, addressing Irish and those of Irish descent in the US, both speeches contained the quote 'and whether we live in Cork or Boston, Chicago or Sydney, we are all members of a great family which is linked together by that strongest of chains – a common past'.[69] Tragically, the final time a reference to Cork was contained in one of President Kennedy's speeches he never got the chance to utter the words:

> *In San José and Mexico City, in Bonn and West Berlin, in Rome and Cork, I saw and heard and felt a new appreciation for an America on the move – an America which has shown that it cares about the needy of its own and other lands, an America which has shown that freedom is the way to the future, an America which is known to be the first in the effort for peace as well as preparedness.*[70]

The speech was due to be delivered on 22 November 1963, the day John F. Kennedy, President of the United States and freeman of Cork, was killed in Dallas, Texas.

ÉAMON DE VALERA

(1882–1975)

Elected as Freeman of Cork on 26 February 1973

Conferred as Freeman of Cork on 31 March 1973

by Pádraig Mac Consaidín

'That the freedom of the city of Cork be conferred on Éamon de Valera, President of Ireland, in appreciation of his lifetime of devoted service to the Irish nation as patriot, soldier, scholar and statesman and in token of the esteem and affection in which he is held by the people of Cork.'

BIOGRAPHY

In his biographical work of de Valera, Tim Pat Coogan comments that 'percolating down to us through a process of selective amnesia, recollections by contemporary admirers (and detractors), the story of Éamon de Valera's childhood and youth comes across as a combination of Aesopian fable and Lincolnesque progression from log cabin to White House'.[1] Almost forty years after his death, the immense influence de Valera has had on the Irish state can still be felt; his position in the annals of history remains a divisive one and his legacy has sparked many a debate throughout the island of Ireland.

Born in New York to immigrant parents – Catherine Coll of Knockmore, near Bruree, County Limerick, and Juan Vivion de Valera, a young man of Spanish descent – Éamon de Valera entered the world on 14 October 1882 in New York's Nursery and Child's Hospital on Lexington Avenue. He was baptised in St Agnes's church near Grand Central Station in December of the same year.[2] A reliable and accurate account of de Valera's early childhood is problematic to compile, even from the records that are available. The difficulty is compounded by de Valera's own accounts of his childhood, which contravene other reports available to historians and biographers, as noted by Tim Pat Coogan. What is known is that the young de Valera was sent to Ireland around the age of two with his uncle Ned to be raised in Catherine's home parish of Bruree.[3]

De Valera was educated at Bruree National School and later at the Charleville Christian Brothers School, where he often made the 14-mile round trip on foot. According to his autobiography, he had his own agenda for wanting to continue his education; he wished to study for a scholarship that would raise him up the educational ladder. He was successful in his endeavour and received an allowance of £20 per year for three years.[4]

His formal education did not include history, and certainly not Irish history, given the time that it was. It would seem that this element of de Valera's education came from Fr Sheehy, the local priest renowned for his nationalist sermons and Land League activities,[5] from whom de Valera would hear stories during his time as an altar boy in the local church.

Securing his next placement in the educational system proved more difficult for the scholarly de Valera. Though he is quoted in many of his obituaries as having said he chose Blackrock College, Dublin, due to its standing as the most competitive school,[6] the reality was he had been rejected by two local colleges, before being accepted into Blackrock.[7] Nonetheless, while attending Blackrock, de Valera excelled academically, securing numerous scholarships and developing an interest in sport, primarily rugby,[8] which would later see him play full-back for Munster and be credited for one of the longest kicks in the history of Munster rugby.[9] It was also while at Blackrock that the young de Valera struck up a lifelong friendship with John d'Alton, later Cardinal d'Alton, also a freeman of Cork. De Valera remained at Blackrock for his third level education, studying for his Bachelor of Arts degree. However, with only one year of his degree remaining, he abandoned his studies and relocated to Rockwell College in Tipperary in order to take up a teaching position at the Munster facility (de Valera would later complete his studies and attain his Bachelor of Arts degree with a pass grade). Despite his scholarly reputation, de Valera would never scale any great heights in academia; he did not achieve his Master of Arts degree, though he attended many lectures under various professors.[10]

Following the attainment of his undergraduate degree, de Valera began a career in teaching. He married Sinéad Flanagan in 1910 and the couple had two children within the first two years of marriage. In 1912 de Valera was appointed part-time lecturer in mathematics and mathematical physics at St Patrick's College, Maynooth. The appointment was made by Dr Daniel Mannix, also a native of Charleville, life-long admirer of de Valera and later, fellow freeman of Cork.[11] De Valera remained active in the Gaelic League, once seeking election to the governing body, but having been defeated by a known Sinn Féin activist, reportedly told his wife that he would never join Sinn Féin.[12] It was around this time that de Valera also joined the Irish Volunteers; he progressed through the ranks rapidly, due to his attention to detail and diligence in all that was asked of him. Later, de Valera would join the IRB, the pre-runner to the IRA, seemingly unaware of the influence the IRB already exercised over the Gaelic League and Irish Volunteers pre-dating his membership of those organisations.[13]

The 1916 Easter Rising, a critical juncture in Irish history, saw de Valera take command of the Third Dublin Battalion of the Irish Volunteers, a command appointment he received from Pádraig Pearse.[14] De Valera acquitted himself with distinction during the Rising, holding his position in the face of superior British troop numbers, while suffering heavy casualties preventing the British march along Northumberland Road. He was also the last Volunteer Commandant to surrender his position. Some argue this may have resulted in his reprieve from the firing squad, avoiding the summary execution of the other rebel leaders, benefiting from a change in British attitudes brought about by public opinion.[15] In June 1917, de Valera secured his release from Dartmoor Prison. His brief career as a soldier ended with the Rising but it was to provide a launching pad for a lengthy political career that would shape a nation.

Returning to a hero's welcome in Ireland, de Valera was installed as the people's favourite and the Volunteers' candidate for a parliamentary by-election in East Clare. Displaying his political prowess even at this early stage, de Valera was the first signatory on a cable to the US President, Woodrow Wilson, promoting the call for a nation's right to self-determination and calling for the President's ideal to be applied to Ireland.[16] Indeed, de Valera was also a member of a travelling party to France in 1919 that – partly under the portents of presenting President Wilson with the freedom of Cork – hoped to have the President press the cause of a free Ireland at the conference in Versailles. It is believed that this request angered the President greatly and, while Wilson may have been predisposed to meeting the contingent, such a meeting became an impossibility due to speeches de Valera made in Ireland which upset the British,[17] America's great ally. Prior to this, however, de Valera was once more a guest at His Majesty's pleasure, this time in Lincoln Prison. Unlike his previous imprisonment, where the grant of freedom came from his jailors, de Valera escaped in a daring scheme that involved Philip Monahan,[18] the future City Manager of Cork, an escape that astonished the British and delighted the Irish.[19]

Following his escape, de Valera set out for New York, travelling as a stowaway. Entering the US illegally, he remained for eighteen months during which time he raised an estimated £6 million for the Republic Bonds, with another £1 million through unspecified means. Like Parnell before him, de Valera was well received on the American circuit and – also like Parnell – fundraising for the Irish effort was a resounding success. Returning to Ireland in 1920, de Valera found one significant change – Michael Collins, a perceived junior member of the 1916 Rising, had become a capable diplomat in his absence, managing the advances of the British effectively and efficiently.[20] De Valera was soon to reassert his dominance, however, negotiating with the British in peace talks that would lead to the truce of 1921 and ultimately the Treaty talks (attended by Collins but not de Valera). Ironically, de Valera opposed the Treaty negotiated by Collins and refused to sign it. The fallout from the Treaty with Britain led to one of the darkest periods in Irish history, the Civil War. De Valera played a pivotal role in the hostilities and, like many, emerged from the conflict with a tarnished reputation, following the despairing reality that had pitted brother against brother and neighbour against neighbour.[21]

During the Civil War, de Valera was busy building the Sinn Féin political position, though some argue that this was interrupted by his imprisonment from 1923 to 1924.[22] In spite of his internment, de Valera continued this pursuit, until an extraordinary Árd Fheis (national conference) of the Sinn Féin party in 1926 saw him resign as President of the organisation he once swore he would never join. One month later, de Valera announced the formation of a new republican party, Fianna Fáil.[23]

During the early years, de Valera devoted much of his time to fundraising, in order to establish a national newspaper that would aid Fianna Fáil's bid for power. This meant further trips to the US until – in 1931, with enough capital raised – the printing presses of *The Irish Press* newspaper began to roll. The enterprise was a success and the ensuing election saw Fianna Fáil returned to the Dáil in significant numbers with de Valera elected President of the executive council.[24] What followed was a sustained period in Irish history of political dominance by one figure, de Valera, and one party, Fianna Fáil.

During the 1930s, and as leader of the Irish Free State, de Valera engaged in an economic war with the British. In the context of a worldwide economic recession, it gave him the opportunity to 'introduce protectionism under the guise of patriotism' as noted by historian Ronan Fanning. De Valera's undisputed power was further illustrated in the drafting of the 1937 constitution, no more so than in the religious article 44 ('The State acknowledges that the homage of public worship is due to Almighty God. It shall hold His Name in reverence and shall respect and honour religion'), which was not seen by anyone until de Valera revealed it to the cabinet; he got it ratified and published the very next day.[25] The next major challenge to face de Valera was leadership of the country during the Second World War. Though de Valera had used rising tensions in Europe to secure financial, trade and defence agreements with Britain in exchange for a guarantee that Ireland would not be used as a base for attacking Britain, this was a bargaining ploy. De Valera was committed to Irish neutrality and was said to be 'glum and sad' on hearing Prime Minister Chamberlain's declaration of war in 1939, remarking to his sons, 'Life will never be the same again.'[26] For many people of this generation, de Valera is probably more readily remembered for the implementation of draconian restrictions during 'the Emergency' (as the Second World War was also referred to in Ireland) and the visit of condolence to the German Embassy on the death of Hitler – the latter engendered a sense of disgust among many.[27]

Though a member of Dáil Éireann for another fourteen years, compared to his earlier exploits, these years were relatively uneventful. In the context of this period, Fanning remarks, 'Even his official biographers give it [the period] a mere 21 of their 500 pages.' Though partition, the IRA and forging Ireland's new independent identity on the global stage were features of his remaining political career as a member of the Dáil, issues of an economic nature featured prominently. Ill at ease with economic matters, de Valera adhered to his protectionist beliefs, advising the Dáil in 1956 that 'we have to tighten our belts', and spoke of Irish people having the choice between the 'humble cottage instead of [being] lackeys partaking in the sops of the big man's house'. These comments resonate with the now infamous 1943 St Patrick's Day radio address in which he alluded to the 'ideal Ireland' of 'cosy homesteads' and 'happy maidens'.

De Valera resigned as Taoiseach in 1959 and, aside from political revolution, 'he left Irish society very much as he had found it' according to John A. Murphy.[28] On the eve of retirement, however, one of his final acts was an attempt to reform the electoral system, in an effort to make securing an overall majority more achievable for a larger party,[29] like Fianna Fáil. While de Valera was subsequently elected President, the referendum to amend the electoral system failed.

A political 'lap of honour' is how Fanning describes de Valera's two terms as President of Ireland. De Valera undertook to avoid commenting on Irish party politics as President, though he was known to support Jack Lynch, especially during the arms trial, when he commented to Desmond O'Malley, 'the disloyalty which Lynch had to suffer is appalling, the worst ever'.[30] Embracing the office's ceremonial duties, receiving visiting dignitaries, such as US Presidents Kennedy and Nixon, was de Valera's role. President Kennedy's visit in 1963 was a particular highlight of de Valera's term in office, though he would travel to the US for the President's funeral later that year, striking an unforgettable figure on Irish television, striding along sightlessly behind the solemn cavalcade as it made its way to Arlington Cemetery.[31] The following year de Valera found himself back in Washington, when a historic opportunity presented itself, becoming the second Irish President, after Seán T. O'Kelly, to address a joint session of the US Congress. De Valera retired from public life on completion of his second term of office in 1973, coincidentally, the same year of Ireland's accession to the European Economic Community (EEC). One could argue that it was somewhat poetic, the symbol of Irish protectionism stepping out of public life at the moment when Ireland was to join an international economic community.

Éamon de Valera, or 'Dev' as he is more commonly referred to, immigrant, teacher, revolutionary, Taoiseach and President of Ireland, 'is often condemned not for what he did as for what he never tried to do' according to Fanning. Yet he will always remain a giant of Irish history. De Valera died in Dublin on 29 August 1975, aged ninety-two.

FREEDOM OF CORK

President Éamon de Valera travelled to Cork on Saturday 31 March 1973 to receive the freedom of the city, arriving slightly late into Kent Station as a result of a stirring reception received in Mallow, the penultimate stop for the State rail coach on its journey.[32]

Alighting from the train, the President was welcomed by the Lord Mayor, Councillor Seán O'Leary, the City Manager, Patrick Clayton, and a number of other local representatives. After the exchange of customary pleasantries, which allowed for a number of photographs to be taken, the President moved along the red carpet to his waiting car, the Austin Princess, which had made the journey down from Dublin the previous day.[33] Travelling in the presidential motorcade as it set out for City Hall were a joint garda and military motorcycle escort and an RTÉ vehicle, which carried a television cameraman to capture the occasion. The streets of Cork, busy with Saturday shoppers, paused briefly to cheer and wave as the cavalcade made its way down St Patrick's Street, on to Grand Parade, along South Mall, before arriving at the City Hall. Journalist Dick Brazil reported that the public reception through the streets was muted compared with the rapturous welcome afforded to

Éamon de Valera in Cobh, County Cork, on 11 July 1938, for the return of naval facilities from British forces. COURTESY *IRISH EXAMINER*

John F. Kennedy ten years earlier. This said, however, a large crowd of well-wishers did assemble at Cork City Hall to greet the President. Waiting to welcome the newly elected freeman, the first since the 1960s, was a sizeable crowd of citizens and the members of the Corporation, clad in their splendid robes of office.[34]

In keeping with tradition and ceremonial procedure, the President's entry to the hall was preceded by the members of Cork Corporation, while he himself was accompanied by the Lord Mayor, along with an entourage that included the Minister for Transport and Power, Peter Barry TD; Jack Lynch, leader of the opposition; and a number of high ranking gardaí and military officers. The hall was bathed in brilliant brightness, emanating from the lights of the television crews that had come to film the occasion for both British and Irish television. On entering the hall, the guest of honour was afforded a standing ovation as he made his way through the crowd towards the specially erected platform, the focal point of the ceremony.[35]

Roll call, the opening prayer and the minutes of the meeting (26 February) in which the President was elected a freeman of the city were read at the beginning of the ceremony. This was followed by the Lord Mayor's address, where Councillor O'Leary chronicled the service President de Valera had carried out for the Irish state, mentioning the 1916 Rising, preserving neutrality during the Second World War and the President's other achievements during his time as Taoiseach and President respectively. Referring to the fight for Irish independence from 1916 to 1930, the Lord Mayor commented, 'For your efforts on behalf of the Irish people in this period alone, you are most deserving of the freedom of the city.'[36] This was a sentiment further expressed in relation to de Valera's time as both Taoiseach and President, with the Lord Mayor advising that for services rendered in both of these positions de Valera would be a worthy recipient of the honour the city had bestowed upon him. In conclusion, the Lord Mayor once more welcomed the President to Cork and made reference to the many opportunities that the city of Cork had to welcome de Valera in the past, specifically reminding the assembled gathering that de Valera had officially opened the 'new' City Hall in 1936.[37] The President was then invited to reply to the Lord Mayor's speech.

Rising to speak, the President recalled how his first glimpse of Ireland was Cork, when the ship that bore him from America sailed into Cork harbour. He recounted that when he asked where he was, seeing the British flags flying over Forts Camden and Carlisle, he was told it was Queenstown (now Cobh), which was 'the first word I heard when I came to Ireland'.[38] It was therefore, with great satisfaction and joy that he was present when the port was returned to Irish control and the tri-colour replaced the British flag over Spike Island. The President then thanked the city for the honour it had bequeathed him, saying '*tá aoibhneas ar mo chroí an saoirse seo a fháil*' ('it delights my heart to receive this freedom'). Then, speaking openly and honestly, the President said that while he had received the freedom of a great number of cities, he did not feel he would ever receive the freedoms of either Cork or Dublin because there remained 'political questions'. Closing his oration, the President thanked the Christian Brothers in Charleville for his early education and the people of Cork for the honour they had awarded him – in the City Hall where he laid the foundation stone. The President was then invited to sign the register of honorary freemen and receive his scroll, encased in a silver casket made by Egans of Cork. The Lord Mayor remarked that the casket was 'an outstanding example of Cork craftsmanship', which carried a new and specially designed hallmark to signify Ireland's recent membership of the EEC.[39]

Thereafter, the ceremony finished and the President made his way to the Lord Mayor's office and then the council chambers for a modest reception and to meet the invited dignitaries, which included the Mayors of Limerick, Waterford and Clonmel; the Bishop of Cork, Cloyne and Ross; the President of University College Cork; the Chairman of Cork County Council; and the Cork County Manager. Before departing from Kent Station that evening, the President had one other engagement; he paid a visit to the Ursuline Convent in Blackrock and the nearby African Missions, where he used to attend mass on prior visits to Cork. At ten past six that evening, Éamon de Valera waved from the State coach as it entered the railway tunnel at Kent Station, bidding a final farewell to Cork as President of Ireland.[40]

ALOYS FLEISCHMANN

(1910–1992)

Elected as Freeman of Cork on 16 January 1978

Conferred as Freeman of Cork on 28 April 1978

> *'Teacher and composer, whose life and energies have been devoted to the development of music and art in the city of Cork, in appreciation of his great and unselfish work and dedication as Director and organiser of the Cork Choral Festival, the Cork Orchestral Orchestra and other institutions, and of his abiding affection and interest in the welfare of our nation and of the people of the city and county of Cork.'*

BIOGRAPHY

Aloys Fleischmann Sr, a Bavarian musician, married Cork-born Tilly Swertz (she was of German extraction) in his hometown of Dachau in September 1905. Aloys had met Tilly in the autumn of 1901 when she came to Dachau to visit relatives. The couple moved to Cork in 1906 where Fleischmann became organist and choirmaster at the Cathedral of St Mary and St Anne, succeeding Tilly's father in that role.[1] In the autumn of 1909, a pregnant Tilly Fleischmann – also a talented musician who gave piano recitals and taught – went to give a concert in Munich. She stayed in Munich for the following months and gave birth to Aloys Jr on 13 April 1910. It has been suggested that her lengthy stay in Munich was because she had a higher regard for the obstetrical skills of doctors in Germany than those in Ireland.[2] The family was united again in Cork in July of that year. As a baby, Aloys Jr was called Bubi (little lad) by his parents and friends but was always referred to as Alfi whenever he visited his father's hometown of Dachau.[3] In later life, Aloys Jr always bemoaned the location of his birth as he felt it interfered with his chances of being considered a native Corkonian.[4]

Aloys' happy childhood was disturbed by the outbreak of the First World War in 1914. Initially, the Fleischmanns were protected in Cork by influential Anglo-Irish friends but Aloys Sr was interned as an enemy alien from 1916 to 1919 in Oldcastle, County Meath, and then on the Isle of Man.[5] He was subsequently deported to Germany and only returned to Cork in the autumn of 1920, having been separated from his wife and young son for nearly five years.[6] One of his first cathedral services after his return was the requiem Mass for the Lord Mayor of Cork, Terence MacSwiney, who had died in October on hunger strike in Brixton Prison, London.[7]

From an early age, Aloys Jr demonstrated brilliance in the area of music. He shared his parents' sympathies for the Gaelic revival and, like them, took a keen interest in all aspects of contemporary Irish life.[8] Having studied with distinction in Christian Brothers College and at St Finbarr's College, Farranferris, he went to University College Cork (UCC), aged seventeen in 1927 to study music, English and German.[9] He received a first class honours BA in 1930, a BMus in 1931 and his MA in 1932 for a thesis entitled 'The Neums in Irish Liturgical Manuscripts'.[10] Later in 1932, he studied composition and conducting in Munich University under the renowned Joseph Haas, before returning to Leeside in 1934 to take up tenure as Professor of Music (initially as acting Professor) in UCC – a position he held for forty-six years until his retirement in 1980. When Fleischmann was made professor in UCC, he was just twenty-four years old and was the second youngest professor in the university (James Horgan became Professor of Law at twenty-three).

Fleischmann became the main driving force behind developing UCC's music department and he went on to found the Cork Symphony Orchestra. He remained with the orchestra for so many years – fifty-six in total – that it won an entry in the Guinness Book of Records.[11] Fleischmann was also co-founder, with Joan Denise Moriarty, of the Cork Ballet Company and he also established the Cork International Choral and Folk Dance Festival, staying as director for thirty-three years.

During his time in UCC, Professor Fleischmann notably helped to foster the careers of Seán Ó Riada, Tomás Ó Canainn and Micheál Ó Súilleabháin. In addition, he was a prolific composer of orchestral and choral works which have been performed in Ireland and abroad. Fleischmann was keenly aware of his position as one of the first groups of native composers to live and work in Ireland.[12] According to Séamas de Barra:

> He [Fleischmann] adopted an Irish pseudonym, Muiris Ó Rónáin, feeling that his German surname was inconsistent with his nationalist aspirations; he wrote songs to Irish texts; and he even persuaded Chester, who published his 1933 Piano Suite, to print all musical directions in Irish as well as Italian.[13]

In his later life, Fleischmann's immense contribution and lasting influence on Irish musical life was recognised through a series of awards and honours. Trinity College Dublin conferred him with the degree of Mus.D. *honoris causa* in 1964 and he received the Officer's Cross of the Order of Merit of the German Federal Republic in 1966.[14] In 1974, the President of Ireland, Erskine Childers, visited UCC's Department of Music to acknowledge Fleischmann's remarkable contribution to the development of music as a university subject.[15] Three years later Fleischmann was presented with the Silver Medallion of the Irish-American Cultural Institute and also with the UDT National Endeavour Award. In 1978 he was made a freeman of Cork.[16]

Fleischmann retired from UCC in 1980, aged seventy, but he was granted the title Emeritus Professor of Music and he continued to work tirelessly. His main work revolved around a research project that had been underway in the Department of Music for nearly three decades – a compilation, with analysis and thematic index, of all the printed sources of Irish traditional music from about 1600 to 1855.[17] He suffered a grave disappointment in 1989 when Irish National Ballet was abolished, leading him to write:

> *Perhaps in the third millennium, someone will again arise with the creative ability, the dedication and the stamina to awaken a lethargic public to the stimulation and delights of dance as a theatrical art form.[18]*

Fleischmann marked his eightieth birthday by once again demonstrating the indefatigable energy with which he lived his life. Accompanied by Senator John A. Murphy and others, he climbed Mount Brandon in Kerry, reportedly wearing a suit and tie hidden by rain gear.[19] Fleischmann was diagnosed with a serious illness in 1992 but he continued to work, refusing palliative medication to do so.[20] He completed the final draft of his magnus opus, 'Introduction to Sources of Irish Traditional Music' three days before he died on 21 July 1992, aged eighty-two. The work was published in New York in 1998.

In January 2010, President Mary McAleese opened celebrations organised by Cork City Council to mark the centenary of the birth of Aloys Fleischmann Jr. The Fleischmann Centenary programme was planned by the Cork City Council's Arts Office and former councillor Máirín Quill chaired the Fleischmann Working Group. In total, 226 commemorative events took place during the year, in all corners of Ireland and in five other countries.

FREEDOM OF CORK

In recognition of his lifetime's work for music in Ireland, Aloys Fleischmann Jr was conferred with the freedom of Cork on Friday 28 April 1978 at a special meeting of Cork Corporation. He had been nominated for the honour by Cork's first Jewish Lord Mayor, Gerald Goldberg. The *Cork Examiner* reported that the ceremony was a moving and colourful one and that the council chamber was packed to capacity, colourfully adorned with yellow and green floral harps and bouquets of flowers.[21] After City Manager Joe McHugh read the council resolution, Lord Mayor Goldberg paid a glowing tribute to Fleischmann. Describing him as a great man, he said that Fleischmann inspired everybody with whom he worked and that his name would always be honoured and treasured in the city. Tribute was also paid to Fleischmann's wife, Anne, and his six children before Cork's newest freeman signed the roll of honour and was presented with his silver casket, containing his scroll.

Fleischmann then addressed the crowd and stated that the honour bestowed upon him was far too generous and out of all proportion to the little he had contributed.[22] He soon turned his attention to one of his favourite subjects – the lack of money available for the promotion of the arts. He even

Professor Aloys Fleischmann (*right*) signs the freedom register on 28 April 1978 while City Manager Joe McHugh (*left*) and Lord Mayor Councillor Gerald Goldberg (*centre*) look on. COURTESY IRISH EXAMINER

found time to criticise the institution that was honouring him, stating that Cork Corporation's arts grant was 'comparatively small'.[23]

Fleischmann described as 'sheerest nonsense' the suggestion that Cork did not have an opera company or professional orchestra due to lack of money. He argued, 'It is not a question of money; it is a question of priorities. We spend £300 million on drink in this country per annum. If 1% of this was saved we would have the financial resources for a permanent opera company.'[24]

Warming to his task, Fleischmann joked that he was going to take full advantage of having a captive audience and he proceeded to criticise the fact that, in his opinion, there was not enough music education in schools. He closed his speech by praising the Lord Mayor and Lady Mayoress, saying:

> *They have been true patrons of the arts and have considerably enriched the city as a result. Cork city historically speaking has many different traditions – Irish, Viking, Norman, English and Jewish – and has a tapestry as rich in its ingredients as any city anywhere, enabling the young people to see visions and us older people to dream dreams.*[25]

Following the conferring ceremony there was a reception at which a specially commissioned portrait of Fleischmann at work in his study was unveiled.

BISHOP CORNELIUS LUCEY

(1902–1982)

Elected as Freeman of Cork on 4 November 1980

Conferred as Freeman of Cork on 19 December 1980

'That the freedom of the City of Cork be conferred on Most Rev. Dr Cornelius Lucey, former Bishop of Cork and Ross, in recognition of his outstanding service to the church and to the city of Cork as Bishop from 1952 to 1980, of his distinguished achievements as a sociologist renowned for his contributions to major issues of the day and particularly, in the sphere of faith and morals, as the first Irish bishop to inaugurate a diocesan foreign mission by adopting a parish in Peru as part of his diocese, as a great builder of schools and churches, as a pastor who preached the fundamental truths, and as a token of the affection and esteem in which he is held by all the people of the city and county of Cork.'

BIOGRAPHY

Cornelius Lucey, the outspoken bishop 'who for so many years ruled the spiritual lives of the people of Cork'[1] was seventy-eight years old when he was conferred with the freedom of his beloved city by the Lee. Born on 15 July 1902 at the family farm at Ballincollig in the parish of Ballinora, his educational path took him to the local national school, to the Presentation Brothers' College, to St Finbarr's Farranferris and to Maynooth College.[2] He graduated from Maynooth in 1927 with a BA degree and was ordained a priest that year also.[3] From there, Lucey went to Innsbruck University in Austria from 1927 to 1929 where he received his doctorate in theology before coming back to Ireland and earning an MA in University College Dublin in 1930.[4] For the next twenty years he held the chair of philosophy and political theory at Maynooth. During this period, Lucey became 'a recognised authority in Ireland and Britain on social questions and lectured in the US.'[5] He served on a government commission on population and emigration from 1948–1954 and showed his independent streak by writing a minority report 'which was a thinly veiled attack on civil servants for possessing too much power and influence over social and economic policy'.[6] Lucey also founded the Christus Rex society for priests and became the joint editor of its journal.[7]

In 1950, Lucey left Maynooth when he was appointed coadjutor to the Bishop of Cork, Daniel Cohalan.[8] The following year, Lucey was ordained Bishop of Cork (and later Bishop of Ross in 1958) and 'he quickly became a highly vocal member of the hierarchy and had forthright views on virtually everything'.[9]

The diocese of Cork inherited by the new bishop 'was growing in population, and particularly around Cork city'.[10] Lucey initiated an extensive building programme of churches and schools in the city's expanding suburbs.[11] His reputation, however, was forged not so much by his building programme but by his staunch public proclamations defending Catholic social teaching. His sermons, especially those at confirmation ceremonies, quickly acquired legendary status. Not only did he speak about matters of faith and morals, 'he also frequently sermonised on issues such as politics and the constitution of the state, the plight of small farmers, government economic policies, emigration, smoking, gambling, alcoholism, and industrial affairs'.[12] Bishop Lucey was not disturbed by controversy and commented once, 'I am not surprised or upset when people are against me. Sometimes, things are got all wrong and it is not right that people should be misled. I don't care what labels are put on me, I say what I think.'[13] In describing Lucey as an 'independent thinker', historian Diarmaid Ferriter warns that 'it would be simplistic to stereotype him as a myopic authoritarian'.[14]

While the public perception of Bishop Lucey was of a stern character, he had a sensitive side as well and 'was regarded with genuine affection by the ordinary people of Cork'.[15] He was 'an advocate of adoption before the political will existed for its facilitation'[16] and in 1954 he founded the St Anne's Adoption Society. Lucey was also heavily involved in the credit union movement, partly because he was determined 'to stamp out the scourge of moneylenders'.[17] He was especially exercised by emigration 'which he felt was more reprehensible and unnatural than partition'.[18] In addition, he spoke out publicly about the dangers of urbanisation and industrialisation and advocated a policy of decentralisation.[19]

Bishop Lucey had a huge personal commitment to the missions and in the mid-1960s 'adopted' four parishes of Trujillo in Peru as extra parishes into the diocese of Cork.[20] One of the most controversial chapters of his career came in 1968 when he barred the theologian Fr James Good from preaching in Cork, 'after Good had criticised the papal encyclical *Humanae Vitae*'.[21] Ferriter records that 'Good was subsequently dismissed from the chair of theology in University College Cork, though the two men were later reconciled'.[22]

Though he led a very full and active religious life, Bishop Lucey had many hobbies and he loved reading, gardening, speaking Irish and attending GAA matches, especially hurling. Interestingly, one of his primary passions was beekeeping; he was vice-president of the Federation of Beekeepers and a founder of the journal, the *Irish Beekeeper*.[23] It says a lot about Lucey that he chose not to devote his time to these leisurely pursuits after his retirement as Bishop of Cork in August 1980. Rather, in his late seventies, he volunteered for mission work in Kenya, desiring as he said 'to make reparation for my sins while I still have the time, not that I have been all that bad a sinner'.[24]

Ironically, during his two years in Turkana, Kenya, Bishop Lucey developed a close friendship with Fr James Good who had been working there for a number of years. In a 2008 article, Fr Good wrote:

I have vivid memories of Bishop Lucey saying Mass under a tree in one of the out-stations, struggling with the very difficult Turkana language, surrounded by a congregation of Turkana people sitting in the sand, most of them women feeding their babies.[25]

In the same article, Fr Good stated, 'In spite of our close relationship he never once referred to my suspension, though he did once say to me that I should go back to my own diocese. I believe that he deeply regretted the suspension but believed that he could not do anything about it.'[26]

Bishop Lucey died on 24 September 1982 in his beloved Cork city. Fr Good claims that Lucey had been suffering from leukaemia before he arrived in Kenya while Ferriter adds that he contracted malaria in the Turkana desert.[27] Bishop Lucey was laid to rest in the precincts of St Mary's Cathedral in Cork.

In 1985, Bishop Lucey was honoured when a park in Cork city centre – bounded by Grand Parade, Tuckey Street, South Main Street and Christ Church Lane – was officially opened by the Lord Mayor of Cork, Alderman Dan Wallace TD, and given the name 'Bishop Lucey Park.' The opening of the park was one of the events organised by Cork Corporation to celebrate 800 years of the city's status since being granted a charter in 1185.[28]

Bishop Cornelius Lucey remains an iconic figure in Cork. Ferriter concludes that his career was 'marked by courage, conviction, and conservatism'.[29] The insightful view of Canon Denis O'Connor, the former administrator of St Mary's Cathedral, is:

Not everybody cheered the points he made, but for all they were compulsive reading, deep truths, simply put in impeccable English. All his sermons and public addresses were written out by himself beforehand and every one contained something fresh and worthwhile.[30]

FREEDOM OF CORK

Five months after his retirement as Bishop of Cork, Lucey was elected as a freeman of Cork city (along with the former Taoiseach, Jack Lynch) at a special meeting of Cork Corporation on 4 November 1980. In the original minutes of the meeting, just seven councillors were named in support of the motion. This was subsequently clarified at a meeting of the corporation on 10 November when the motion was re-stated and passed unanimously with an order that the minutes reflect the fact that there were no dissenting voices.[31]

The conferring ceremony for Bishop Lucey and Jack Lynch took place in a packed Concert Hall (in the City Hall) on 19 December 1980. The Lord Mayor, Alderman Toddy O'Sullivan, described the granting of the freedom of the city as a 'rare and distinguished privilege'[32] and said that the occasion was unique in that, for the first time, two men were being honoured in a joint ceremony.

Bishop Cornelius Lucy signs the freedom register on 19 December 1980. COURTESY *IRISH EXAMINER*

Cork's newest freeman Bishop Cornelius Lucey accepts a standing ovation in Cork City Hall. COURTESY *IRISH EXAMINER*

Writing in *The Irish Times*, Dick Hogan noted:

For the 2,000 or so people who packed City Hall, the ceremony marked the end of an era, and few who were present yesterday could doubt that both men, each in his own sphere, packed a weighty punch and commanded the kind of respect and loyalty that can only be described as intense.[33]

The Lord Mayor gave an account of Bishop Lucey's career, highlighting his long service, his outspoken statements on many problems and his work on behalf of the poor and underprivileged. He praised him for founding the St Anne's Adoption Society and his instrumental role in introducing Cork to the credit union movement. In particular, the Lord Mayor complimented Bishop Lucey on the 'extraordinary step'[34] of adopting the four parishes of Trujillo in Peru into the diocese of Cork. In ending his speech, the Lord Mayor posed the question, 'Could it be that it is here (Peru) that Bishop Lucey's most lasting memorial is being built daily?'[35] On behalf of the corporation and the people of Cork, the Lord Mayor then presented Bishop Lucey with a silver casket containing the scroll of the freedom of the city.

Having accepted the casket and signed the freedom roll, Bishop Lucey replied, 'This is really one of the greatest moments of my life.'[36] He added that it was a particular honour to receive the freedom of Cork as:

Cork is no run of the mill city. It is a city of distinction. It is a city of character with its own accent and charm. It is a growing and busy city. It is a city to be proud of. Cork is my own place and its people my own people. For me, there is no place like Cork and no people like Cork people.[37]

In delivering his speech, Bishop Lucey spoke modestly and asserted that he had received credit for the churches and schools built in and around Cork over the last thirty years but that the praise 'should in all fairness go to others'.[38] In this regard, he highlighted the people who had provided the money for the buildings and the public authorities who had accommodated the church with suitable sites. He added, 'Nowhere that I have been have I seen council houses as good as the council houses in Cork.'[39]

Bishop Lucey concluded his speech, not untypically, by making a couple of recommendations to the members of Cork Corporation. He called for more trees in and around the city, 'in particular a few groves of chestnut trees where the youth of Cork can get their supply each year for the chessie season'.[40] He offered to pay for the trees once the corporation planted them. Secondly, Bishop Lucey asked the councillors to consider 'a city master street from Shandon on the north via the Grand

Parade to, roughly, the Red Abbey on the south side'.[41]

After Bishop Lucey's speech, the freedom of Cork was conferred on Jack Lynch, who stated:

> *For me the honour is enhanced in that I share this day and this ceremony with Most Rev. Dr Lucey, Bishop of Cork and Ross for so many years, whose steadfastness, courage and dedication to the material as well as the moral well-being of his flock have set him apart as one of the outstanding members of the Irish hierarchy in this country.*[42]

At the end of the joint ceremony, both new freemen received a sustained standing ovation.

JACK LYNCH

(1917–1999)

Elected as Freeman of Cork on 4 November 1980

Conferred as Freeman of Cork on 19 December 1980

by Pádraig Mac Consaidín

'That the freedom of the city of Cork be conferred on Mr Jack Lynch, BL, LL D, formerly Taoiseach and head of successive governments of the Republic of Ireland from 1966 to 1973 and from 1977 to 1979; one time chairman of the Council of Ministers of the Council of the European Community, Teachta Dála for the constituency of Cork City since 1948; exemplar and upholder of the democratic rights of man and rule of law, who devoted himself to the establishment of a better way of life for his fellow countrymen, to the fullest expression of the Irish ideal and culture at home and abroad, whose sincerity, dedication and unselfish devotion to his people, his country and his fellow citizens, whose wise counsel, dignified restraint, firmness and humility, at all times, placed him in the forefront of great leaders and endeared him, not only to those of his friends who knew him best but also to the nations of the world among whom he is loved and respected and admired; sportsman extraordinary and holder of the greatest awards which can be won in the field of Irish national games; as a Corkman Jack Lynch has brought honour to the City of his birth and has set a goal for all Irishmen to follow for generations to come. For all this and much more.'

BIOGRAPHY

On the second floor of a corner house, practically under the bells of the landmark Cork clock-tower known as the 'four faced liar', on 15 August 1917[1] one of Cork city's most famous sporting and political figures was born. The family home of Dan and Nora Lynch in St Anne's Churchyard, Shandon, which still stands to this day, bears a plaque honouring the birthplace of their son, John Mary Lynch; he is more commonly referred to in the annals of Irish history as Jack Lynch. The Lynch family moved to this well-appointed property, owned by Nora's grandmother, from their first home a short distance away at 67 Dominick Street,[2] in an area of Cork that was severely disadvantaged and where many of Cork city's citizens lived in 'undesirable conditions'.[3] Despite being raised surrounded by, but not living in, poverty,[4] Jack Lynch recalled; 'We were comfortable enough for the time. There was always enough on the table, and we were well-dressed with our father a tailor.'[5]

Jack, the youngest of the Lynch boys, had a reputation as a 'wilder', known to 'get away with murder at home'.[6] As free-spirited as he may have been, Jack had a close relationship with his mother, Nora, who was known to bring some of her children to the Cork Opera House on Thursday nights to witness the Abbey Theatre players perform or hear some variety of concert or other. However, it was with Jack that she shared her love of music in particular,[7] a passion he held for the rest of his life and an affinity with the Cork Opera House he would never forget. This close relationship with his mother meant Jack was deeply affected by the tragic and unexpected passing of Nora when he was just fifteen. Jack was at home when a nurse from the North Infirmary Hospital, which was located around the corner from the family home, knocked on the door to deliver the fateful news. Many years later, Jack summed up his feelings at the time, 'I was absolutely shattered. I walked around the streets in a daze for hours before coming back home and for years later I was deeply affected by the loss.'[8] Despite the tragedy, Dan Lynch managed to keep the family together and having completed his Primary Certificate, Jack competed for a Cork Corporation scholarship for his second level education in the Christian Brothers-run North Monastery School. With only ten scholarships available, Lynch was tied for the tenth and final scholarship but, as luck would have it, the corporation made an additional grant available so that both boys who tied for the final position each received a scholarship.[9]

Despite his reputation as a 'wilder' in his younger days, Lynch was a model student. It was while attending the North Monastery that Jack's prowess on the playing field came to the fore. Lining out in both hurling and football, Lynch played with the North Monastery, his local club Glen Rovers and her sister club St Nicholas' Football Club. Having progressed through the underage ranks, Jack made his senior hurling debut for Glen Rovers in the 1934 county championship semi-final against Seandún. The following year he commenced his inter-county career with Cork in a national League game against Limerick, lining up directly opposite the legendary Mick Mackey.[10]

In 1936, Jack sat his Leaving Certificate examinations. Unsure of his career path, he also sat examinations for the civil service, teacher training college and the Electricity Supply Board. However, in a fortunate turn of events, his brother Finbarr became aware of a temporary position in the Dublin District Milk Board. Coincidentally, the chairman of the Board was also the chairman of the Civil Service Hurling Club, which was on the lookout for new talent. Jack Lynch, Cork hurler, was ideal for the position.

Lynch accepted the temporary position but, not long after, moved to the civil service in Dublin when he was offered a job there. His sojourn in Dublin seemed destined to become a long-term arrangement but this was not the case. As it turned out, by December 1936 Lynch was home, assigned to the court service in the State Solicitor's Offices in Cork.[11] For the next several years, Jack worked in the circuit court, developing a knowledge of and interest in law and legal proceedings[12] that would ultimately lead him to University College Cork to study law. When Lynch registered in 1941, he made up one half of the law class in University College Cork for that year; he continued his legal studies later in King's Inns[13] in order to become a barrister.

During this time, as he worked for the courts service and continued his education, Jack remained a feature of the Cork senior hurling and intermediate football teams as well as lining out for his beloved club, Glen Rovers. One of the proudest moments of his inter-county career was possibly in 1939 when he was made captain of the Cork hurling team, the first to reach an All-Ireland final in eight years. Though Cork lost the game, the match has gone down in GAA folklore as one of the most memorable in history. Played on the day war was declared in Europe[14] and in stormy conditions that were almost unplayable,[15] the game has been more commonly referred to since as the 'thunder and lightning' final, due to the inclement weather conditions.[16]

Jack Lynch was more than simply a hurler and footballer though, he was an athlete. On one occasion, Lynch played three matches in a single day – first, he played for the civil service in the morning, then in a Railway Cup hurling semi-final that afternoon, before finally lining out for the Munster footballers in the evening. He scored in all three games.[17] Lynch was a member of the Cork team that won the historic four-in-a-row All-Irelands beginning in 1941 and was selected as captain once more in 1942. When Cork missed out on the opportunity for their fifth successive All-Ireland title in 1945 it was still a successful year for Lynch who helped the county footballers to All-Ireland glory over Cavan and, in the process, ended a thirty-four-year famine for the Sam Maguire cup in the county. The following year, Jack won his fifth and final All-Ireland hurling medal, though he would contest one more All-Ireland final before he retired. Glen Rovers were once more crowned Cork county hurling champions in 1950 with Jack in the starting team, though this was to be the end of his competitive career as a hurler and footballer.[18] Declining an invitation to play once more with the club in 1951, Jack Lynch brought down the curtain on an illustrious playing career that yielded five All-Ireland hurling medals, one All-Ireland football medal, ten county senior hurling medals, two county senior football medals and a Dublin senior football title with the civil service.[19] This roll of honour will always see Jack Lynch remembered as one of the GAA greats; today, his impressive medal collection is on display in the GAA Museum in Croke Park, Dublin.[20]

Personal reasons meant 1943 was an important year in the life of Jack Lynch for it was then he would meet his future wife, Máirín. From Dublin, Máirín was holidaying with a friend in Glengarriff, County Cork. Máirín met and developed an interest in the future Taoiseach, unaware of his sporting fame and achievements. However, before the courtship developed into something more serious, Máirín's mother, an administrator with the Irish Industrial Development Association, subjected Jack to the 'buy Irish' test, in keeping with her steadfast belief in supporting Irish businesses. On their first meeting, Mrs O'Connor offered to take the young man's hat, to see if it was foreign or Irish made – Jack passed the test. Not only was his hat Irish, it was made in Cork by T. O'Gorman's Cork Cap Factory, located at the time across the road from the old Lynch family home in Shandon.[21] Indeed, Jack remained a patron of many Cork businesses his entire life; O'Gorman's for his hats and Fitzgerald's on St Patrick's Street for his shirts.

Jack and Máirín were wed in 1946 and began their life as a married couple in Cork, renting a small flat on the South Mall while Jack was forging a career as a recently qualified barrister. Jack's status as a sporting icon ensured a trail of political suitors calling to his door but he was not to enter the political arena until the general election of 1948.[22] Standing for Fianna Fáil in the Cork Borough Constituency, Lynch was the second candidate to be returned on the eleventh count of a closely contested ballot.[23] When the Dáil reconvened soon after, Fianna Fáil had lost power to a multi-party coalition and Jack Lynch entered the national parliament as an opposition backbench Teachta Dála (TD).[24] Between 1948 and 1951, Lynch established a reputation as an effective parliamentarian, contributing to national debate on many issues while also bringing problems that faced his constituency in Cork to national attention. Two such matters were emigration and youth unemployment, which would also play a prominent role in the subsequent 1951 general election, following the fall of the coalition government amid the Mother and Child controversy.[25]

That 1951 election was to be another successful campaign for Jack Lynch; Fianna Fáil, supported by a number of independents, formed the new government on 13 June 1951, with Éamon de Valera as Taoiseach.[26] Lynch, arriving at Leinster House for the meeting of the new Dáil was summoned by de Valera who informed him that he was to be appointed parliamentary secretary with special responsibility for the Gaeltacht and Congested Districts.[27] Lynch committed himself to the added duties with his usual diligence, while also attending meetings of Cork Corporation as often as he possibly could in his capacity as Alderman from 1950 until his resignation in 1957.[28] Before he was to resign from the corporation, however, Lynch faced into his third general election in six years.

From 1954, he had to be content once more with a seat on the opposition benches, while also returning to Cork in an attempt to revive his legal career. Though his spell as an Alderman was relatively short, in reality Lynch was more effective as a national parliamentarian than as an elected member of local government. Despite being in opposition, Jack continued to question the then government on issues that affected the nation and his borough in Cork, garnering a reputation as a strong constituency advocate.[29]

Elected once more in the 1957 general election, Lynch received a call from the Taoiseach while working in his office on St Patrick's Day; he was to make his way to Dublin at his earliest convenience. It was during this meeting that Lynch was offered his first ministry, though it would take two further meetings and consultation with Máirín before he would accept. This promotion signalled an end to Lynch's career at the bar and his position on Cork Corporation. Lynch brought a range of skills and experience to the position of Minister for Education. As a young man, a former civil servant and a fluent Irish speaker, Lynch was afforded a warm welcome by those in his new department, especially his Private Secretary, Jim Dukes (father of the future Fine Gael leader, Alan Dukes), with whom he developed both a strong working and personal relationship. Lynch did not remain in the ministry for a great deal of time but probably the most substantive impact he had during his stewardship was removing the marriage bar on employing married women as teachers at primary level.[30]

A number of events conspired in 1959 that would see Lynch change ministries. Dr Ken Whitaker, secretary of the Department of Finance, had penned his Economic Development document, the forerunner to the White Paper on Economic Expansion. De Valera had stepped down as Taoiseach, to be elected President, with Seán Lemass becoming Taoiseach. Recognising the need to address Ireland's stagnant economy, Lemass appointed the erudite Lynch to the key ministry of Industry and Commerce to assist in the implementation of his and Whitaker's plan to develop the Irish economy and adopt a policy of free trade.

During his tenure as Minister for Industry and Commerce, Lynch was also keen to extol the virtues of Cork as a destination for new industry in Ireland while assisting with the expansion of existing companies in the county. This was evident in Lynch's speech at the opening of the Whitegate Oil Refinery in September of 1959 when he spoke of Irish Steel's expansion, the imminent arrival of Goulding's fertiliser plant and the new airport, which was still under construction. Lynch promised that the future of Cork in terms of employment was becoming more attractive. Another matter Lynch alluded to during his speech was the Cork Opera House rebuilding project.[31] This project was close to Jack's heart – no doubt remembering the days his late mother would bring him to see shows at the theatre – and he sought to help the project as best he could. In all, Lynch served as Minister for Industry and Commerce from 1959–1965, where he toiled to change a department which knew nothing but protectionism. He began the tentative steps of preparing Ireland for membership of the then EEC, while gaining experience and making allies that would be invaluable to him in years to come.

The year 1965 saw another general election and Fianna Fáil once more returned to government, this time winning seventy-two seats in the new Dáil.[32] Lemass used the opportunity when forming his new government to promote younger members of the party to key positions. One promotion, though not of the new generation, was Jack Lynch to the finance portfolio.[33] Here, Lynch would work closely with Ken Whitaker and further develop a relationship and friendship he would call upon later at critical junctures in the nation's history. Lynch's early months in his new assignment were challenging to say the least. The national finances were in disarray and requesting his ministerial colleagues to cut expenditure was one of the first tasks Lynch undertook as minister. In the following months, he would introduce a budget that would endear him to neither his government colleagues nor the people of Ireland. But Lynch did what was required of him, though it would not be enough to stem a growing deficit that would require a supplementary budget and intense confrontations with some members of cabinet.[34] It could be argued that Lynch did not have adequate time as Minister in the Department of Finance to effect the necessary changes to the national finances; however, in late 1966 a challenge of a new kind presented itself to the Shandon native.

Lemass implied prior to the 1965 general election that it may be the last he would lead his party in to. The financial difficulties of the state, along with defiant younger members of the party meant that by late 1966, Lemass was ready to hand over the mantle of leadership to a successor. Sensing an impending change in leadership, Charles Haughey and George Colley bolstered support for a possible contest, even before Lemass had officially resigned his position. Possibly bearing this in mind and keen to avoid a power struggle within the party, Lemass favoured an agreed successor and he wanted Jack Lynch.

At that point in time, a leadership contest was seen as a two-horse race between Haughey and Colley but Lynch allowed his name to go forward and was elected leader of the party and, by extension, Taoiseach. Before Lynch took control of the affairs of state, he first returned to Cork and a hero's welcome. The first Corkman to become Taoiseach in the history of the state, he was greeted by large crowds – bands roused the crowds with musical renditions and the processional route was illuminated by bonfires and burning tar barrels,[35] reminiscent of when a young Jack Lynch caught his first glimpse of political campaigning in 1932 when de Valera held a rally in Blackpool and Shandon.[36] Indeed, Lynch took de Valera's old route to enter the city; down Dublin Hill, past the Glen Rovers Hall, up Gerald Griffin Street before descending Shandon Street, across the river Lee and into the city centre.[37] This route unquestionably held more sentiment for Lynch than de Valera; he was travelling through the areas where he grew up. The 'wilder' from St Anne's Churchyard was returning home, the conquering political hero, leader of his country.

In the context of his predecessors and, indeed, some of his successors, Lynch was a modern leader and modernising Taoiseach.[38] Yet his time as Taoiseach would be challenging; within two years of taking leadership he faced the threat of a resurgent Irish Republican Army and subsequent fragmentation of Northern Ireland under violence, which ironically began from a campaign seeking civil rights. Though the tragedy of the Northern Ireland situation had been foreseen by Lynch, his government was ill-prepared when the warnings became reality. Despite this criticism, Lynch was unwavering in his commitment to democratic institutions, as illustrated during the arms crisis. When presented with evidence that senior ministers were involved in a plot to import arms for distribution in Northern Ireland, they were removed by Lynch. Their overnight sackings will be remembered as one of the most significant acts in the history of the state.[39] The Northern Ireland issue is, without question, the single greatest matter that dominated Jack Lynch's time as Taoiseach, therefore, perhaps his greatest legacy from this period was preserving peace on the island of Ireland as a whole. Lynch also realised a process he helped begin in the early 1960s in his capacity as Minister for Industry and Commerce, which he continued as Minister for Finance and completed as Taoiseach; Ireland's accession to the EEC.

Lynch's reign as leader of Fianna Fáil also proved challenging. An unprecedented building boom during the period offered opportunities for large profit-making for both speculators and building developers. Fianna Fáil, in government since 1957, contained within its ranks a number of ministers who exuded arrogance. Others grew uneasy at the relationships that were forming between government ministers and the building industry. Lynch, recognising this growing association, decided that the process of political donations to the party needed to be made transparent. According to

Des Hanafin who became the controller of the fundraising operation, Lynch had no hesitation in returning any donation he felt could be compromising to the party.[40] Another challenge Lynch faced as party leader was how to deal with insubordinate senior members of the party, often government ministers. He encountered these issues too often as Taoiseach during a critical period in the state's history, from the Haughey-Boland-Blaney disorganised leadership challenge of 1971 and the unruly Árd Fheis, to the arms crisis and the political fallout thereafter.[41] Also during this period, Fianna Fáil, though a formidable campaign force at election time, was in need of modernisation as a party. Lynch began this undertaking during the party's period in opposition from 1973 to 1977 but despite any reforms he would subsequently make – as a result of the 1977 general election when he returned to power – both he and his party would ultimately be held responsible for the type of auction politics that exemplify general elections in Ireland today.[42]

During his time as Taoiseach, Lynch continued to travel to Cork as much as possible and often holidayed with Máirín at the couple's retreat near Ballydehob in west Cork. One instance that demonstrates Jack's bond with his native city can be seen in his dedication to saving Skiddy's alms-house in Shandon. Standing only yards from where Lynch was born, the building was destined to be demolished. On hearing this, he took a personal interest in the matter, assigning the parliamentary secretary of the Department of Finance to report to him on developments concerning the issue and hold public hearings on the matter. Lynch's intervention in the process eventually saved the building from destruction and he was present at its reopening some years later.[43]

On 5 December 1979 Jack Lynch resigned as Taoiseach and leader of Fianna Fáil. His decision followed months of disquiet within the party and further attempts to remove him as leader. A catalyst to Lynch's decision may have been the loss of two by-elections, when even *The Irish Times* intimated that Lynch was no longer the political power he once was.[44] Despite his modest and unassuming manner, these setbacks must have been difficult to endure for the man Liam Cosgrave, leader of the opposition, once described as the most popular politician in Ireland since Daniel O'Connell.[45] Lynch embraced his retirement and stepped back completely from national politics. He remained active in business and sporting endeavours, serving as a director for a number of companies and as President of the Glen Rovers Hurling Club. He continued to travel to Cork, often entertaining guests at the Lynch holiday home in west Cork.

Lynch and his wife also continued to travel extensively, visiting Russia, China, Turkey and their favourite destination, Italy. Lynch's death in 1999 left Cork with a sense of great loss for their native son, their 'real' Taoiseach. Thousands attended his funeral at the North Cathedral in Shandon, with many thousands more lining the route of his funeral procession through the city to St Finbarr's Cemetery. Jack Lynch's memorial stone in the cemetery holds the inscription, 'Happy is the man who finds wisdom'. Jack Lynch found more than wisdom during his years, he found success in almost everything he undertook.

FREEDOM OF CORK

Jack Lynch was elected as a freeman of Cork, along with the recently retired Bishop of Cork, Cornelius Lucey, at a meeting of Cork Corporation on 4 November 1980 – although the nominations had to go again before the meeting on 10 November due to a confusion about the earlier procedure when only seven councillors were present (see the profile of Bishop Lucey). The conferring ceremony was held in Cork's City Hall on 19 December 1980 and the Lord Mayor, Alderman Toddy O'Sullivan, began by commenting on the fact that history was being made as 'the badge of freeman was being conferred on two great Corkmen'.[46]

The conferring of Bishop Lucey was first and then the Lord Mayor spoke in tribute to Jack Lynch. He said that there were certain key words which could be used to set out Lynch's career and he proceeded to list 'North Monastery', 'Glen Rovers' and 'Politics'.[47] Lord Mayor O'Sullivan then highlighted Lynch's unique distinction of winning six senior All-Ireland medals in a row, for hurling in 1941, 1942, 1943, 1944 and 1946 and football in 1945. Chronicling Lynch's political career, the Lord Mayor praised him especially for leading Ireland into the EEC.

He concluded by linking Lynch's sporting and political skills, saying that, as a player, Lynch was 'clean, skilful, and determined' and that as a politician he also exhibited these characteristics and had always 'acted with dignified restraint, firmness, humour, and humility'.[48]

Rising to accept the honour, Jack Lynch addressed the estimated crowd of 2,000 people and delivered a typically eloquent and humble speech which drew a minute-long standing ovation at its conclusion. He began by saying:

> In olden times, I understood when the freedom of the city was conferred one was given the keys of the city. Even if there were no city gates to unlock the keys were regarded as symbolic. Apart from the very high honour they signify, the keys are more than just symbols. They are in fact real keys, real in the sense that they do fulfill the function of keys; they unlock the box of one's memories. Memories that are today unlocked for me are very special ones, which now that I look back upon them, help me to realise how much Cork has shaped me.[49]

He then reserved special praise for his wife, Máirín, for her 'influence, courage and support'[50] before paying tribute to the men he had played with and against on the GAA pitches of Ireland, adding, 'they have all left their mark on me and I use that phrase in both senses'.[51] Lynch stated that his contentment on this day stemmed from being back in a place that was a safe harbour for ships. Maintaining the theme, and with an apparent reference to decentralisation, he commented, 'Perhaps when I was at the helm of the ship of state I should have steered it here to permanent anchorage'.[52]

Lynch ended his speech by saying that the day was enhanced for him by virtue of the fact that he was sharing the conferring ceremony with Bishop Lucey; he then praised the Lord Mayor and the members of Cork Corporation:

You, Lord Mayor, have already distinguished yourself in the high office you hold and you deserve the esteem in which, I know, you are held by the citizens. The fact that you, a member of a political party other than my own, initiated and proposed the conferring of this honour makes me doubly indebted to you, as well as to the Aldermen and councillors of all parties and of none.[55]

Jack Lynch will always be remembered as a scholar, sportsman, politician, leader, peace-maker, devoted husband and freeman of Cork.

Facing page: Jack Lynch signs the freedom register in Cork City Hall on 19 December 1980.
COURTESY *IRISH EXAMINER*

THOMAS 'TIP' O'NEILL

(1912–1994)
Elected as Freeman of Cork on 11 February 1985
Conferred as Freeman of Cork on 16 March 1985

by Pádraig Mac Consaidín

'In recognition of his outstanding achievements over many years in the political life of his native country, in testimony of the honour which he brings to Ireland, the country of his ancestors, through his love for this country and its people, an affection which he continually demonstrates through his work and actions on our behalf and for his steadfast belief in and concern for democracy at home and in all parts of the world especially where freedom and human rights are under threat.'

BIOGRAPHY

'I knew I was Irish even before I knew I was American.'[1] Tip O'Neill was born into an American-Irish family on 9 December 1912 – his father was a mason and local organiser and a member of the Cambridge Elks Lodge, Knights of Columbus and the Democratic Party. His mother, a homemaker, passed away while he was still an infant, her dying wishes that the family not be divided. Thomas P. O'Neill Jr, or 'Tip' as he was more commonly known, grew up to become a giant of American politics. He was a colossus who brushed shoulders, and in some instances locked horns, with US Presidents Dwight D. Eisenhower, John F. Kennedy, Lyndon B. Johnson, Gerald Forde, Jimmy Carter and Ronald Reagan. An emissary of the United States of America, he carried his nation's message to Mikhail Gorbachev and the Soviet Union during the Cold War. However, despite his exalted position, O'Neill remained a champion of working people throughout, truly believing politics and government could make a difference in people's lives.[2]

Tip was educated in the local Catholic school and because his father was keen that his children would also maintain links to their Irish heritage, the O'Neill children were enrolled in a 'Gaelic School', which held classes on Sunday afternoons. There, the children learned Irish language phrases, songs and step dances. During his spell in the 'Gaelic School', O'Neill was taught by the sister-in-law of Terence MacSwiney. However, after the death of MacSwiney, O'Neill was no longer welcome at the school. This was due to Mrs MacSwiney's reservations about not only O'Neill's but other children's claims to be Irish, as their parents were born in America and not Ireland. Such people were referred to at the time as 'narrowbacks'.[3]

O'Neill went on to attend St John's High School in Cambridge where, by his own admission, he was never the best student in the class. He was, however, recognised as a talented debater, taking a position on the school's team. One nun stated O'Neill could 'talk you deaf, dumb and blind'. O'Neill earned a reputation as a likeable fellow while at school, where he also developed an appreciation for sport. O'Neill would spend much of his free time playing or watching athletics, while also enjoying basketball, baseball, football and golf. Indeed, he was even in a position to profit from his leisure pursuits, working as a caddy at the Arlmount Country Club.[4]

Following his graduation from high school, O'Neill secured employment with a construction company as a truck driver. This contrasted greatly with his siblings who both enjoyed success academically. His brother attended Harvard Law School on scholarship and his sister became a teacher and later the first female principal in the Cambridge public school system. O'Neill's education was to continue though – one day while driving his truck he was noticed by one of his former teachers, Sr Agatha, who knew that while he had not been the best student in the class, he still had the potential to be more than simply a truck driver who loitered with friends in his spare time. O'Neill later recounted Sr Agatha saying to him, 'Thomas, you should be going to college to make something of yourself.' Thereafter, O'Neill enrolled in Boston College where he studied a number of subjects such as mathematics, Latin, history and English. While a senior at college, O'Neill also ran for a seat on the Cambridge City Council, one of the forty-eight candidates for eight seats – he polled ninth. This was O'Neill's first attempt to run for an elected position; it was the only election he ever lost.[5] Though, as he states himself, it was not his first foray into politics: this began in 1928 when he worked for Al Smith's presidential campaign.[6]

O'Neill believed he learned his most important political lesson in the last days of his first campaign. One of his neighbours advised him that she would vote for him, though he had not asked her to. O'Neill was surprised at this, believing that he did not have to ask for a vote but his neighbour reassured him that people like to be asked and, indeed, thanked for their vote. This once more underlines why O'Neill placed so much emphasis on the motto 'all politics is local'. As if to emphasise the point, before leaving the house every polling day, O'Neill would ask his wife Millie for her vote – he would say, 'Honey, I'd like your vote.' To which Millie would reply, 'Tom, I'll give you every consideration.'[7] In 1937, O'Neill began the first of his fifty years in public service. He built for himself a reputation as an independent-minded legislator, known for his hard work and integrity. It was a reputation that would see him re-elected a number of times and to serve a total of sixteen years in the Massachusetts House of Representatives. In 1952 O'Neill was elected to Congress for the first time, retaining the seat for the Democrats after the incumbent had vacated the seat to run for the Senate.[8] The incumbent in question was John F. Kennedy, who O'Neill befriended. (Though not a man given to rumour and conjecture, O'Neill was highly sceptical of the official Warren Report into the 1963 Kennedy assassination, having heard first-hand accounts of events in Dallas from those who were with Kennedy the day he was shot.[9])

To try and catalogue the accomplishments of a man who served in the US House of Representatives for thirty-four years is a daunting task. There are many highlights of a long and distinguished career worth mentioning though. In 1958, O'Neill – along with Edward Boland – introduced legislation that led to the establishment of the Cape Cod National Seashore. In 1970, O'Neill co-sponsored a reform bill that ended the practice of unrecorded voting in the US House of Representatives: this meant Congressmen were now accountable to their constituents for their actions in the House. In 1971, O'Neill became the Majority Whip and part of the House leadership. Two years later, he became the Majority Leader, where he played a key role in the impeachment of President Richard Nixon in 1974. O'Neill became the Speaker of the House in 1977 and retained the position until 1987, the longest continuous term of the Speakership in the history of the United States of America. During the 1980s, O'Neill was seen domestically as the man who ensured the excesses of the Reagan Revolution were kept in check. During this period he championed the cause of the aged and less advantaged citizens, when social programmes to help these members of society came under threat of massive scale backs from the Reagan administration. O'Neill decided against running for a further term in 1986 and retired from public life in 1987.[10]

In retirement, O'Neill wrote his autobiography, *Man of the House*, which became a national best-seller. He appeared in numerous television commercials and public service announcements on the subject of colon cancer, an illness from which he suffered late in his life. Boston College remained close to his heart. He worked tirelessly on behalf of the college out of a debt of gratitude he felt towards the institution, for the opportunities it afforded him as a result of his education there. The esteem in which Boston College holds one of its favourite alumni is clear to see and O'Neill's legacy lives on to this day – the library at the college is named after him, along with a scholarship, a distinguished citizenship award and an endowed position in the Political Science Department. Tip O'Neill passed away on 5 January 1994. An American-Irish descendent of Cork who achieved political greatness in the most powerful nation in the world, O'Neill is remembered as a beloved Speaker of the House, a prominent and powerful champion of the working classes and as a man who loved people most of all.[11]

FREEDOM OF CORK

Anticipation ordinarily reserved for the arrival of All-Ireland winning Cork hurling or football teams gripped Kent Railway Station, Cork, on Saturday afternoon, 16 March 1985. The City Manager, Thomas McHugh, waited patiently on the platform for the next scheduled arrival at platform one. Then, shortly after four o'clock a familiar sound echoed from the railway tunnel that marks the entrance to Cork's main rail terminal. The short, sharp, blast of the klaxon signalled the appearance of the train carrying the Speaker of the United States House of Representatives, Tip O'Neill, along with a large party of Congressmen, their wives and a potent security detail. Irish, American and British journalists covering Speaker Tip O'Neill's sentimental return to his roots prepared to document the occasion that was about to unfold. Following the official greeting by the City Manager on the station's platform, the visiting party made its way to the waiting transport. They were then whisked to Cork City Hall under official garda escort for the freedom of Cork ceremony. Awaiting the distinguished guests at the doors of City Hall were Cork's first citizen, the Lord Mayor, Alderman Liam Burke TD, and his wife the Lady Mayoress, Noreen Burke.[12]

The ceremony in the main concert hall was a colourful affair. The members of Cork Corporation, wearing their official red robes of office, were joined in the concert hall by 300 guests as they awaited the commencement of the event. The assembled mass rose as Speaker Tip O'Neill entered the hall accompanied by the Lord Mayor and City Manager. They were led to the stage by the mace bearers to take their seats for the proceedings. Opening the ceremony, the Lord Mayor read the special motion which conferred the freedom of the city of Cork on Thomas P. O'Neill Jr, citing the various reasons the ancient honour was being bequeathed to the esteemed guest. Following the reading of the motion, O'Neill was then invited to reply to the Lord Mayor and address the capacity attendance. The audience, which included two bishops, the Minister for Foreign Affairs, Ministers of State, local TDs and Senators, MEPs and visiting members of Congress from the United States, waited in anticipation to hear the oration from the man who held the title of Mr Speaker. He began by saying, 'I am now a Corkman … I want to tell you I have been a Corkman all my life. I learned at my grandfather's knee that there are two classes of people, those from Cork and those who wished they were.'

The Speaker, who had earlier said the honour being bestowed upon him was the biggest thing to ever happen to him, described how, on the train journey to Cork he knew he was home once the train came to a stop in Mallow. It was undeniably an emotional and special event in the life of the Speaker when the famous statesman alighted from the train in Mallow during its scheduled stop and kissed the ground to spontaneous applause from both those on the platform and the remaining passengers on the train. The Speaker said he felt a special sense of joy in returning home.[13] Continuing on, O'Neill declared that being granted the freedom of the city of Cork was indeed a special honour for him, not least because his good friend, predecessor in the US House of Representatives and later President of the United States, John F. Kennedy, received the honour on his visit in 1963. On the subject of previous recipients, the Speaker commented on the fact that only five Americans, including himself, had ever received the award, Presidents Woodrow Wilson and John F. Kennedy, Cardinal Cushing and Mayor Pat Collins of Boston. He went on to point out that four of the recipients were from Massachusetts.[14] On the subject of his home state at another juncture in his speech, the Speaker remarked that having met with the councillors of the corporation earlier in the day, whose names were familiar to him because they were the same names as those borne by neighbours, friends and acquaintances in the part of Boston he grew up in, it was little wonder his childhood neighbourhood was nicknamed 'Cork'. This elicited an enthusiastic standing ovation from the audience that lasted a number of minutes.[15]

O'Neill continued by saying that this ceremony was special to him: he spoke of other conferrings and honours bestowed upon him in his fifty years of public life. He made special mention of Boston College naming a library in his honour, one of the best libraries in the world costing $30 million. But today was special because he was back to his roots. The Speaker alluded to Cork's rich heritage. Cork city, which dates back to the sixth century and its establishment by St Finbarr, offered – according to the Speaker – an historic tapestry with many diverse cultural influences, from the Danes, Normans and English to the Celts, which was the beauty of his race, the fact that his heart swelled with the Celtic blood that flowed through his veins.

For those of Irish American ancestry, Cork would always hold a special place, for many could trace their grandparents to the city and county and many more had ancestors who came from Ireland and journeyed from the harbour of Cobh aboard the steamships that brought them to the United States, often with no prospects of seeing their native land again, added the Speaker:

America owes so much to the strength, wisdom and faith of these people who left Cork and came to the United States. Their children will always remember the land of their birth and the bells of Shandon will always ring the sweet music of home.

Before the Speaker resumed his seat, he made special mention of Congressman Ed Boland who was one of forty congressmen and their wives who had made the trip. The Speaker advised that this was the second freedom of Cork ceremony the Congressman had attended, having been in the Kennedy party that called on the city in 1963. The Speaker once more thanked the assembled guests and concluded his address by saying he was privileged to be made a freeman of Cork. The audience was once more on its feet for a long-lasting applause.[16]

With the speeches complete, the lavish banquet got underway. Cork's newest freeman mixed freely with the guests, conversing with fellow freemen Jack Lynch and Aloys Fleischmann while the ambience was enriched by the Ballyphehane GAA choral group, which provided a selection of traditional Irish songs.[17] The Speaker remained in Cork for a number of days, taking a seat as a special guest on the viewing platform for the Lord Mayor's parade (St Patrick's Day parade) the following Monday, before an emotional farewell to Cork at Kent station as he made his way back to the United States.

Thomas 'Tip' O'Neill (*left*) receives his freedom casket from Lord Mayor Alderman Liam Burke TD (*right*) on 16 March 1985.
COURTESY IRISH EXAMINER

SEÁN Ó FAOLÁIN

(1900–1991)

Elected as Freeman of Cork on 13 June 1988

Conferred as Freeman of Cork 9 July 1988

'In recognition of his literary ability and creative imagination; in appreciation of his energetic devotion to his vocation and his outstanding contribution of ten volumes of short stories, three novels, a play, numerous prose works including literary criticism, five biographies as well as travel essays and an autobiographical memoir; in acknowledgement of his contribution to the political, social and cultural currents of Irish life and his abiding affection and interest in the welfare of our nation and of the people and city of Cork; in gratitude for his assistance to and encouragement of young writers when as editor of The Bell *he greatly influenced such writers as Brendan Behan and James Plunkett while publishing the best Irish writers of the time.'*

BIOGRAPHY

The 'short story writer, novelist, historian, dramatist, biographer, critic, and man of letters'[1] Seán Ó Faoláin was born on 22 February 1900[2] in the family home overlooking Nicholas O'Connor's pub on the corner of Half Moon Lane in Cork city.[3] On one side his home 'looked over the River Lee at the city's most famous landmark, Shandon Tower',[4] on the other side was the back of the Opera House. In his autobiography, Ó Faoláin wrote:

> *Our house on the corner of Half Moon Street looked across the River Lee flowing or ebbing between deep limestone quays. Except for the seagulls and the fishermen nothing ever happened in this part of the river, which was always empty except for a couple of moored rowboats spotted by seagulls' droppings.*[5]

Ó Faoláin's parents, Denis Whelan and Bridget Murphy, were 'pious Catholics, ambitious for their three sons'.[6] He was educated at the Lancasterian School from 1905 to 1912 and then at Presentation Brothers' College (aka Pres) until 1918.[7] They proved to be contrasting experiences – he subsequently described his primary school as 'crazy-happy' but wrote that 'Pres was a fake in every respect except two; it provided some sort of pseudo-religious education and it was a useful cramming factory'.[8]

The summer of 1918 was a pivotal one for Ó Faoláin as 'he began to learn Irish and met Eileen Gould, whom he would marry; in the autumn they went to Ballingeary to study Irish'.[9] It was in Ballingeary, a place he loved and visited very summer for the next eight years, that John Whelan (as he was christened) became Seán Ó Faoláin.

Ó Faoláin entered University College Cork in October 1918 to study in the Faculty of Arts – 'When I went to UCC, it was a new world. When I was a boy it was a wonderful world and I thought of it as one that was made for me.'[10] His biographer, Maurice Harmon, records:

> *He let his hair grow long, wore a black hat, Irish tweeds and a long overcoat that hung loosely from his lanky frame. Like any full-blooded, intelligent and inquisitive young man, discovering the delights of being free of parental and teacher control, he took advantage of his freedom.*[11]

In the summer of 1921, Ó Faoláin completed his final university exams and received a second class Honours grade. He shared first place with another student and won the Peel Memorial Prize for the most distinguished student of the year.[12] He returned to University College Cork in 1924 to do an MA in Irish and in 1925 to complete an MA in English and gain a Higher Diploma in Education.[13] They were difficult years in Ireland and Ó Faoláin took the republican side in the Civil War and was an active IRA member for six years. He was 'a committed nationalist, a Gaelic Leaguer, active in a number of literary activities, and interested in becoming a writer'.[14] It was in this period of his life that Ó Faoláin met the Cork writer, Frank O'Connor, and they developed an interesting relationship as 'friends and rivals'.[15]

In 1926, Ó Faoláin went to study in Harvard University, having been awarded a fellowship. Harmon states that Ó Faoláin had mixed feelings about moving to America – the opportunity provided him 'with an escape from Cork's provincialism, an intellectual challenge, variety, and an expansion of personal life at all levels' but it also threatened what he clung to: 'the subjective, inner world of the writer and the haven of the familiar'.[16] Despite these initial concerns, Ó Faoláin prospered in America; he was awarded an MA in modern languages in 1928 and then taught modern-Irish literature at Boston College.[17] He also married Eileen Gould and the young couple lived in Cambridge, Massachusetts. In the same year his story 'Fugue' was published in *Hound and Horn*, having been approved by Edward Garnett, a noted English writer, critic and editor. Harmon claims that 'the relationship with Garnett was the most important in Seán's literary life'.[18]

Seán and Eileen Ó Faoláin moved to London in 1929 and remained there until 1933, with Seán working as senior lecturer in English and literature at St Mary's Training College, Strawberry Hill. During these four years in England his writing career flourished under the generous guidance of Garnett. Ó Faoláin's short stories about revolution were published in *Midsummer Night Madness* and he also wrote his first novel, *A Nest of Simple Folk*.[19] His daughter, Julia, was born during this period (June 1932) and she would go on to become a well-known short-story writer and novelist also.

In July 1933, 'Seán and Eileen realised their dream of returning to Ireland'[20] and lived in Killough House in County Wicklow. From this point, Ó Faoláin dedicated himself to writing and that is how he made his living. He stated in his autobiography, 'After our return to Ireland in 1933, to live in that rustic ramshackle retreat grandiloquently called Killough House, Kilmacanogue, I produced nine books in six years almost without taking breath.'[21] Among the books written by the prolific Ó Faoláin during these six years were biographies of Countess Constance Markievicz and Daniel O'Connell as well as the controversial novel *Bird Alone*. Of the latter book, he wrote in his autobiography that 'it was banned at once by the Irish government as "obscene and indecent" presumably because the heroine had a baby out of wedlock'.[22]

In 1938, the Ó Faoláin family moved to Knockaderry in Killiney and this was where their son, Stephen, was born.[23] Ó Faoláin worked as editor of *The Bell*, a creative fiction magazine, from 1940 to 1945 but he eventually grew disillusioned. Harmon explains that 'he [Ó Faoláin] had grown weary of attacking the bourgeoisie, the Little Irelanders, chauvinists, puritans, stuffed-shirts, pietists, Tartuffes, Anglophones, and Celtophiles'.[24] He resigned as editor of the magazine and went to Italy to write a travel book, *Summer in Italy*.[25] Ó Faoláin returned to Ireland refreshed from his travels and he later described the ten years, 1946 to 1956, as 'the crucial turning point in my life'.[26] He was commissioned by Penguin Books to write *The Irish* (1947) and he adopted a 'pioneering revisionist approach' to analyse 'what successive peoples and particular events had brought to the creation of modern Ireland'.[27] The 1950s was a fruitful decade for the writer; his earnings improved, he travelled to America a good deal to present lectures and seminars and he published *The Vanishing Hero – Studies in Novelists of the Twenties* (1956) and *The Finest Short Stories of Seán Ó Faoláin* (1957).

With his stories now enjoying greater success, Ó Faoláin took on a variety of other roles – he was the President of the Irish Association of Civil Liberty from 1953 to 1957 and he served as director of the Irish Arts Council from 1956 to 1959.[28] He also received an honorary degree from Trinity College Dublin in 1957 (he received one as well from the National University of Ireland in 1978). Later in life, he continued to have an impressive literary output with his novel *And Again* (1979) and *Collected Stories* (1980). His autobiography, *Vive Moi!*, was published posthumously in 1993.

Seán Ó Faoláin died on 20 April 1991, at the age of ninety-one. Harmon states that the writer had accepted death – 'he had lived long enough; he thought there was so much time allotted to each person. He had no belief in the afterlife. It was just baloney.'[29] Many tributes were paid to Ó Faoláin after his death, led by his fellow freedom of Cork recipient, President Mary Robinson.

Seán Ó Faoláin has a deserved place at the top table of Irish literary greats but his personal life came in for scrutiny in March 2013 when his daughter, Julia (who received the freedom of Cork on his behalf), published her memoir, *Trespassers*. In the book, she describes the full extent of her father's numerous affairs, including those with the writers Elizabeth Bowen and Honor Tracy, as well as the American socialite, Kick Erlanger.[30] She adds, 'With hindsight, his marriage to my mother strikes me as providing a small but telling illustration of how people in de Valera's Ireland felt obliged to live.'[31]

The Lord Mayor of Cork Councillor Tom Brosnan (*right*) presents the freedom casket to Seán Ó Faoláin's daughter Julia (*left*). The writer was too ill to attend the conferring ceremony in person. COURTESY *IRISH EXAMINER*

FREEDOM OF CORK

Seán Ó Faoláin was elected a freeman of his native city on 13 June 1988, with the conferring ceremony taking place the following month on 9 July. It was an unusual ceremony insofar as the celebrated writer was too ill to accept the award personally and his daughter, Julia, did so on his behalf. The Lord Mayor of Cork, Councillor Tom Brosnan, commenced proceedings and said that the award of freedom represented a 'welcome home' to Ó Faoláin who had a love-hate relationship with the city. He described Cork's latest freeman as 'among the greatest short story writers the world has known'[32] and praised him for his massive contribution to Irish literary life.

Accepting the city's freedom casket and certificate on her father's behalf, Julia Ó Faoláin said:

> *Everyone Irish knows that freedom is not granted but grasped. My father grasped the freedom to practice his craft within this city's confines, with perhaps, at times, a little friction and local opposition. There is a very satisfying elegance and symmetry in this freedom now being made official.*[33]

She continued by stating that having his name added to the distinguished list of freemen and freewomen of Cork offered her father 'a kiss of peace'.[34] She noted, 'Seán is a man of fiction, a realist sliced with a romantic, who mythologised Cork and turned it into a dream place. It is fitting that this mythical city is presenting him with a metaphorical freedom.'[35]

Though a relatively low-key event, conducted in the absence of the recipient, the Seán Ó Faoláin conferring ceremony was poignant and moving. Amongst those who attended were the Auxiliary Bishop of Cork, John Buckley; the President of University College Cork, Professor Tadhg Ó Ciardha; well-known local TD Peter Barry (who was made a freeman in 2010); and member of the European Parliament, Gene Fitzgerald MEP.

PERIOD 4
HIGH ACHIEVERS –
1990 TO 2013

The recipients of the freedom of Cork covered in this chapter are:

MARY ROBINSON

MAURICE HICKEY

MAUREEN CURTIS-BLACK

GEORGE MITCHELL

JOHN HUME

SONIA O'SULLIVAN

ROY KEANE

MARY MCALEESE

MICHAEL FLATLEY

JOHN MAJOR

Mary Robinson speaking in Cork City Hall. Behind her is the city crest, which was made from over 6,000 red, white and pink carnations that had been grown in the corporation's nurseries. COURTESY *IRISH EXAMINER*

MARY ROBINSON

(1944–)

Elected as Freewoman of Cork on 17 December 1990

Conferred as Freewoman of Cork on 23 February 1991

'In recognition of her outstanding achievements in advancing civil rights and social justice in Ireland; in recognition of her achievement of being the first woman to attain the highest office in the land, that of Uachtarán na hÉireann, and as a token of the high esteem in which she is held by the people of Cork, for all this and much more.'

BIOGRAPHY

Mary Robinson, Ireland's first female president, was born in Ballina, County Mayo, on 21 May 1944. She was the only girl out of five children born to her parents, Aubrey Bourke and Tessa O'Donnell, both of whom were qualified medical doctors. The Bourke family lived in Victoria House in Ballina and the five children enjoyed a privileged upbringing. They attended Miss Ruddy's private school rather than the public national school and had a nanny at home, Anne Coyne.[1] Even as a young girl, Robinson felt constrained by Ballina, 'I couldn't wait to escape to boarding-school. I couldn't wait to escape to college. I couldn't wait to escape.'[2] Robinson did manage to escape in that she went to Dublin for her second-level education in the elite Mount Anville School run by Sacred Heart nuns. Robinson was a good student who queried everything and she attended a finishing school in Paris for a year after completing her studies in Mount Anville. The year in Paris was a formative one for Robinson who came to question her Catholic faith:

She never felt more at home than she did in Paris, more comfortable with being the outsider, more comfortable with a culture that encouraged her to question everything. It was there that she made the first big decision of her life. At the age of seventeen-and-a-half she stopped going to mass regularly because she could no longer intellectually justify it.[3]

Nonetheless, Robinson had been baptised a Catholic which meant that her father, Dr Aubrey Bourke, had to get special permission from the Archbishop of Dublin, John Charles McQuaid, to allow her to attend the Protestant-dominated Trinity College in Dublin. Permission was granted and Robinson studied law in Trinity before continuing her legal education at King's Inns Dublin and Harvard Law School, to which she won a fellowship in 1967.[4] Robinson joined the Trinity Law Faculty as an academic in 1968 and, the following year, at the age of twenty-five, 'became Ireland's youngest professor of law when she was appointed Reid Professor of Constitutional and Criminal Law at Trinity'.[5]

These were heady times for the new professor who successfully contested the Seanad Éireann election of 1969. Her maiden speech, delivered on 2 December 1969, highlighted the lack of direction in government policy and the gross under-use of the Senate by government.[6] Robinson's election came as a surprise to many and her biographers note that 'a new voice had entered politics, an awkward voice asking questions'.[7]

One year later, in December 1970, she married Nicholas Robinson, 'a lawyer, conservationist, and an authority on eighteenth-century caricature'.[8] The next twenty years of Mary Robinson's life were extremely busy as an academic (Trinity Law Faculty 1968–1990), legislator (senator 1969–1989) and barrister (1967–1990, senior counsel 1980, English Bar 1973).

In a short period of time, Robinson 'gained a reputation as a strong advocate for human rights, campaigning to eliminate discrimination against women in Irish society'.[9] She was to the forefront of efforts to repeal laws banning the sale and importation of contraceptives in Ireland and she worked as a legal advisor in the campaign for reform of homosexuality laws. In the early 1970s she was appointed by the European Commission as the Irish representative on the Vedel Committee to advise on the enlargement of the European Parliament.[10]

In her legal work, Robinson always 'sought to use law as an instrument for social change, arguing landmark cases before the European Court of Human Rights (including the Josie Airey case in 1979) as well as in the Irish courts and the European Court in Luxembourg'.[11] A committed European, she also served on the International Commission of Jurists, the Advisory Committee of Interights, and on expert European Community and Irish parliamentary committees.[12]

On the political front, Robinson had entered the Senate as an independent but joined the Labour Party in 1976 before leaving the party in 1985 due to her objection to the Anglo-Irish Agreement. She failed in 1977 and 1981 to win a seat in Dáil Éireann as a Labour candidate but she did serve on Dublin Corporation between 1979 and 1983.[13]

In 1988, Robinson and her husband, Nick, founded the Irish Centre for European Law at Trinity College. The following year she announced that she would not be seeking another term as a senator. Instead, her career took a different direction when the Administrative Council of the Labour Party selected her as their nominee for the office of President of Ireland, running as an independent candidate in the 1990 election.[14] Prior to 1990 there had never been a female candidate for the presidency and Robinson was considered an outside bet. She faced two opponents – Brian Lenihan of Fianna Fáil, Tánaiste and Minister for Defence, and Austin Currie, a Fine Gael TD.

An opinion poll in the first week of October, a month before the election day, showed that Robinson was doing well with 33 per cent, which put her comfortably ahead of Currie (16 per cent) but significantly behind Lenihan (51 per cent).[15] Something needed to change and it did when Lenihan became engulfed in a scandal concerning a phone call he had made eight years earlier in an attempt to stop the President from granting the Taoiseach, Garret FitzGerald, a dissolution of the Dáil to hold a general election. Lenihan denied making the call but was caught in a lie when a taped interview emerged during which he had admitted to the call. Lenihan was forced to go before the television cameras to change his story 'on mature reflection'; he was also fired from cabinet by Taoiseach Charles Haughey. The momentum had shifted and although Lenihan received the most first preference votes, Robinson was elected after benefiting from the transfers of the eliminated Currie. In her victory speech that night, the President–elect spoke of the women of Ireland, 'Mná na hÉireann who, instead of rocking the cradle, rocked the system'.[16]

Robinson was inaugurated in Dublin Castle as the first female President of Ireland on 3 December 1990 and concluded her speech on the day by recalling the words of William Butler Yeats, 'I am of Ireland … come dance with me in Ireland.'[17] Robinson proved to be an inspirational choice of president and she transformed the office, moving away from the perception of the presidency being a comfortable retirement home for aged politicians. Historian Tim Pat Coogan records that the new President 'successfully resisted a number of efforts Haughey made to prevent her making public statements on issues of her choosing'.[18] For example, she met the Dalai Lama, despite Haughey's expressed objections.

Robinson's authorised biographers, Olivia O'Leary and Helen Burke, note:

> Mary blossomed in the presidency. Those who knew her as a reserved, often abrupt lawyer were astonished at the real warmth with which she responded to people, the new confidence that public affection gave her. She took risks, trusting that the people wanted her to be generous. They backed her when she visited famine-stricken Somalia, when she broke taboos and visited the Queen, when she visited Northern Ireland and, most controversially, when she visited republican West Belfast and shook the hand of Sinn Féin's Gerry Adams.[19]

Ireland's politicians found it hard to curb Robinson, even though the office of Head of State in Ireland is a weak one. Taoiseach Albert Reynolds (who succeeded Charles Haughey) once famously remarked, 'You can't argue with popularity ratings of 92 per cent.'[20] She is also fondly regarded for reaching out to the Irish Diaspora and remembered them by placing a symbolic light in the kitchen window of Áras an Uachtaráin.

In March 1997, Robinson announced that she would not be seeking a second term as president and she resigned in September, two months before the official end of her term, to take up a new post in Geneva as High Commissioner for Human Rights at the United Nations. She held the post until 2002 and her current job, since March 2013, is as a special envoy (United Nations) to the Great Lakes region of central Africa.

Mary Robinson has been the recipient of many honours and awards during her career, with one of the most notable moments coming in 2009 when she was awarded the Presidential Medal of Freedom, the highest civilian honour bestowed by the United States. She has three children, Tessa (born 2 October 1972), William (born 11 January 1974) and Aubrey (born 3 May 1981).

FREEDOM OF CORK

The seventh President of Ireland, Mary Robinson, was conferred with the freedom of Cork on 23 February 1991. On the day of the ceremony, the *Cork Examiner* ran a headline 'No lavish fête for Robinson' over an article containing a quote from Lord Mayor, Councillor Frank Nash, that 'the days of five-course celebration dinners are long dead'.[21] Yet, the *Cork Examiner* headline on the Monday after the ceremony (which was held on the Saturday) read '1,000 attend lavish event'.[22]

Whether lavish or not, the conferring ceremony was an historic occasion as it was the first time that a woman had received the honour. The President arrived on schedule to City Hall at 2.30 p.m., wearing a dark green coat to protect herself against the inclement weather.[23] Accompanied by her husband and children, the Lord Mayor Councillor Frank Nash, and the City Manager Tom Rice, Robinson entered the hall behind mace bearers John Kenneally and Seamus Keane. She was met by a magnificent scene with the stage backdrop of the city crest made from over 6,000 red, white and pink carnations which had been grown in the corporation's nurseries.[24] The *Cork Examiner* commented that 'the entire affair was conducted with a great degree of dignity and sophistication'[25] while noting that two councillors, Dave Buckley (independent Fianna Fáil) and Tom Brosnan (Fianna Fáil), 'had declined to attend as a protest against the conferring of the honour'.[26]

The Lord Mayor, Councillor Frank Nash, spoke after the official citation was read aloud and the *Irish Independent* stated that 'he did the city proud with a warm, crisp address'.[27] The Lord Mayor ended his words by turning to the President and stating:

> *It had been written of you that if you spent the last twenty years preparing yourself to be President, there has been little sign of it. Rather, it would be more correct to say that Ireland has spent these same twenty years preparing itself for Mary Robinson.*[28]

After the Lord Mayor's speech, the names of previous recipients of the freedom of Cork were read before there was 'an impressive interlude with music, poetry and song'.[29] First to perform was Patricia Moynihan, a young flautist from Cork (who won the 1990 Brass and Woodwind final of the RTÉ Musician of the Future competition), performed a recital, accompanied on piano by her music teacher Evelyn Grant. She was followed on stage by poet Marie Bradshaw who read her commissioned piece, 'First Citizen/Free Woman'. Finally, Cara O'Sullivan sang three songs composed by Aloys Fleishmann, a freeman of Cork who was in the audience with another freeman, Jack Lynch.

Lord Mayor Councillor Frank
Nash presents Mary Robinson
with her freedom casket in Cork
City Hall on Saturday 23
February 1991.
COURTESY *IRISH EXAMINER*

Following the presentation of her freedom casket, the President of Ireland, 'visibly touched by it all',[30] stood to speak. She began by saying that receiving the freedom of Cork was, and would always be, one of the special moments of her life. She added that this was especially so because Cork was a city of great integrity and a place 'with such a great sense of itself'.[31] Robinson remarked that upon entering the City Hall, seeing the large crowd and feeling the atmosphere, she felt a great sense of happiness and it made her want to dance and sing. In a light-hearted and humorous speech, during which she regularly appeared to depart from her prepared script, Robinson commented favourably on Cork's 'magnificent community spirit, camaraderie, dynamism, vitality and sense of place'[32] which enabled it to surmount difficult times.

She drew attention to Cork's writers such as Frank O'Connor and Seán Ó Faoláin (a freeman of Cork) who had made major contributions to Irish society by 'questioning and rebelling and even at times causing offence'.[33] In doing so, they constantly attacked any tendency to close-mindedness. In addition, Robinson highlighted the vibrant arts scene in the city and the academic achievements of institutions such as University College Cork and the then Regional Technical College (now Cork Institute of Technology). As a native of Mayo living in Dublin she expressed particular gratitude at being so warmly embraced as a citizen of Cork. She ended her speech by stating that the outward freedom of a city conferred on people takes its meaning from the inner freedom of citizens and in Cork that freedom came from the relationship between music, writing, art, and the locale.[34]

MAURICE HICKEY

(1915–2005)

Elected as Freeman of Cork on 11 May 1992

Conferred as Freeman of Cork on 13 June 1992

Lord Mayor Councillor Denis Cregan (*left*) presents Maurice Hickey (*right*) with his freedom casket on 13 June 1992.
COURTESY *IRISH EXAMINER*

'In appreciation of his extraordinary contribution to Irish medical practice; in recognition of his pioneering work in the field of thoracic surgery; in particular gratitude for his life saving efforts in the campaign against tuberculosis; in admiration for his selfless dedication and great personal kindness to the sick; in respect for a life dedicated to the care of others; as a token of the high esteem and affection in which he is held by the citizens of Cork; for all this and much more.'

BIOGRAPHY

Maurice Hickey, born in Cork city on 11 June 1915, is the first (and, to date, only) surgeon to receive the freedom of Cork. He was the fifth of nine children born to Maurice Hickey and Hannah Joan (née Hickey) and the family lived on Western Road in Cork.[1] Young Maurice demonstrated exceptional abilities while in education. After studying at Presentation Brothers College and Rochestown College, he graduated from University College Cork with a first class honours degree in medicine in 1941.[2] Biographer Turlough O'Riordan notes that Hickey displayed 'a clear aptitude for surgery'[3] and he won the Peel Memorial Prize for the outstanding University College Cork graduate of the year, the Pearson Medal in surgery and the Blayney scholarship and bursary in surgery.[4] He graduated with a Masters in Surgery (M.Ch.) in 1943 and then trained at Nottingham General Hospital and Nottingham City Hospital.

While working in Nottingham, Hickey married fellow Corkonian, Dr Mary Bourke, on 23 August 1945 and soon afterwards he moved to the London Chest Hospital, 'where he trained under Thomas Holmes Sellors, the leading British thoracic surgeon of his generation'.[5] While in London, as an assistant surgeon, Hickey was 'exposed to the front line of thoracic surgery and the surgical treatment of tuberculosis (TB) in Britain'.[6]

Hickey's next career move was to return to Ireland. He later explained:

> *In August 1948, I relinquished my appointment as Junior Surgeon at the London Chest Hospital and took up my duty as the first local authority Cardio Thoracic Surgeon of the twenty-six counties, Dublin Corporation being the employing authority. This appointment was initiated by Dr Noel Browne. He was then a young and intensely dynamic Minister for Health and had only been a few months in his office.[7]*

The Irish Times subsequently noted that the Minister for Health recognised Hickey as 'the right man, in the right place, at the right time'.[8] Browne and Hickey 'hit it off immediately'[9] and it was reported that the minister gave instructions to his department officials to 'give Mr Hickey whatever he wants'.[10] Hickey operated on patients throughout the country and had an enormous workload, dividing his time between three newly opened thoracic surgery suites in Rialto in Dublin, Mallow in County Cork and Castlerea in Roscommon. He said himself, 'I realised the huge task facing me. Thoracic surgeons were a very scarce commodity then. I would be travelling the roads of Ireland day and night when not in the operating theatres.'[11] O'Riordan records, 'Offered a chauffeur-driven car by the department (of Health), he declined the offer, yet managed a significant surgical and administrative workload, driving hundreds of miles each week between the three surgical units.'[12] In a later speech, Hickey stated that in his first year's work back in Ireland, he operated on a hundred cases in Dublin, a hundred at Mallow and sixty-five at Castlerea.[13] His results 'set new standards'[14] and he kept up with the latest international surgical techniques. Hickey became the first surgeon in Ireland to operate successfully on blocked mitral heart valves and he was also renowned for repairing the hearts of 'blue babies'.[15]

With therapeutic drugs for TB emerging in the 1950s, Hickey increasingly focussed on cardiac surgery and in 1956 he moved to the newly opened St Stephen's Hospital in Glanmire, County Cork.[16] The following year, at St Finbarr's Hospital in Cork, he performed the first surgery in Ireland to close the holes in the hearts of young children.[17] Hickey spent the remainder of his working life building St Stephen's Hospital into one of the best centres in Ireland for cardiac surgery. He was supported in this endeavour by Dr Desmond Gaffney, the chief anaesthetist with whom he had 'a superb symbiotic relationship'.[18] Hickey and Gaffney visited specialist cardiac units in America and Europe and 'they married considerable laboratory work with clinical and surgical innovation'.[19] St Stephen's became a teaching hospital for University College Cork in 1964 and Hickey was appointed to a lectureship in thoracic surgery in the university in 1966.[20]

Awarded the West Cork Man of the Year in 1972 and the freedom of Cork in 1992, Hickey spent his retirement primarily living in Limerick but regularly travelled to the family's holiday home in Baltimore, County Cork. He died at the age of eighty-nine in Limerick on 16 May 2005, survived by his wife and their two daughters and two sons.[21] Ireland's leading chest surgeon was laid to rest in Douglas in Cork in the cemetery adjoining St Columba's Church.

The obituary for Maurice Hickey in *The Irish Times* noted:

He had a most imposing appearance – a larger-than-life figure, well over 6ft., carefully groomed, broad shouldered, with trademark centre parting of his huge head of hair. Nothing but the best was good enough for his patients. He was dogmatic, ruthless, not particularly popular with colleagues and often rubbed people up the wrong way. He was a fervent Catholic and was charitable about others. He was an indulgent father, greatly loved by his family. He did not make, nor did he seek to make, a lot of money in private practice.[22]

O' Riordan's judgement of Hickey is:

He combined first-rate surgical and clinical ability with a relentless work rate, diligently seeking the best outcomes for all his patients, and eschewing the rewards offered by private practice. His dedication and work ethic made a significant impact in improving patient outcomes. Kind and considerate with patients, he was effective in navigating and managing Irish medical bureaucracy in the interests of his patients, emanating from his prioritisation of patient needs and his championing of public access to specialised surgery and treatments.[23]

FREEDOM OF CORK

At the meeting of Cork Corporation on 11 May 1992, it was unanimously agreed that the freedom of the city should be conferred on Maurice Hickey and Fr Roch Bennett – a Capuchin priest who had worked tirelessly on behalf of the marginalised in Irish society, especially young people. The joint conferring ceremony took place on Saturday 13 June and the Lord Mayor, Councillor Denis Cregan, recited the opening prayer before the Deputy City Manager, Niall Bradley, read the resolution of the corporation conferring the freedom of Cork on Maurice Hickey. The Lord Mayor then addressed the crowd and described Hickey as 'an extraordinary man'[24] who had confronted the dreadful disease of TB against all the odds and eventually had beaten it. The Lord Mayor stated that the surgeon 'gave himself willingly and totally to the service of those who were ill'[25] and that thousands of families had every reason to be grateful for his medical skills.

Accepting the honour, Hickey described it as 'one of the greatest moments of my life'.[26] He continued his speech by summarising his career, concentrating on the period after 1948 when he returned to Ireland to fight TB and perform cardiac surgeries. The new freeman of Cork concluded by saying that the honour was enhanced by the fact that he was sharing the day and the ceremony with Fr Roch Bennett. He thanked the members of Cork Corporation again for the 'special honour and privilege'[27] before gratefully receiving his casket and signing the city's historic freedom register.

MAUREEN CURTIS-BLACK

(1910–1999)

Elected as Freewoman of Cork on 26 April 1993

Conferred as Freewoman of Cork 19 June 1993

'In appreciation of her extraordinary commitment to social justice; in admiration of her pioneering work in the establishment of Cork Citizens' Advice Bureau and in the development of similar advisory services elsewhere; in recognition of her immense contribution to the welfare of women, particularly those widowed or disadvantaged as manifested in the founding of the Cork Widows' Association; in acknowledgement of her courage and role in winning Free Legal Aid for those not in a position to fight for legal entitlement and of the huge national and international significance of that campaign; in respect for a life dedicated to the service of others, particularly those with no voice; as a token of the high esteem and affection in which she is held in this city.'

Maureen Curtis-Black enters City Hall for her conferring ceremony, accompanied by Lord Mayor Councillor Micheál Martin.
COURTESY *IRISH EXAMINER*

BIOGRAPHY

Maureen Curtis-Black, founder of the Cork Widows' Association and the Cork Citizens' Advice Bureau, created history in 1993 as the first Cork woman to receive the freedom of the city. Described as 'a bright, intelligent girl'[1] she was a member of 'a distinguished Cork family'[2] and daughter of a long-time city councillor, Patrick Curtis. Patrick's story is a remarkable one. He served as a councillor for thirty years and was twice the agreed candidate to become Lord Mayor but never assumed the office. As Sandra McAvoy records in her 1994 article on Maureen Curtis-Black:

> *Tragically, on the night of his first election, his young wife died in childbirth. At the time of his second election, his second wife, Maureen's mother, was pregnant. Given the conventions of the time, she felt this would inhibit her carrying out the duties of Lady Mayoress and, in deference to her, he stood down.*[3]

Maureen won a scholarship to University College Cork in 1930 and she graduated with a BA in languages and a Higher Diploma in Education in 1933.[4] With jobs in short supply locally, she went to England and, after teaching spells in Ipswich and Hartlepool, she obtained a post 'teaching languages in St Bernard's Convent for girls, Westcliffe-on-Sea'.[5] In the early years of the war, Maureen married Jack Black and subsequently gave birth to her son, Brian. Tragedy struck, however, when Jack died while Brian was still a baby, leaving Maureen Black (as she was now called) to raise her infant son alone.[6]

Black spent the bulk of her teaching career at St Bernard's and rose to the position of head of modern languages.[7] She retired back to Cork in 1965 partly due to ill health but also because her son, Brian, was an undergraduate student in University College Cork. McAvoy claims that the 'move marked a new and important phase in Black's life'.[8] She joined a range of societies and organisations, including the Cork Women Graduates' Association and the Federation of Women's Organisations. Through her involvement in these organisations, Black 'saw with fresh eyes the difficulties and problems faced by many different groups and individuals'.[9] Motivated to help people solve their problems she founded (with the help of the Federation of Women's Organisations) the Citizens' Advice Bureau in Cork. The offices of the centre were opened in 1972 and the Cork centre, the first in Ireland, became a model for others to follow later.[10] Interviewed by Sandra McAvoy in 1994, Black claimed that of all the projects she was involved in during her life, this was the most important. Within twenty years of the opening of the Citizens' Advice Bureau in Cork, the centre was handling 8,000 cases per year and was staffed by 48 volunteers.[11]

McAvoy states that the Cork Bureau 'was more than an advice centre'[12] and that support was actively given to clients. The best example of this was the Josie Airey case. Josie Airey's husband 'had ceased to support his family but she could not afford the legal representation necessary to bring the case to court'.[13] With the support of Maureen Black over the course of a prolonged process, Josie Airey – as a private citizen – took her case to the European Court of Human Rights. Her case was partly based on the fact that 'at that time only those who were well off in Ireland could afford to seek justice in the High Court, contrary to the Convention on Human Rights'.[14] Black travelled to Strasbourg on a number of occasions, at her own expense, to support the case and to offer guidance to Josie Airey who found the process intimidating.[15] With Mary Robinson as counsel, Josie Airey won her case in 1979. It was regarded as a landmark judgement which 'established the rights of ordinary citizens to gain justice in Europe, and led to the establishment of free legal aid in Ireland and ultimately in the countries that had signed the Convention on Human Rights'.[16]

Black also founded the Cork Widows' Association as she had been a young widow herself and understood the difficulties involved. Additionally, as chairwoman of the Cork Amenity Council, 'she worked hard to retain the character of the city and succeeded in doing so'.[17] Black's steadfast work in promoting social justice ultimately paved the way for the establishment of the office of Ombudsman in Ireland. Her efforts on behalf of the underprivileged earned her the Hanna Sheehy Skeffington Peace Prize; she was awarded the Person of the Year award in 1975, and, of course, she received the freedom of her native city. She continued to be outspoken on social issues well into her eighties and regularly argued that the Irish Constitution 'belonged to another era'[18] and was 'essentially anti-woman'.[19] Upon her death in 1999, *The Irish Times* noted:

She had vision, courage, leadership, a sense of justice, and above all, compassion. She was not intimidated by the system. It seemed unlikely that she was intimidated by anyone, or anything … Maureen wasted none of her life. She lived it fully and generously … Maureen Curtis-Black was a woman who recognised that there are many ordinary people who cannot make themselves heard. She worked tirelessly to give them a voice, and we are all in her debt.[20]

FREEDOM OF CORK

Maureen Curtis-Black was elected a freewoman of Cork on 26 April 1993 and was conferred with the honour on 19 June of the same year. Though she tended to use her married name, Maureen Black, she asked Cork Corporation to confer her as Maureen Curtis-Black in tribute to her father Patrick, the long-serving councillor and twice Lord Mayor-elect.[21]

The Lord Mayor, Councillor Micheál Martin, paid tribute to Maureen Curtis-Black at the commencement of the conferring ceremony, praising her for her 'extraordinary commitment to social justice'[22] and he added that she occupied 'a unique place in the evolution of Irish social history'.[23] The Lord Mayor then spent some time describing the Josie Airey case which he said 'broke new ground'.[24] He continued his speech as follows:

In many ways, from the early 1960s onwards, there was a quiet revolution happening in Cork society which was to have national and international ramifications. It was a most formative period in our social history. Many groups and organisations emerged, firmly rooted within the community and committed to the defence of the advancement of the cause of the less well-off in our community. People were empowered through greater access to information and knowledge. Institutions, both national and European, were taken on, and age-old inhibitions and fears of those in higher positions were eradicated and wiped out. In the midst of all these developments shone one figure like a beacon, the indefatigable Maureen Black.[25]

In accepting the freedom of Cork city, Maureen Curtis-Black said that she was 'deeply touched and honoured'[26] to have been chosen to join such a select group of people. She said that she did not think in terms of achievement; 'If I saw something that needed doing, I did it.'[27] The new freewoman of the city concluded:

I am happy to see that there has been some progress made with regard to women's rights. However I feel that we have a long way to go before women's work is acknowledged the way it should be. Now that the barriers are broken I hope that more women will be awarded the honour [freedom of the city] in the future.[28]

GEORGE MITCHELL

(1933–)

Elected as Freeman of Cork on 14 September 1998

Conferred as Freeman of Cork on 28 November 1998

'In recognition of his exceptional commitment to the cause of lasting peace, justice, and harmony in Northern Ireland; in appreciation of his willing acceptance of the invitation of President Clinton to find a formula for the ending of violence and community fragmentation; in acknowledgement of his deep concern for the wellbeing and prosperity of all sections of the community; in admiration of his extraordinary commitment as Chairman of the All-Party Talks which led to the historic Good Friday Agreement of 10th April 1998; in honour of his qualities of leadership, negotiation, integrity, wisdom and common sense which made it possible for him to draw together for the first time different and deeply divided political opinions; as a token of the high esteem and affection in which he is held by the people of Cork.'

BIOGRAPHY

The former US Senate majority leader, George Mitchell, was born in Waterville, Maine, on 20 August 1933. He was the fourth of five children born to Mary Saad (who had emigrated from Lebanon to America aged eighteen) and George Mitchell (the orphaned son of Irish immigrants). While both parents lacked education they greatly emphasised its importance for their children.[1] Mitchell acknowledged this in an interview conducted in Dublin in June 2002 by the American Academy of Achievement:

My parents had no education. My mother couldn't read or write English. She worked nights in a textile mill. My father was a janitor at a local college in our hometown. But they were part of that generation of Americans who had a very deep commitment to the education of their children. They had, really, an exaggerated notion of the value of education. But their life's goal was to see to it that their children received the education that they never got, and in that, they were successful. They had five children, all of whom went on to graduate from college, and several of us have graduate degrees as well.[2]

Buoyed by his encouraging parents, Mitchell graduated from high school at the age of sixteen and then attended Bowdoin College in Maine from where he graduated in 1954, having majored in history. The following two years were spent in military service, mainly based in Berlin in the US Army Counter-Intelligence Corps.[3] On his return, Mitchell worked as an insurance adjuster and studied by night at Georgetown Law School. He also had other jobs while at college, including driving a truck. He claimed that he learned a very strong work ethic from his parents and that working and studying at the same time 'wasn't really anything out of the ordinary'.[4] He graduated with a law degree from Georgetown in 1960 and then worked for a couple of years as a trial lawyer in the Justice Department in Washington.[5]

From 1962 to 1965, Mitchell worked as an assistant to Democratic Senator Edmund Muskie of Maine. Muskie eventually became the most influential person in Mitchell's life (after his parents) and sparked an interest in politics.[6] While practising law in Maine, Mitchell became increasingly involved in politics and he worked on Muskie's vice-presidential campaign in 1968 and his presidential campaign in 1972.[7] Mitchell's own career was on the rise and in 1977 he was appointed US Attorney for Maine before becoming US District Judge for Maine in 1979.[8]

The year 1980 marked a significant turning-point for Mitchell as Muskie resigned from the Senate to become Secretary of State, creating a vacancy which the forty-six-year-old Mitchell filled after much soul searching. He described his career shift as follows:

It was a very difficult decision. I enjoyed practicing law. I was the United States Attorney for Maine for three years, and then was appointed a federal judge. Those are appointments for life, of course, and so I thought this is it for me, and I truly loved doing it. And then just six months later, Senator Muskie was appointed Secretary of State of the United States, and it created a vacancy.[9]

Mitchell took his seat in May 1980 and it proved to be the start of a fourteen-year career in the Senate. He was elected as a Democrat for full terms in 1982 and 1988 and, in the latter election, received 81 per cent of the votes cast – the highest percentage ever received by a candidate in a state-wide election in Maine history.[10] At the opening of the next Senate session after the 1988 elections, Mitchell was elected as majority leader, 'the second most powerful elected office in the United States'.[11] As majority leader for the next six years, 'he was closely associated with free trade and environmental legislation and with aid to housing and education'.[12] Remarkably, for each of these six years he was voted 'the most respected member of the Senate' by a bipartisan group of senior congressional aides.[13]

In the spring of 1994, Mitchell announced that he was not seeking re-election to the Senate; he claimed that he had made the decision twelve years earlier that he would do the best he could for a limited time. He completed his existing Senate term in 1995, working hard to try and secure health care reform. His commitment to this cause led him to decline a Supreme Court nomination by President Bill Clinton in 1994.

However, in 1995, he answered President Clinton's call to go to Northern Ireland for a short mission, which actually lasted three years. Mitchell himself chronicled this period as follows:

So much later, he [Clinton] asked me to go to Northern Ireland as his representative for a short-term and rather limited mission. As they say, one thing led to another, and, ultimately, the British and Irish governments asked me to serve as chairman of the peace negotiations. There had been more than a quarter century of bitter sectarian war, thousands killed, tens of thousands injured. Every previous effort to reach an end to the conflict failed, and there was little prospect of success. Negotiations lasted for two years, during which there was virtually no progress and widespread predictions of failure. In a sense, we had 700 days of failure and 1 day of success. But through the courage of the political leaders of Northern Ireland and the Prime Minister of Britain, Tony Blair, and of Ireland, Bertie Ahern, and President Clinton's tenacity and perseverance, we ended up with a peace agreement.[14]

In his 1999 book, *Making Peace*, Mitchell wrote:

From February 1995 through May 1998 I spent most of my time going to, coming from, and working in Northern Ireland. It was the most difficult task I have ever undertaken, far more demanding than the six years I served as majority leader of the United States Senate. But it was well worth the effort; the outcome was the most gratifying event of my public life.[15]

The Good Friday Agreement in Northern Ireland stands as the defining legacy of George Mitchell and it was achieved as a result of his charm, patience and quiet determination.[16] In *Making Peace*, he noted, 'If the Good Friday Agreement endures, it will be because it is fair and balanced. It is based on the principle that the future of Northern Ireland should be decided by the people of Northern Ireland, and it seeks to promote tolerance and mutual respect.'[17]

Despite declaring himself 'overcome with exhaustion and emotion'[18] at the end of the Northern Ireland peace process, Mitchell accepted an invitation from President Clinton, Prime Minister Barak of Israel and Chairman Arafat of the Palestinian Authority to chair an 'International Fact Finding Mission' on the crisis between Israel and the Palestinian Authority.[19] He presented his report to President George Bush in 2001. Subsequently, in 2008, President Barack Obama appointed him as a Special Envoy to the Middle East.

George Mitchell, who returned to private life in 2011, is also a noted businessman. He has served as a director of many companies including Walt Disney, Federal Express, Xerox, Unilever and the

Boston Red Sox. In 2004, he was selected as the Chairman of the Board of Walt Disney and in 2006 was asked by the Commissioner of Baseball to lead an investigation into the use of performance-enhancing drugs in the sport.[20] He is also attached to a number of law firms, serves as the Chancellor of Queen's University Belfast and as President of the Economic Club of Washington.[21] He is the recipient of many honours such as the Presidential Medal of Freedom, the Philadelphia Liberty Medal, the Truman Institute Peace Prize, the German Peace Prize and the United Nations (UNESCO) Peace Prize.[22] He is also the author of four books.

Mitchell was divorced from his wife, Sally, in 1987 after twenty-six years of marriage; they had one daughter, named Andrea. In 1994, he married his second wife, Heather, with whom he had two children, Andrew and Claire. *Making Peace* ends with a reference to Andrew as follows:

I have a dream to return to Northern Ireland in a few years with my young son, Andrew. We will roam the countryside, taking in the sights and smells and sounds of one of the most beautiful landscapes on earth. Then, on a rainy afternoon (there are many in Northern Ireland) we will drive to Stormont and sit quietly in the visitors' gallery of the Northern Ireland Assembly. There we will watch and listen as the members of the Assembly debate the ordinary issues of life in a peaceful democratic society: education, health care, agriculture, tourism, fisheries, trade. There will be no talk of war, for the war will have long been over. There will be no talk of peace, for peace will by then be taken for granted. On that day, the day on which peace is taken for granted in Northern Ireland, I will be fulfilled.[23]

FREEDOM OF CORK

George Mitchell was conferred with the freedom of Cork in the City Hall on Saturday 28 November 1998. In opening the proceedings, Lord Mayor Joe O'Flynn praised Mitchell for his 'remarkable and courageous commitment to all the people of this island'[24] and thanked him for staying a long time in Northern Ireland 'to encourage, cajole and pressurise the inheritors of sectarian division to write the first pages of a new history'.[25] After concluding his speech, the Lord Mayor presented Mitchell with his freedom scroll and a specially commissioned casket by silversmith, Chris Carroll.

Mitchell opened his remarks by saying that he had travelled widely through every continent and many countries but had never felt more at home than in Cork.[26] He delighted the large crowd by declaring 'in a real sense I am home'[27] before tracing his roots back to his paternal grandparents, Michael and Bridget Kilroy, who left Cork for Boston where in, 1900, his father was born.[28] The new freeman of the city continued by explaining that he accepted the recognition not as an individual but as a representative of the many men and women who devoted their lives to the cause of peace in Northern Ireland, many of whom gave their lives in the process.[29]

George Mitchell (*left*) receives his freedom casket from the Lord Mayor Councillor Joe O'Flynn (*right*). COURTESY *IRISH EXAMINER*

Later that day, after a reception in City Hall, Mitchell went to University College Cork where he was the recipient of an honorary Doctorate of Laws by the university's President, Dr Michael Mortell.

Over the course of a busy weekend in Cork, Mitchell too delivered the tenth Annual 'Open Mind' guest lecture on RTÉ Radio 1 and referred to the fact that he had been on the verge of quitting the Northern Ireland peace process in the spring of 1997 when there was a lengthy break in negotiations:

Then on 16 October 1997, a transforming event occurred in my life, my wife gave birth to my son. On the day my son was born, I telephoned my staff in Belfast and asked them to find out how many babies had been born in Northern Ireland on that day. There were sixty-one and I became seized with the thought of what would life be like for my son had he been born in Northern Ireland or for those sixty-one babies had they been born Americans. A few days after my son's birth, I left to return to Belfast and at that point, I committed myself to the talks until the end and promised I would redouble my efforts to bring the negotiations to a successful conclusion.[30]

JOHN HUME

(1937–)

Elected as Freeman of Cork on 26 April 2004

Conferred as Freeman of Cork on 8 May 2004

'In recognition of his exceptional commitment to the cause of reconciliation on this island and for being a living testament to that fundamental principle of peace – respect for diversity; in recognition of the pivotal role he played in securing the historic Good Friday Agreement of 10th April, 1998 and his unwavering commitment to the fundamental principles of democracy; in admiration of his qualities as a man of honour, generosity, integrity and courage, but above all else, in recognition of his lifelong commitment to the cause of lasting peace; for his exhortation that we spill sweat together instead of blood and his conviction in the futility of violence; as a token of the high esteem and affection in which he is held by the people of Cork; for all this and more.'

BIOGRAPHY

Nobel Peace Prize winner John Hume was born in Derry on 18 January 1937. His parents, Sam Hume and Annie Doherty, had married the previous year and 'like many another Derry couple had to live in one room of the family home, then on the northern outskirts of the city, between Rosemount and the Glen'.[1] Sam Hume had a great belief in education and regularly told his eldest son John, 'Stick to the books, son, it's the only way forward.'[2] This advice served young Hume well and he commenced his education at primary school in St Eugene's Boys. Hume records in his intimate 1996 memoir, *Personal Views*:

Despite growing up in an area of great poverty, I was one of the lucky ones who benefited from the introduction of free public education. At the age of ten, I passed what was called the Eleven-Plus examination. This enabled me to receive a government scholarship which paid my fees to attend St Columb's College in Derry.[3]

Biographer Barry White confirms Hume's lucky break by explaining that before the state stepped in, the Hume family – with seven children between the ages of ten and two – would not have been able to afford the annual fee of £7 per year to attend St Columb's which was the local Catholic boys' grammar school: 'If John had been born a year earlier, he would have been destined to follow his father's footsteps, a clever child forced into a job below his capabilities or exiled for life.'[4]

After finishing school, Hume studied for three years to be a priest at Maynooth College but he gave it up and instead did a degree in French and History. His father, though disappointed, was philosophical about his son's change in direction, 'It takes a good man to enter the priesthood – and an even better one to leave it.'[5] Hume then went to Paris to study at the Institut Catholique. In his own words, 'After university and my studies in France, I came back to Derry an educated man.'[6]

Hume immediately became involved in the credit union movement and founded the Derry Credit Union on 30 October 1960 with four people and £7. By 1996, it had 14,000 members and £21 million.[7] Also in 1960, Hume married Pat Hone after a nine-month engagement. Hume enjoyed his credit union work and, as a twenty-seven-year-old, became the President of the Credit Union League of Ireland.

At that point in his life, Hume's main focus was to continue working in the credit union movement but he became increasingly drawn to the world of politics, mainly due to the discrimination he witnessed and the shortages of both jobs and houses. In *Personal Views* he explains:

> *Only a third of the population of Derry in the early 1960s was Protestant, but they were able to govern the city through a process of gerrymandering. This was achieved by dividing the city into three wards, and, since they controlled public housing, they were able to put all the Catholics into one ward and then give that ward just eight seats while the other two wards had six seats each. In this way, even though there were more Catholics in the city, the Protestants always won the elections by twelve seats to eight.*[8]

Following the credit union model, Hume formed the Derry Housing Association in 1964 and, in the first year, one hundred family homes were built. He next planned an ambitious development of 700 houses but local politics intervened:

> *The local politicians wouldn't give us planning permission because it would upset the voting balance in their gerrymandered system, and that led me straight into politics, led me straight into the civil rights movement. And of course, in the 1960s, civil rights was very much in the international news because of the leadership of Martin Luther King in the United States, and that had a very major influence on people like myself, and we got involved in the civil rights movement, seeking equality of treatment for all sections of our people, and of course, my involvement in the civil rights movement led me straight into politics.*[9]

Hume and his associates knew that progress could only be achieved through changing the political and electoral systems and they tried to do so through the Northern Ireland Civil Rights Association.

They pursued the Martin Luther King philosophy of non-violence but frequently met with violent resistance. In 1968, 'while trying to defuse a confrontation between demonstrators and the British Army, Hume was repeatedly knocked down with a fire hose and finally arrested for "obstructing Her Majesty's forces"'.[10] Hume was fined £20 but refused on principle to pay – he 'appealed his case all the way to the House of Lords in Westminster, where his conviction was overturned'.[11] The civil rights movement achieved success when the British government announced, in November 1968, that Derry Corporation would be abolished and replaced by an appointed development commission. A five-point reform plan was outlined, 'tacitly admitting that the civil rights case was proved'.[12] Central to the reform plan was a fair system of house allocation and the establishment of an Ombudsman to investigate citizens' grievances.

By 1969, 'Hume's sights were set on Stormont'[13] (the Northern Ireland Parliament) and he announced his candidacy as an independent. Hume was elected and, the next year, founded the non-sectarian Social Democratic and Labour Party (SDLP). Hume's vision for the party was that it would deal with 'real politics, with housing, with jobs, with voting rights, and not flag-waving'.[14] His long-held conviction was that there was a common ground and that if people worked together on the common ground issues, divisions in society would end. Housing remained a big issue and the British government responded to the SDLP demands in 1971 by taking public housing out of the hands of the local authorities and establishing the independent Northern Ireland Housing Executive. While this represented a step forward in reforming the flawed housing system other issues had superseded it; in particular, 'armed extremists on both sides of the conflict had embarked upon a devastating cycle of murder and retaliation'.[15] In 1972, the British government shut down the parliament at Stormont and returned to direct rule from London.

With the Northern Ireland Parliament no longer in existence, 'Hume increasingly looked to the example of European unity for a solution to the politics of Northern Ireland'.[16] Britain and Ireland both joined the EEC (forerunner to the European Union) in 1973 and Hume won a seat in the European Parliament in the 1979 elections. Hume consistently repeated his belief that the European Union is the best example of conflict resolution in the world's history:

I always tell the story of the first time I went to Strasbourg in 1979, to the European Parliament. I went for a walk across the bridge from Strasbourg in France to Kehl in Germany. And I stopped in the middle of the bridge and meditated – 1979 – that if I had stood on this bridge thirty years ago, I thought, at the end of the Second World War, and at the end of the first half of that century, which was the worst in the history of the world, two world wars, and about a hundred million people slaughtered, who could have dreamt then that in the second half of that century, those same peoples would unite in a European Union? But, they did.[17]

Hume was successful in persuading his European partners to agree to special regional aid for Northern Ireland. A community-wide survey strengthened Hume's negotiating position when it found that Northern Ireland was the second poorest of 131 regions, finishing just above Calabria in Italy.[18] Hume savoured another positive electoral result in 1979 when he was selected as leader of the SDLP (a position he held until 2001) – even though Hume had founded the party in 1971, Gerry Fitt became leader, with Hume as his deputy.

In 1983, Hume was elected to the House of Commons at Westminster from the constituency of Foyle. He became a leading figure in developing a Northern Ireland peace process and played a role in the drafting of the Anglo-Irish Agreement in 1985, the first time since the 1920s that the governments of Britain and Ireland had reached a major agreement over Northern Ireland.[19] Hume recollects:

> We [the SDLP] strongly welcomed the Anglo-Irish Agreement when it came out, because it was the first time that there was any such agreement between the two governments to commit themselves to working together. We pointed out that the Agreement was not a solution, but the framework within which a solution could be found. We have been working on that framework ever since.[20]

Determined to use the Anglo-Irish Agreement as a stepping stone towards a long-lasting peace process, 'Hume now undertook one of the most delicate actions of his career, initiating private talks with Gerry Adams, the leader of Sinn Féin'.[21] When Hume and Adams issued their first joint statement in 1993 they 'were subjected to ferocious criticism, and physical attacks were made on the homes of SDLP members'.[22] The Sinn Féin party was 'ostensibly committed to unconditional unification of Ireland, by violence if necessary'[23] while the SDLP had always been strongly opposed to violence. The joint statement proved to be an important catalyst on the road to peace. British Prime Minister John Major and Taoiseach Albert Reynolds agreed an outline for negotiations in 1995 and Bill Clinton demonstrated his support by becoming the first American President to visit Belfast and Derry. Other pieces of the jigsaw were put in place when David Trimble, the leader of the Ulster Unionist Party (UUP), significantly agreed to participate in the talks and George Mitchell accepted an invitation from the British and Irish governments to chair those negotiations.

The historic culmination of the efforts of all involved was the Good Friday Agreement of 1998. The Agreement (sometimes referred to as the Belfast Agreement) states the two governments:

> affirm that any change in the status of Northern Ireland would only come about with the consent of a majority of the people of Northern Ireland;

> recognise that the present wish of the majority of the people of Northern Ireland is for no change in the status of Northern Ireland;

declare that, if in the future a majority of the people of Northern Ireland clearly wish for and formally consent to the establishment of a united Ireland, they will introduce and support in the respective Parliaments legislation to give effect to that wish.[24]

The Good Friday Agreement 'marked a significant normalisation in the north–south and British–Irish relationships'[25] and on 29 November 1999, 'for the first time in twenty-five years, Northern Ireland regained a power-sharing executive. Direct rule ended the following day when Westminster approved devolution orders transferring power from London to Belfast'.[26]

The important roles in the process played by Hume and Trimble were recognised in 1998 when they jointly received the Nobel Peace Prize. With Trimble as First Minister of the new Northern Ireland Assembly, Hume served in Stormont for three years. He also continued his work in the UK and European parliaments before announcing his retirement, for health reasons, from elected office in 2004.

Hume has rightly been lauded nationally and internationally for his part in the Northern Ireland peace process. As well as being a co-recipient of the Nobel Peace Prize, he was presented with the Gandhi Peace Prize and the Martin Luther King Award – he is the only person to have been awarded these three major peace awards.[27] Former US President Clinton has described Hume as 'Ireland's most tireless champion for civil rights and its most eloquent spokesman for peace'.[28] In 2010, in a massive public vote organised by RTÉ, Hume was voted the 'Greatest Person in Irish History' ahead of Michael Collins, James Connolly, Bono and Mary Robinson. In 2012, he was made a Knight Commander of the Papal Order of St Gregory the Great by Pope Benedict.[29]

FREEDOM OF CORK

John Hume was elected as a freeman of Cork on 26 April 2004, following the proposal of Lord Mayor, Councillor Colm Burke, and seconded by Councillor Jim Corr. Hume was accompanied to the conferring ceremony on Saturday 8 May by his wife, Pat, and they were joined by 400 invited guests. Lord Mayor Burke explained to the audience that Hume was being recognised for his pivotal role in securing the Good Friday Agreement of 1998 and 'for his unwavering commitment to the fundamental principles of democracy'.[30] Before Hume was presented with his freedom casket, Cork poet Thomas McCarthy read his poem 'A Medallion for John Hume' and music was played by the local traditional group, Meitheal.[31]

Beginning his acceptance speech, Hume said that he was humbled and honoured to receive the honour from the people of Cork, especially in light of the people who had received the freedom of the city in the past:

John Hume (*right*) receives his casket from Lord Mayor Councillor Colm Burke. COURTESY *IRISH EXAMINER*

It is an honour, and quite emotional for me, to be included on a list with great people like John F. Kennedy, who inspired the world, and Senator George Mitchell who worked tirelessly for peace in Northern Ireland.[32]

Hume then spoke of the links between Cork and Derry and paid tribute to two great Corkmen, Jack Lynch and Peter Barry, for prioritising the Northern Ireland issue. Continuing, the new freeman of Cork recalled his time working in the credit union movement and said that the movement was never more important than at that time. He reserved a special mention for the newly enlarged European Union as a great example of conflict resolution and said that it was a cause of frustration to him that poor health had recently forced him to step down from the European Parliament. The ceremony concluded with an emotional Hume giving a rousing rendition of 'Derry Air' ('Danny Boy') with the large audience joining in.

Hume and his wife, Pat, then joined the Lord Mayor, the City Manager (Joe Gavin) and the leaders of the political parties in council for a celebratory dinner.

SONIA O'SULLIVAN

(1969–)

Elected as Freewoman of Cork on 23 May 2005

Conferred as Freewoman of Cork on 14 June 2005

In recognition of her extraordinary achievements in the field of athletics during the course of her remarkable career at both national and international level; for her capacity to uplift her nation with feats of extraordinary brilliance, determination and single-mindedness; in admiration of her courage in the face of adversity; for her unshakeable commitment to competing at the highest level without augmentation and for her devotion to the promotion of athletics particularly among the young; for her Olympian spirit, her indomitable will to succeed and for holding us enthralled by her inspiring feats on the track and field – all wrought from a unique talent and a steadfast resolve; in recognition of her untiring work for humanitarian and charitable causes; as a token of the high esteem and affection in which she is held by the people of Cork.'

BIOGRAPHY

Cobh-born Sonia O'Sullivan is the third woman to receive the freedom of Cork and the first person from the world of athletics to be honoured. Born on 28 November 1969, O'Sullivan's initial involvement with athletics came after she started secondary school. She explained in a 2007 interview with Tina Ryan, 'There was an athletics club, Ballymore-Cobh, based just next to my school. When I was about twelve, some friends and I realised that if you belonged to the club, you got to go away on weekends. We thought that sounded exciting, so we joined for the trips away.'[1] Though she did not excel immediately, O'Sullivan won a cross-country race at the end of her first season and this gave her the confidence to continue and to work hard at running. Recalling this time in her life, O'Sullivan stated in the aforementioned interview:

Without really thinking about any fixed goals I realised I needed a training schedule. That was probably the first important step I took. I'd heard of a coach, Sean Kennedy, who was well known for his punishing programmes, so I called him. He used to write me a programme every two weeks and drop it through my letterbox – it was during that time that I thought I could be good.[2]

During her school years, Sonia developed quickly as a runner with the encouragement and guidance of Sean Kennedy and in 1987 she was rewarded with a four-year athletics scholarship to Villanova University in the United States. In her autobiography, *My Story*, O'Sullivan wrote that she went through customs at JFK airport 'rail-thin and saucer-eyed'[3] and admitted that she had no idea what to expect: 'I'd never been to America before in my life. Cobh was my oyster. Running was just a career option.'[4] Despite struggling for her first two years in America due to a series of injuries, O'Sullivan asserts that 'America made me into a real athlete'.[5] Her times and performances improved during her final two years at Villanova and her first major international competition came in the 1990 European Championships in Split where she finished eleventh in the 3,000 metres. The following year saw O'Sullivan win the gold medal for the 1,500 metres at the World Student Games in Sheffield; she also claimed a silver medal in the 3,000 metres.

It was an Olympic year in 1992 and O'Sullivan headed to Barcelona in fine spirits, having improved her personal best times over the summer. She ran a courageous race in the 3,000-metres final, before being passed on the home straight and finishing in fourth place. She describes the final stages of the race in her autobiography:

We come around on to the final straight and we are beyond thought and tactics now. Our guts are busting, our hearts are pumping. I can feel their breaths on my shoulders. One hundred metres to an Olympic medal. Ninety metres. Just down that track. I can see the glory … No! … Romanova and Dorovskikh and Chalmers have all gone past and my face is just like that painting, 'The Scream' by Edvard Munch. I look like I am crying but I am just screaming. I'd just watched my death.[6]

The year after the Olympics, Tetyana Dorovskikh – who finished second – tested positive for drugs and received a ban which effectively ended her running career. The gold medal winner from Barcelona, Yelena Romanova, died alone in a flat in Volgograd in January 2007 at the age of forty-three 'of causes which have never been properly explained'.[7]

Over the next few years, O'Sullivan established herself as a top female middle distance runner. She went to the 1993 World Championships in Stuttgart as favourite for both the 3,000- and 1,500-metre races. Things did not go as planned and she finished fourth in the 3,000-metre final behind three Chinese athletes – Qu Junxia, Zhang Linzi and Zhang Lirong. O'Sullivan says of the race, 'And that was it. My first 3,000 metre defeat in almost a year. Another fourth place for my collection. Another big lesson learned. I'd have to grow up from here. Again.'[8] She responded positively to this disappointment by collecting a silver medal less than a week later in the 1,500-metre final, behind Liu Dong of China.

O'Sullivan ran superbly throughout 1994 and was crowned 3,000-metre champion at the European Championships in Helsinki. She states in her book, 'It seems a small enough deal now, looking back on it, and I went to Helsinki expecting to win and expected by others, but that was my first major championship victory. At the time it seemed like it would be the first of many.'[9] O'Sullivan went one better the following year when she became the first ever women's 5,000-metre world champion in Gothenburg when she sprinted past Portugal's Fernanda Ribeiro. As a world and European champion, everything was gearing up for O'Sullivan to confirm her supremacy at the 1996 Olympic Games in Atlanta. Unfortunately, Atlanta turned out to be the low-point in her career. In the 5,000-metre final, O'Sullivan, feeling 'heavy-limbed and sluggish and hot'[10] faded badly in the second half of the race and did not complete the race:

With four laps to go I felt like I was running under the surface in a pool of hot water . . . I kept going. The Irish voices that had been calling to me in the din were quiet now. I was becoming invisible. I took a lap to think about what I wanted to do. I made a decision. With two laps remaining I came around the back bend and slipped straight out of the stadium down the exit tunnel. Just like that. Race favourite gone. Vanished. 83,000 spectators and a worldwide television audience left to wonder.[11]

There was to be no redemption for a weakened O'Sullivan in the 1,500-metre competition and she failed to qualify for the final, finishing tenth out of eleven runners in her heat. She later described Atlanta as 'a bad and surreal experience'[12] and said her body betrayed her in the broiling humidity. The Irish nation was in mourning after O'Sullivan's Atlanta disaster and the athlete cried herself to sleep every night for two weeks.[13]

The Atlanta Olympics cast a long shadow over O'Sullivan during the 1997 season and she ran well below her best. She disappointed at the World Championships in Athens, finishing eighth in the 1,500-metre final and she did not qualify for the 5,000-metre final to defend her title. To the outside world, O'Sullivan was an athlete in decline but she answered her critics with some astonishing running in 1998. In March, at the World Cross Country Championships in Marrakech, she won the short course (4 kilometres) and long course (8 kilometres) events on successive days. Unsurprisingly, these triumphs gave O'Sullivan much-needed confidence after her disappointments over the previous eighteen months:

Marrakech changed a lot of things for me. Or, more correctly, I suppose I was very much changed by the time Marrakech happened. I learned to enjoy victories just as much as I had tortured myself in defeats.[14]

A rejuvenated O'Sullivan headed to the European Championships in Budapest later in the year in great spirits and dramatically won both the 5,000- and 10,000-metre titles, a staggering achievement given that she had never run the latter track event before. Recalling the joy of her Budapest victories, O'Sullivan notes in her book that two years of pain had been purged.[15]

The twenty-nine-year-old O'Sullivan took a break from competitions in 1999, giving birth to her daughter Ciara on 10 July. In typical fashion, O'Sullivan returned to training just ten days after Ciara's birth, essentially beginning her preparations for the Sydney Olympics in 2000. Sydney provided O'Sullivan with what she has described as her greatest sporting moment, claiming a silver medal in the 5,000-metre final after a thrilling battle with Romania's Gabriela Szabo. In becoming the first Irish track-and-field Olympic medallist since John Treacy won silver at the Los Angeles Olympics in 1984, O'Sullivan also set a new Irish national record with a time of 14:41:02. During an indepth interview with the *Irish Examiner* in April 2013, O'Sullivan described her mindset at the end of the race:

The first thing that happened at the end was I asked myself a question, 'Are you happy?' I put my hands on my knees and put my head down and I definitely had to think about it and kind of decided that I was. I had a quick think about things, it's very difficult because you are in this emotional state and how you react is how you are always going to feel about that moment. I realised though that I'd done the best I could in that race and on the day probably got the best possible result I could've got.[16]

O'Sullivan also competed in the 10,000-metre final at the Sydney Olympics, finishing sixth in a personal best time that set a new Irish national record. In October she made her marathon debut, winning the Dublin event in fine style.

O'Sullivan gave birth to her second daughter, Sophie, on 23 December 2001 but she did not bring the curtain down on her illustrious athletics career and returned to action in 2002, claiming silver medals at the European Championships in Munich for the 5,000- and 10,000-metres. Despite her fine efforts in Munich, O'Sullivan's career was indisputably in decline and there were few highlights over the next few years. Of course, 2004 was an Olympic year and O'Sullivan qualified for the final of the 5,000 metres but – suffering from illness – finished last in a field of fourteen runners. However, she showed great commitment and resolve to complete the race, though cut adrift from her fellow runners. In her book, she notes:

But on that lap something happened, people just started clapping me and I started waving back. [...] I was given almost a hero's reception by the crowd as I jogged around my last lap. It was so poignant and lovely. The way to say goodbye. [...] You can't change things. You can't unring a bell. That was how it was supposed to end.[17]

In January 2006, not yet fully retired from competitive running, the thirty-six-year-old O'Sullivan successfully applied for dual citizenship of Ireland and Australia. She was then selected by Australia for the 2006 Commonwealth Games in Melbourne but was not able to compete due to a hamstring injury.

Sonia O'Sullivan is still actively involved in running and was appointed Chef De Mission for the Irish Olympic team at the 2012 games in London; earlier in the summer she had the honour of carrying the Olympic flame onto St Stephen's Green in Dublin. In April 2013, the University College Cork race track at the Mardyke Sports Grounds was renamed the Sonia O'Sullivan Athletics Track.

O'Sullivan lives in Australia with her husband, Nic Bideau, and their two daughters, Ciara and Sophie.

FREEDOM OF CORK

Sonia O'Sullivan was conferred with the freedom of Cork in a joint ceremony with soccer player, Roy Keane, on 14 June 2005. They had both been elected on 23 May, following a proposal by Lord Mayor, Councillor Seán Martin, which was seconded by Councillor Terry Shannon. On the day of the conferrings, hundreds of people gathered outside Cork's City Hall to catch a glimpse of their sporting heroes as they arrived and there was a festive atmosphere to the proceedings. The Lord Mayor commenced by describing the recipients as 'two of the greatest sportspeople Cork, or Ireland, have ever produced'.[18] He said that O'Sullivan, through her long career, 'had married an unassuming manner with the "sterner stuff" of competition'.[19]

After the Lord Mayor's speech, O'Sullivan and Keane were treated to some video highlights of their careers. The *Irish Examiner* reported that both awardees 'looked a little embarrassed as moments from their sporting pasts were replayed on a screen in the concert hall'.[20] This point was echoed by *Inside Cork* reporter Graham Lynch who wrote, 'And truth be told both looked somewhat embarrassed by it all.'[21]

Cork City Council had commissioned local writer and poet Theo Dorgan to compose a poem in honour of O'Sullivan and he read aloud 'Running with the Immortals' which focused on the athlete's hometown of Cobh, 'the uphill and downhill capital of Ireland'.[22] The poem ended with the following verse:

I turn my face to the climbing sun, remembering another world,
a tall girl surging to the line. I want to find that child's soul and say:
talent is not enough, belief is not enough in this world;
you must push out into the lonely place where it all falls away—
and then, if you're lucky and blessed, the friend at your shoulder,
keeping pace, will be long-legged clear-eyed Artemis herself.

After receiving her casket and signing the freedom register, O'Sullivan spoke briefly and humbly, acknowledging the affection of Corkonians throughout her career. She stated that she now found it easier to assess the medals and titles she had won over the years because she knew how hard she had worked for them. O'Sullivan concluded her speech by paying tribute to her fellow recipient, Roy Keane, and to her partner, Nic Bideau (whom she married later in the year).

Sonia O'Sullivan and Roy Keane with their Freedom of Cork caskets in City Hall, Cork, on 14 June 2005.
COURTESY *IRISH EXAMINER*

Facing page: Sonia O'Sullivan and Roy Keane on the stage in Cork City Hall with Lord Mayor Councillor Seán Martin.
COURTESY *IRISH EXAMINER*

ROY KEANE

(1971–)

Elected as Freeman of Cork on 23 May 2005

Conferred as Freeman of Cork on 14 June 2005

'In recognition of the position which he has occupied for more than a decade at the pinnacle of Premiership and international football and for his contribution to that sport on the local, national and international stage; in admiration for his unwavering commitment to excellence in his chosen sport; for his leadership, skill and courage as captain of both Manchester United and the Irish national squad; for the exceptional pleasure and pride which he has engendered in the hearts of Irish and most especially Cork men and women during the course of his remarkable career; in recognition of his extraordinary and most often anonymous work for charity; as a token of the high esteem and affection by which he is held by the people of Cork; for all this and more.'

BIOGRAPHY

Soccer legend Roy Maurice Keane was born at Ballinderry Park, Mayfield, a suburb of Cork city, on 10 August 1971. During a long and distinguished playing career, 'he would win more medals, garner more headlines, and divide loyalties of Irish fans like no player ever before'.[1] Keane was born into a staunch soccer family and, while at school, he did not shine academically. He wrote in his autobiography, *Keane*:

> *I didn't shine in the classroom. I was quiet, happy not to be noticed. For me and my friends it was sport rather than education that really mattered in our lives. Life began when the bell began to signal the end of the school day.[2]*

Keane joined Rockmount AFC as a boy, a very successful local club. As a nine-year-old he played on the under-11 team and was voted 'Player of the Year' at the end of his first season. Over the next few years playing with Rockmount, Keane developed a reputation as whole-hearted player who was fully committed in every game. He noted of this time in his life:

'When the ball was there to be won I didn't hold back. Being small, I made a point of establishing my ball-winning ability as early as possible in every game. A lot of those big guys didn't like it when the studs were flying. And although I was small, my studs were as big as anyone else's.'[3]

Keane was fortunate to be a part of 'one of the most gifted schoolboy outfits the city of Cork had ever seen'[4] and scouts from England were regularly at Rockmount matches. However, while some of his colleagues were given trials at English clubs, Keane was frequently overlooked due to concerns over his size and temperament. Respected writer Dave Hannigan recalls, 'A legion of scouts tracked that Rockmount team season after season and none ever saw fit to take a chance on Keane. The letters he wrote to every English club begging for a trial never elicited a single plane ticket.'[5]

The turning point for Keane came in 1989. The Irish government, in partnership with the Football Association of Ireland, established a FÁS football course for elite young footballers, with one place on offer for each of the twenty-four League of Ireland soccer clubs. Keane signed as a semi-professional with second-tier Cobh Ramblers on the condition that the club gave him a place on the FÁS football course. Keane played with Ramblers at the weekends and then travelled to Dublin for a tough training regime which opened his eyes to what he could expect as a professional footballer. Benefiting from the training in terms of fitness and strength, Keane played for Cobh Ramblers youth team in a high-profile cup game against Belvedere Boys in Dublin in February 1990. Ramblers lost 4–0 but, in his own words, Keane played 'like a man possessed – by that strange compound of anger, frustration and personal pride'.[6] Noel McCabe, a scout from Nottingham Forest, was at the game and he was impressed enough to offer Keane a trial at the City Ground. Keane did well during his trial and signed a contract with the legendary Forest manager, Brian Clough.

Keane's aim for the 1990/1991 season was to establish himself in the reserve team but, remarkably, he was included in the first team squad for the second match of the season – away to Liverpool at Anfield. Keane thought he was going to Anfield to make up numbers in the squad but famously before the game, 'He was trying to look busy in the dressing room, helping to put the jerseys out when Clough turned to him and said "Irishman, put the number seven shirt on. You're playing".'[7] Keane acquitted himself well on his debut; Forest lost 2–0 but the young Irishman had taken a major step forward in his professional career. It is staggering to think that only six months had passed between Keane playing for the Cobh Ramblers youth team on 18 February and making his first team debut for Nottingham Forest at Anfield on 28 August, having just turned nineteen.

Keane was now up and running: 'Over the next few months the transformation of my life was complete. Week in week out I was playing against clubs and players I'd been watching on *Match of the Day* the previous season.'[8] Later, Brian Clough said of his gamble on Roy Keane, 'People said I'd flipped my lid but he did well and after that even Enid Blyton couldn't have written a better script.'[9]

Nottingham Forest was a strong side at the start of 1990s and made a determined push for the 1991 FA Cup. Along the way, Forest played Crystal Palace at the City Ground and Keane gave away a goal with an under-hit back-pass to his goalkeeper. Forest won the game but the drama did not end there:

When I walked into the dressing room after the game, Clough punched me straight in the face. 'Don't pass the ball back to the goalkeeper,' he screamed as I lay on the floor, him standing over me. I was hurt and shocked, too shocked to do anything but nod my head in agreement. My honeymoon with Clough and professional football was over ... He never said sorry, but the following week I was given a few days off to go home to Cork.[10]

Forest made it all the way to the FA Cup final at Wembley but there was to be no fairytale ending to Roy Keane's first season as a professional footballer, with Tottenham Hotspur winning 2–1 after extra time. Before departing on his post-season holidays, Keane played his first full international game for Ireland under manager Jack Charlton in a friendly against Chile at Lansdowne Road. Keane describes the occasion as not being a memorable one, partly because 'Charlton's approach to football was profoundly at odds with the game we played at Forest. Passing the ball was not a priority.'[11]

Keane returned to Wembley twice the following season with Nottingham Forest, tasting defeat to Manchester United in the League Cup final but securing victory in the Zenith Data Systems Cup final over Southampton. This was Keane's first medal in English football but plenty more would follow. Keane's third season with Forest, 1992/1993, was a disastrous one and the club was relegated despite Keane showing good form and emerging as the hottest young prospect in the English game. He agreed a deal with Kenny Dalglish to join Blackburn Rovers and was ready to sign a contract but the deal had been struck on a Friday afternoon and the staff at Ewood Park had left for the weekend. Dalglish told him not to worry, the contract form could be signed on Monday and the pair shook hands.[12] Keane went home to Cork for the weekend and received a phone call from Alex Ferguson, the manager of Manchester United, at Sunday lunchtime. They agreed to meet in Manchester the following day and Keane was persuaded to join Manchester United after Ferguson said to him. 'Roy, Manchester United are going to dominate the domestic game with or without you. With you we can win in Europe.'[13] Keane rang Blackburn's Kenny Dalglish to tell him he had changed his mind. Not surprisingly, Dalglish 'went crazy'.[14] Keane signed with United for a fee of £3.75 million, which was a British transfer record at the time.

The Corkman would stay at the Old Trafford club for over twelve years winning honour after honour. He broke into the Manchester United team, gradually replacing the aging and frequently-injured Bryan Robson. On his Manchester United Premier League home debut, Keane scored twice in a 3–0 win over Sheffield United and instantly became a favourite of the fans. He recalls, 'From that night on the burden of being the game's most expensive player eased. Soon it ceased to matter.'[15]

United won both the Premier League and the FA Cup in 1994, the club's first ever 'double', and Keane established himself as a regular starter. The following season saw United finish second in the Premier League and lose the FA Cup final but the Red Devils bounced back in 1996 and again won the 'double'. The league title was retained in 1997 and Keane took over as club captain in the summer after the departure of Eric Cantona. However, he missed most of the 1997/1998 season with a cruciate knee ligament injury after an attempted tackle, for which he received a booking, on Alfie Haaland of Leeds United.

Without Keane for much of the season, Manchester United lost the Premier League title in 1998 but the following campaign proved to be an historic one with the Red Devils winning an unprecedented 'treble' of Premier League, FA Cup and UEFA Champions League. In the second leg of the Champions League semi-final, against Juventus in Turin, Keane delivered a virtuoso performance to inspire United to recover a two-goal deficit and win 3–2. Unfortunately for the Manchester United captain, a yellow card for a trip on Zinedine Zidane meant that he missed the final where the Red Devils scored two late goals to stun Bayern Munich. In his autobiography, *Managing My Life*, Alex Ferguson describes Keane's display in Turin:

> *It was the most emphatic display of selflessness I have seen on a football field. Pounding over every blade of grass, competing as if he would rather die of exhaustion than lose, he inspired all around him. I felt it was an honour to be associated with such a player.*[16]

Three further Premier League titles followed for Keane in 2000, 2001 and 2003 but there was plenty of controversy along the way. In the 2001 Manchester derby, Keane received a straight red card for a dangerous tackle on Alfie Haaland. The Manchester United captain received a three-game suspension but five more games were added to the suspension after the publication of his autobiography, in which he admitted that he set out to hurt Haaland and had been waiting for the moment for three years. In August 2002, Keane received another FA suspension, and a large fine from Alex Ferguson, for elbowing Sunderland's Jason McAteer, a colleague of his on the Irish national team.

The last trophy that Keane lifted for Manchester United was the FA Cup in 2004. The following season United lost the FA Cup final on penalties to Arsenal and on 18 November 2005, Keane left Old Trafford by mutual consent. The thirty-four-year-old club captain was recovering from injury and had made a number of appearances on Manchester United TV (MUTV) criticising the performances and attitudes of some of the team's players. Keane had enjoyed a very close relationship with Alex Ferguson but the pair had argued at the team's pre-season training camp in Portugal and an outburst on MUTV in November proved to be the final straw for the club's management. Keane felt bitter about his hasty departure from Manchester United (he trained on the Friday morning before his contract was suddenly ended by lunchtime) and later stated, 'The day I left United I should have stopped playing. I lost the love of the game that Friday morning. I left Old Trafford and thought "football is cruel, life is cruel".'[17]

Keane did not stop playing after being let go by Manchester United. Instead, he signed for Celtic in January 2006 and won the Scottish Premier League and Scottish League Cup before finally hanging up his boots six months later.

On the international stage, Roy Keane won sixty-seven caps for the Republic of Ireland between 1991 and 2005, playing at the 1994 World Cup in the US and helping his country to qualify for the 2002 World Cup in South Korea and Japan. Keane, however, famously did not play in the tournament. Upset by the training conditions in Saipan and what he regarded as an unprofessional approach in the Irish camp, Keane returned home before the tournament began after a major row with manager Mick McCarthy. Keane vowed never to play for his country again while McCarthy was in charge but he did later make a short-lived comeback when Brian Kerr took over as manager of the national team. Hannigan notes that 'the saddest element of Keane's departure from Saipan was that it cost him his last chance of playing in a World Cup at somewhere close to his peak'.[18]

Shortly after retiring as a player, Roy Keane took over as manager of Championship side Sunderland in August 2006 and took them from the foot of the table to the league title. He helped Sunderland stay in the Premier League in 2007/2008 but left the club in December 2008 after a poor start to the season. He was appointed manager of Ipswich Town in April 2009 but was fired after twenty months with the club near the bottom of the league, having suffered seven losses in the previous nine games.

Keane now works as a football analyst on ITV and is as outspoken and controversial as he was during his playing career. He lives with his wife Theresa [Doyle] and their five children in Woodbridge, near Ipswich. Keane has engaged in a lot of charity work and is most closely associated with the Irish Guide Dogs, with whom he has had a long relationship.

FREEDOM OF CORK

Roy Keane was elected as a freeman of Cork on 23 May 2005 and was conferred with the honour, alongside athlete Sonia O'Sullivan, on 14 June – six months before his dramatic departure from Manchester United. Keane entered the City Hall through a side entrance as chants of 'Keano, Keano' rang out from the large crowd gathered outside.[19]

In his opening address, the Lord Mayor, Councillor Seán Martin, praised Keane and O'Sullivan as two of the country's greatest ever sportspeople. He referred to the Saipan controversy as Keane's 'most courageous performance'[20] as the player had more to lose than anyone else involved. After the Lord Mayor's speech, the large audience of approximately 700 people was treated to some video highlights of the careers of Keane and O'Sullivan, with both stars looking somewhat embarrassed as they sat and watched.

O'Sullivan was first to be presented with her freedom casket and before Keane took to the podium the newly-written 'Ballad of Roy Keane' was performed by composer Con Fada Ó Drisceoil. Writing in the *Irish Independent*, Miriam Lord noted that 'by the third of seven verses, the audience was singing along'[21] and enjoying the refrain of:

Keano! Keano! On stand and on terrace they're chanting his name.
Keano! Keano! All Corkmen are proud of his glory and fame.

The song also referred to Keane as 'the antidote to the hucksters and chancers, posers and bluffers'.[22]

When Keane took to the podium to receive the freedom of Cork, the *Irish Examiner* stated that 'he kept his words as tight as his haircut'.[23] He began by congratulating his fellow recipient, Sonia O'Sullivan, and then said, 'I am tremendously proud more than anything else to be honoured in my home town and I am deeply moved by the occasion.'[24] With his hands behind his back, Keane delivered a typically modest speech in which he stated that he had been very lucky during his career and he thanked everybody associated with Rockmount, Cobh Ramblers, Nottingham Forest, Manchester United and the Irish national team. He concluded by commenting that he had especially enjoyed the ballad composed and sung in his honour by Con Fada Ó Drisceoil.

MARY McALEESE

(1951–)

Elected as Freewoman of Cork on 8 May 2006

Conferred as Freewoman of Cork 30 May 2006

> '*In recognition of her leadership in promoting greater understanding and building bridges between all the peoples of this island; in recognition of being the first woman to attain a second term in the highest office in the land, that of Uachtarán na hÉireann; in recognition of her outstanding personal and academic achievements, and as a token of the high esteem in which she is held by the people of Cork, for all this and much more.*'

BIOGRAPHY

Mary McAleese, the eighth President of Ireland, was born in the Royal Hospital, Belfast, on 27 June 1951. She was the eldest of nine children born to Paddy Leneghan and Claire McManus who were married the previous year in Holy Cross Church, Ardoyne – a mainly Catholic area of Belfast. McAleese's parents 'were reasonably devout people' and no one in the house would be allowed to miss Sunday mass.[1] She attended the Convent Primary School of the Sisters of Mercy and later went to St Dominic's High School, 'a famous grammar school run by the Dominican nuns on the Falls Road'.[2] Growing up in the 1960s was an interesting experience for McAleese as old certainties were being questioned, especially in areas such as 'the role of women, the authority of the Church, authority in general, sexuality and personal responsibility'.[3] Unfortunately it was also a time when there was a lot of violence and the Catholic McAleese family was one of many adversely affected by the 'Troubles'.[4]

In August 1969, eighteen-year-old McAleese watched in horror from the top of Ardoyne as violence broke out, which became 'the genesis of thirty years of Troubles'.[5] During the riots of that month, Catholic houses were burned out and some residents living on the Shankill side of the Crumlin Road were forced to move out of their homes.[6] Later in life, looking back as this time period, McAleese noted:

> *I was a Northern Catholic from Ardoyne, my family had lost our home, our business: having actually physically suffered during the Troubles. People didn't want to know that. Nobody wanted to face up to it, and I think still don't really, to the ghastly meandering war*

on their doorsteps. They would have preferred if I with my personal witness had gone away.
And because I refused to, their way of dealing with me was to stick me in a box and label it:
maniacal nationalist, ultra-Republican – neither of which I was.[7]

After graduating in law from Queen's University Belfast in 1973, McAleese was called to the
Northern Ireland Bar in 1974 but she moved to Dublin the following year when she was appointed
Reid Professor of Criminal Law, Criminology and Penology at Trinity College, following in the
footsteps of Mary Robinson. She was glad to leave Belfast because of the bigotry and violence but
found Dublin a harsh place, partly because of 'the glazed-over look when you started to talk about
the problems in the North and in particular when you started to recite the things that happened to
you personally'.[8]

McAleese held her position in Trinity until 1979 when she joined RTÉ as a journalist and
presenter. McAleese enjoyed presenting the current affairs show, *Frontline*, and – not long after taking
the role – she interviewed lawyer Mary Robinson on the subject of Diplock Courts in Northern
Ireland.[9] Married to Martin McAleese, an accountant, since 1976, the couple were living in Dublin
and making a comfortable living on their two salaries. The situation changed somewhat in the spring
of 1980 when Martin announced that he wanted to return to university to study dentistry. Reduced
to a one-salary family, McAleese opted to return to the Reid professorship in Trinity while retaining
some part-time work in RTÉ.

In the February 1987 general election she contested a seat with Fianna Fáil in the Dublin South-
East constituency but was unsuccessful.[10] Following this disappointment, McAleese returned to
Queen's University as Director of the Institute of Professional Legal Studies. In 1994, she became
the first female Pro-Vice Chancellor of the university.[11] During this period of her life she also held
a variety of other positions including being a Director of Channel 4 Television and of Northern
Ireland Electricity.[12]

In 1997, McAleese received the Fianna Fáil nomination, defeating Albert Reynolds, to contest
the presidential election. She faced an unusually crowded field with four other candidates – Mary
Banotti (Fine Gael nominee), Adi Roche (Labour Party nominee) and two independents, Rosemary
'Dana' Scallon and Derek Nally. Her biographer, Ray Mac Mánais, states that the election campaign
had an insipid start:

The four women were friendly and polite, too friendly and too polite, perhaps, for the taste of
an Irish public that was reared on more piquant political fare. Almost from the start the
campaign was styled as a contest between the heart and the head – the heart of Adi Roche
and the head of Mary McAleese – a generalisation that was unfair to both women.[13]

McAleese ran a steady campaign as Roche, the early leader in the polls, faltered. As a native of Northern Ireland with a nationalist outlook, McAleese was not popular in all quarters and *The Irish Times* ran an opinion piece by Eoghan Harris in October 1997 entitled 'Why Mary McAleese Must be Stopped'. In the article he referred to her as a 'tribal time bomb'.[14] Despite these concerns, McAleese was a comfortable victor in the election, taking 45 per cent of the first preference votes and defeating Mary Banotti in the second count.[15]

Mary McAleese was inaugurated as the eighth President of Ireland in Dublin Castle on 11 November 1997. During her speech she quoted the fifth President, Cearbhall Ó Dálaigh, who had stated at his inauguration in 1974, 'Presidents, under the Irish constitution don't have policies. But … a president can have a theme.'[16] McAleese then announced that the theme of her presidency would be 'Building Bridges' and that these bridges would demand patience, imagination and courage.[17] She concluded her inaugural address as president by saying:

Ireland sits tantalisingly ready to embrace a golden age of affluence, self-assurance, tolerance and peace. It will be my most profound privilege to be President of this beautiful, intriguing country. May I ask those of faith, whatever that faith may be, to pray for me and our country that we will use these seven years well, to create a future where, in the words of William Butler Yeats, 'Everything we look upon is blest'.[18]

The new President caused controversy early in her term by receiving Holy Communion with her family during an Anglican service in Dublin. A public opinion poll showed that 78 per cent of people approved of her actions but she was heavily criticised by the Archbishop of Dublin, Cardinal Desmond Connell. He said that Catholics receiving communion in a Protestant church were engaging in a 'sham' and a 'deception'.[19] McAleese received strong support from the Taoiseach, Bertie Ahern, who said it was ironic that the Church was condemning an act of reconciliation and bridge-building between the denominations.[20]

In 1998, during an official visit to the United States, McAleese met with the now disgraced Cardinal Bernard Francis Law, the former Catholic Archbishop of Boston, who berated her for her support of the ordination of women priests and stated he 'was sorry for Catholic Ireland to have you as President'.[21] McAleese responded that she was the 'President of Ireland and not just Catholic Ireland' and the two became engaged in a heated argument.[22]

McAleese was returned unopposed for a second seven-year term in office in 2004 and she was re-inaugurated on 11 November. She stated that she was 'proud to represent one of the world's most successful and dynamic countries, with a rags to riches, conflict to peace story that I know inspires many in a troubled world'.[23] There were many highlights during her second term as president, none more so than the historic and symbolic visit by Queen Elizabeth II to Ireland in May 2011. On President McAleese's final day in office, 10 November 2011, she published a piece in *The Irish Times* under the headline 'My personal thanks to Ireland'. Referring to herself and her husband, Martin, she wrote:

> *We made friendships across all sorts of ancient estrangements and differences of politics, ethnicity, faith and perspective. We shook thousands of hands at Áras an Uachtaráin and relished the pleasure that a visit to that house brought to so many people. We were particularly heartened by the people who came as tentative and distrustful strangers but who gradually grew more comfortable. Their willingness to engage allowed us to believe that a future of good-neighbourliness and partnership was possible. The happy and healing visit of Her Majesty Queen Elizabeth II showcased the extent of the mutual desire for a new and healthier relationship between our countries and how far we have travelled in creating it.*[24]

McAleese has been very active since leaving office. She started studying canon law in Rome and in October 2012 she published her latest book, *Quo Vadis? Collegiality in the Code of Canon Law*. In March 2013 it was announced that she would go to Boston College in the autumn as the Burns Library Visiting Scholar in Irish Studies.

Mary and Martin McAleese have three children, Emma, born in 1982, and twins Justin and SaraMai, born in 1985.[25]

FREEDOM OF CORK

Mary McAleese, President of Ireland, was conferred with the freedom of Cork on 30 May 2006 during her second term in office at a special meeting of Cork City Council. She had been proposed for the honour by the Lord Mayor, Councillor Deirdre Clune, and seconded by Councillor Damian Wallace at a meeting on 8 May. In starting the conferring ceremony in the City Hall, the Lord Mayor stated:

> *It stands to reason that the person to whom this award is given must be exceptional or have achieved greatness in some particular field. I don't think there can be anybody present here today who would argue that President McAleese more than meets those criteria. If it were not enough to be the only elected Head of State in history to succeed another female Head of State, the aims the President has set for both of her presidencies have not only been met, they have largely been surpassed.*[26]

The Lord Mayor continued by praising McAleese for the success of her 'Building Bridges' theme and added:

It has been a hallmark of her period in office that the door to the President and to the Presidency has never been more open or inviting to the marginalised, disenfranchised and excluded. Community workers, schoolchildren and volunteers, especially those involved with the Special Olympics World Games which were such a resounding success, found the door to the Áras open and welcoming at all times during her presidencies.[27]

The Lord Mayor then invited the President of Ireland to sign the register and accept her freedom casket. Having completed the formalities, Mary McAleese commenced her speech by paying tribute to the city of Cork:

Between the Heineken Cup and the Palme D'Or [with reference to the successful film 'The Wind that Shakes the Barley'], Cork's credentials as the 'real capital' of Europe, whatever about Ireland, have never been stronger!!! When I gave Sean Óg O'hAilpín a distinguished graduate award at his alma mater, DCU, a few weeks ago, he told me disarmingly and seriously that he would next shake my hand in September at Croke Park. It is that 'Cork-sureness' so often mistaken by the ignorant as 'cocksureness' that is the driving spirit of the people of this city and county. It is also the very attitude, the pose which gives the rest of us not born near 'the banks' a lifelong inferiority complex. For most of us that accident of birth over which we had no control, is unalterable, unchangeable. We are destined to go through life apologising for not being from Cork, and being starved spectators at the feast that is Corkness. But for a very small and lucky band, history can be rewritten and today I am privileged to have conferred on me the freedom of this mighty city. Now at least, if I cannot say I was born in Cork, I can say I am a freewoman of the city of Cork, an honorary citizen. When explaining in future that, without my consent, my parents chose Belfast as the city of my birth, I can now say proudly that Cork chose me.[28]

McAleese went on to say that the award of the freedom of Cork meant that her CV was now complete[29] and that Cork was blessed in its people, in their ambition for their city and in their energy in working for her and her future.[30] She reserved special praise for Cork City Council which had been crowned 'Local Authority of the Year' in 2005, and then quoted from John FitzGerald's song, 'I have roamed through all climates, but none could I see, like the green hills of Cork and my own lovely Lee'.[31]

Cork's fourth freewoman concluded her well-received speech in a typically light-hearted way, saying, 'You'll be relieved to hear I won't be back next week with a few Dublin sheep and cows to graze in the Lee Fields. The shock of what they have been missing all these years might be too much for the unfortunate animals.'[32]

MICHAEL FLATLEY

(1958–)

Elected as Freeman of Cork on 10 April 2007

Conferred as Freeman of Cork on 2 June 2007

'In recognition of his personal achievements as a world-class dancer, musician, performer and as a person of outstanding artistic talent and capability; in recognition of his exceptional vision and achievement of raising the profile of Ireland abroad by bringing Irish dance and music to a new level and to a worldwide audience through the phenomenal international success of his shows; in recognition of his pursuit of pushing boundaries and passion for his heritage; and as a token of the high esteem in which he is held by the people of Cork, for all this and much more.'

BIOGRAPHY

The acclaimed Irish-American dancer Michael Ryan Flatley was born in Chicago on 16 July 1958 to Irish parents. He claims in his autobiography, *Lord of the Dance* (published in 2006), that dance is in his very first memory and he describes being taught a few steps as a four-year-old.[1] He credits his grandmother, Hannah Ryan, as a hugely positive influence in his early years:

> *I learned my first steps in my grandmother's kitchen . . . My grandmother taught me more than just to dance. She told me you could get everything you wanted if only you concentrated and worked hard. She explained that we were descendants of the High Kings of Ireland and that it was in my blood to be a great leader. She said that one day I would be famous – and more than that. 'You will be the King of Ireland some day, Michael,' she told me. 'You'll live in a castle. You must work hard and believe in yourself and your bloodline.'[2]*

Flatley did not start official dancing lessons until he was eleven but he was soon winning championships all across the United States. He sprang to prominence in Dublin in 1975 when he became the first non-European to win the World Championship for Irish Dance. Showing his vast array of talents, Flatley also won the Chicago Golden Gloves boxing championship and the All-Ireland Concert Flute championship in Donegal in the same year.

After graduating from Brother Rice High School in Chicago, Flatley immediately opened a dance school. He notes in his autobiography:

It isn't easy making a school pay, especially if you're young and inexperienced. But I had the advantage of being a world champion and that was better than an advertising campaign. On the opening evening, hundreds of kids and their parents were lined up to study with me. Soon I was taking down a fortune in cash.[3]

While the dance school was a success and the money was good, Flatley grew frustrated over time as he wanted to perform rather than teach. Accordingly, he closed the school and commenced a tough period in his life, working as a labourer during the day and dancing by night.[4]

In the early 1980s, Flatley received a phone call that changed his life. It came from Joe Whitston, the manager of the legendary Irish traditional group, the Chieftains. The group had seen Flatley dancing in New York and wanted him to tour with them. Flatley was understandably delighted to accept the offer:

I didn't have the words to tell him [Whitston] just how interested I was. At that point, the Chieftains were the only band playing traditional Irish music on the international stage. Their offer was to make me the first ever professional Irish dancer. My first night out, I got a standing ovation. I came off the stage, breathing heavily as I made my way to my tiny, beat-up dressing room. I looked into the cloudy mirror and thought, 'This is it. I'm never going back [to labouring]. This is what I want to do.'[5]

Flatley made the most of his big break with the Chieftains. While he retained the basic structure and spirit of Irish dance he also 'incorporated new and exciting ideas that helped make the dances become less rigid, adding flowing arm movements and exciting rhythms to the traditional steps'.[6] His fame and popularity spread and he was invited to perform some solo dance concerts at prestigious venues including New York's Carnegie Hall and the Hollywood Bowl.[7] With his career already on the rise, he 'exploded on the public consciousness'[8] on 30 April 1994 when he led the inspired dance act (which he had created and choreographed himself) during the interval of the Eurovision Song Contest.

Flatley retains fond memories of the Eurovision performance:

I felt I had 800 years of Irish repression on my back. And below me, buoying me up, my thirty-five years of hard work. I was dancing for Ireland, for my parents, for my fellow dancers, and for myself. When I finished it felt like scoring the winning goal in the World Cup. The greatest feeling of triumph I'd ever had. Even before the audience broke into applause, I knew I'd done what I'd set out to do.[9]

It is fair to say that the interval act outshone the song contest itself and, taking advantage of the moment, Flatley extended the routine (and Bill Whelan's musical score), with Moya Doherty and John McColgan, into a longer dance show and began touring with *Riverdance*. McColgan had been sitting in the Eurovision audience and noted that at the end of the interval act, the audience did not break into a cheer 'but a primeval roar'.[10] He knew that he had a potential massive hit on his hands and when *Riverdance* opened at Dublin's Point Theatre in February 1995 it was 'watched by millions on television worldwide, before transferring to London, where it was equally well received'.[11] Flatley was the undoubted star of the phenomenal show but his association with it ended abruptly in October 1995 due to a contract dispute about artistic control, rather than money. He also had suffered physically from performing eight shows a week – as well as his choreography responsibilities – and had collapsed backstage at the Point Theatre.

The end of Flatley's relationship with *Riverdance* came sharply on 2 October 1995 when lawyer Robert Lee rang the dancer and told him, 'You're out, Michael. They do not want a star. They want a show where everyone can be replaced.'[12] Flatley's primary dancing partner on the show, Jean Butler, later stated, 'Michael leaving the show affected me enormously. I felt I was losing my right hand.'[13]

Not one to rest on his laurels, Flatley began work on another production called *Lord of the Dance*, which opened in the Point Theatre. The production showcased Flatley's rich dancing talent to the full 'and was hugely acclaimed by critics, with all performances sold out for weeks on end'.[14] *Lord of the Dance* played mostly in big arenas and stadiums as opposed to the traditional theatre-style venues. For example, the show sold out for four consecutive weeks and set a new record for the Wembley Arena in London.[15] In the same year, 1997, Flatley and his dancing troupe performed at the Academy Awards ceremony before a massive global audience. Flatley and his dancers received a standing ovation at the ceremony, with Lewis Segal, dance critic of the *Los Angeles Times*, writing, 'The Academy Awards made the milestones of film history into a mere backdrop for Flatley.'[16]

Flatley continued to be driven by an insatiable hunger for success. After the triumph of the Academy Awards, he notes in his autobiography:

I loved the success I'd worked so hard for. But I knew I could not just sit back and count the cash. I had to retain my focus. We were flying fast and getting faster. The suites got bigger, the girls prettier, the cars faster – but the dance was still the main thing. There was still a long way to go, still lots of places and people to conquer.[17]

He danced in the last performance of *Lord of the Dance* in Dublin in June 1998 and soon afterwards opened a new show, *Feet of Flames*. The premiere performance was in front an audience of 25,000 people in London's Hyde Park and the show, once again, was a big success for Flatley.[18] Despite announcing his retirement from touring in 2001, Flatley continues to perform and he launched his new show *Celtic Tiger* in July 2005. Since then he has performed in new versions of *Feet of Flames* and *Lord of the Dance* and released a flute album in 2011. Flatley divides his time between living in America and Ireland. Though he has no family roots in Cork, he spends a lot of time in the county, having purchased and refurbished Castlehyde, one of the finest examples of Georgian architecture in Ireland, a stately home overlooking the Blackwater River, outside Fermoy. Local Cork historian Pat Bartley visited the Castlehyde estate in 2006 and noted:

> *I knew the house and grounds in the year 2000 and to see them now is unbelievable. When Michael Flatley moved here the house was derelict and the grounds were a wilderness. Now, it is a sight to behold. The splendour of it is breathtaking; the 800-year-old Norman castle still stands guarding this historical place and Michael; the peacocks and pheasants strut around the river and woodland walks and the lawns and avenues. There are very few people who could have achieved this.*[19]

Michael Flatley has been married twice. His first wife was Polish-born Beata Dziaba and they divorced in 1997 having been married in 1986. In 2002, he was briefly engaged to model Lisa Murphy before marrying Niamh O'Brien in 2006. The couple have one son, Michael St James Flatley, born in April 2007.

FREEDOM OF CORK

Saturday 2 June 2007 was the day that Michael Flatley was conferred with the freedom of Cork city, having been elected a freeman at the council meeting of 10 April. Flatley was accompanied to the ceremony by his Sligo-born father, Michael, his Carlow-born mother, Elizabeth, and his wife, Niamh, who the *Irish Examiner* noted, 'looked radiant in a classic but simple navy and brown polka-dot pinstriped cream suit from designer Karen Millen'.[20] There was a festive atmosphere inside the City Hall and 'the audience lightly sang to the background playing of "Red Rose Café", waiting for the slightly late entrance'.[21]

The ceremony began with the roll call of council members, some of whom – according to the *Irish Examiner* reporter, Cornelia Lucey – 'didn't look too delighted to be there on the bank holiday weekend'.[22] After the initial formalities were completed, poet Thomas McCarthy took to the stage and recited his poem 'A Dance at Castlehyde' which referred to Flatley as the 'new Fred Astaire'. There followed a traditional music performance from Geraldine O'Callaghan, Johnny McCarthy, Flaithrí Neff and Brian Hanlon which set '400 feet tapping to the rhythm'.[23]

In his speech, the Lord Mayor, Councillor Michael Ahern, congratulated Flatley and his wife Niamh on the birth of their son the previous month. He also praised Flatley for the refurbishment of Castlehyde and expressed the wish that, 'Maybe your son will bring the McCarthy Cup or the Sam Maguire, or both, back to Castlehyde some day.'[24] The Lord Mayor added:

Lord Mayor Councillor Michael Ahern (*left*) presents Michael Flatley (*right*) with his freedom casket. COURTESY *IRISH EXAMINER*

In honouring Michael we are honouring someone who has taken a traditional Irish cultural and artistic form and re-invented it for the new millennium without losing any of the skill, tradition or heritage of the form. He has brought Ireland and Irishness centre stage and no doubt inspired many others to do likewise.[25]

Rising to respond and accept his freedom casket and certificate, the new freeman of Cork 'gave a speech which brought tears to several of those present'.[26] He praised the spirit of the Irish people and re-emphasised the words of John F. Kennedy – 'Ireland, your time is now'. In dedicating the award to his father, Flatley said:

It is a great honour to be granted the freedom of Cork city, proud capital of the county which is now home to Niamh, Michael St James and myself. It is humbling to join such a distinguished list of freemen and I will carry the honour with pride. I am grateful to Lord Mayor Ahern, the city council and the people of Cork.[27]

JOHN MAJOR

(1943–)

Elected as Freeman of Cork on 12 May 2008

Conferred as Freeman of Cork on 20 June 2008

'In recognition of his contribution to the process which led to the establishment of
a lasting democratic solution in Northern Ireland, equally respectful of the hopes
and aspirations of both communities; in honour of his qualities of leadership,
integrity, negotiation, and common sense in so doing; for his statesmanship,
diplomacy, energy and commitment to the initiative despite the prevailing climate
at the time and his unfailing and unwavering belief in the value of the process; for
all this and much more.'

BIOGRAPHY

John Major, the British Prime Minister from 1990 to 1997, was born in the Worchester Park suburb
of southwest London on 29 March 1943, 'the youngest son of Thomas Major and Gwendolyn Minny
Coates'.[1] By the time John was born, his parents were relatively elderly and 'beyond the period of
fanciful exertions'.[2] His father, whose colourful earlier life 'had taken him to the United States and
South America where he worked in circuses and music halls',[3] now supported his family through a
small business manufacturing garden ornaments. However, when John was a young boy, his father's
business failed and the family hit bad times, moving to a cramped two-room flat in Brixton. John
was not an especially conscientious student and he later acknowledged that 'he lacked motivation
and bridled against school discipline'.[4] With only O-Levels to his name he left school at the age of
sixteen and worked in a variety of clerical and labouring jobs for the next few years.

Aged nineteen, Major spent nine months unemployed before he got a job at the London
Electricity Board which laid 'the foundation for his eventual entry into a position with the Standard
Chartered Bank'.[5] It was during this period that his political career took off. Having joined the Young
Conservatives in 1965, he was elected to the Lambeth Borough Council in 1968, 'where he
eventually became Chairman of the Housing Committee'.[6] Major was politically ambitious and
by the early 1970s he 'was enthusiastically pursuing a parliamentary seat'.[7] He was foiled in the
1974 general election but won a seat at the 1979 election, 'which saw Margaret Thatcher replace
the Callaghan government and institute a radical right agenda for the new Conservative
administration'.[8] Major's 1979 electoral win was in the constituency of Huntingdon and he held
the seat comfortably until his retirement from the House of Commons in 2001.[9]

Major rose swiftly in the Conservative Party and he held various positions over the years which followed – Parliamentary Private Secretary in 1981, Assistant Whip (1983–1985) and Under-Secretary of State for Social Security (1985–1986). By 1986, he 'had become a Minister of State at the same department [Social Security] and was being widely cited as future cabinet material'.[10]

Following the 1987 general election, Major's inevitable promotion to cabinet occurred when he was appointed Chief Secretary to the Treasury. Major initially harboured some self-doubts 'over his capacity to take on the demanding role of controlling public expenditure'[11] but the doubts were soon dispelled 'by the familiar formula of a prodigious work rate and an ability to lower the resistance of those around him through genial informality and expectations of mutual support'.[12] In a surprising cabinet reshuffle in July 1989, Prime Minister Thatcher appointed Major as Foreign Secretary to succeed Geoffrey Howe. In his book, Michael Foley describes the appointment as 'an astonishing promotion for a minister who had yet to run a department'.[13] For Thatcher, the promotion of Major was part of a succession strategy as she subsequently admitted in her book, *The Downing Street Years*:

A modest man, aware of his inexperience, he [Major] would probably have preferred a less grand appointment. But I knew that if he was to have a hope of becoming Party leader, it would be better if he had held one of the three great offices of the state … I had simply concluded that he must be given wider public recognition and greater experience if he was to compete with the talented self-publicists who would be among his rivals.[14]

Neither Thatcher nor Major realised how quickly things would move and that the leadership of the Conservative Party would change sixteen months later. Major served as British Foreign Secretary for the grand total of three months before being appointed Chancellor of the Exchequer in October 1989 after the shock resignation of Nigel Lawson.[15] Foley states that 'in appearance, Major was a middle-ranking minister in a senior position because of good fortune and a dependency upon an unpredictable patron [Thatcher] who had a track record of breaking out of formal hierarchies of policy consultation and decision-making'.[16] Yet, a little over one year later, Major became Prime Minister after defeating Douglas Hurd and Michael Heseltine in the Conservative Party leadership contest that followed Thatcher's departure.

As Prime Minister, Major 'had no wish to try and emulate Thatcher's forceful leadership'[17] and opted for the consultative consensus building approach that had served him well up to this point. Having assumed power just after Saddam Hussein had invaded Kuwait, 'Major gained a reputation for toughness, through his support for the Gulf War in 1991'.[18] In December of the same year, Major negotiated the European Union Maastricht Treaty, obtaining an 'opt out' from the Euro to maintain Sterling as an independent currency.[19] He successfully guided the Conservative Party to victory in the 1992 general election, 'even though his overall majority was narrow and disappeared during the course of that term in government'.[20]

The period in government from 1992 to 1997 was a difficult one for Major and the Conservative Party. On the positive side, Prime Minister Major worked with Taoiseach Albert Reynolds (and later John Bruton) to seek a solution to the troubles in Northern Ireland and this work paved the way for the historic Good Friday Agreement of 1998. On the negative side, Major struggled with political in-fighting over Britain's place in Europe and a variety of damaging 'sleaze scandals' emerged involving some of his government colleagues. Major was a Prime Minister under pressure and he stood down as leader of the Conservative Party in 1995 (while retaining his role as Prime Minister) in order to force the hands of his opponents and contest a new leadership battle. It turned out to be a politically smart move and Major was re-elected leader, heavily defeating John Redwood. However, while his authority within the Conservative Party was temporarily bolstered, 'failures seemed to outnumber successes'[21] for the beleaguered government.

It was, therefore, not surprising when the Conservative Party was defeated in the general election of May 1997, which brought Tony Blair and the Labour Party to power. Foley explains that things had gone full circle for Major:

In 1990, John Major had been the youthful option. At that point he had the distinction of being the youngest prime minister of the twentieth century. He had injected new blood into the party and effectively rejuventated the government. Now he was confronted by an opposition leader [Blair] ten years his junior who was making his party and his administration look grey, outmoded and worn out.[22]

Following the election defeat, Major was replaced as party leader by William Hague in June 1997, and he stayed as a parliamentarian until 2001 when he retired from the House of Commons before that year's general election. Since leaving public office, Major has maintained a relatively low profile, indulging two of his main passions – writing and cricket. He has written three highly acclaimed books, starting with *John Major – The Autobiography* in 2000. In 2008, *More Than a Game* was published – in the book, Major provides a detailed history of cricket with a focus on the game's early development. In 2012, Major paid homage to his father with *My Old Man: A Personal History of Music Hall* and the book was shortlisted for a Theatre Book Prize.

Major married Norma Johnson (now Dame Norma Major) in October 1970 and the couple have two children, James and Elizabeth. The marriage survived the scandal that broke in 2002, which revealed Major's four-year affair with Edwina Currie between 1984 and 1988. At that stage Currie was a Conservative Party backbencher and Major was a whip in Thatcher's government.[23]

FREEDOM OF CORK

The names of John Major and Albert Reynolds went before Cork City Council on 12 May 2008 in a proposal from Lord Mayor, Councillor Donal Counihan, that both men should receive the freedom of the city. Following a fractious debate in the council chamber, the motion was passed by 21–6, with three Sinn Féin councillors, two from the Labour Party and one from the Socialist Party opposing. Reporting on the meeting in the *Irish Examiner*, Eoin English noted:

> *Councillors usually agree unanimously to the nominees. But this joint proposal split the council. After weeks of behind-the-scenes talks to secure a two-thirds voting majority, councillors voted last night to accept a straight majority. They then voted 21 to 6 in favour.*[24]

The opposition to the joint election of Major and Reynolds as freemen of Cork was entirely centred on Major. Sinn Féin councillor Jonathan O'Brien described the former British Prime Minister's role in the peace process as one of 'obstruction, dishonesty and cover-ups' and added that he had to 'be dragged kicking and screaming' to the negotiating table.[25] Labour councillor Michael O'Connell stated that Major had been a member of Thatcher's cabinet that had 'waged war on the trade union movement in England'.[26]

The protests against Major were also apparent on the day of the conferring ceremony, Friday 20 June. A crowd of about twenty people, led by members of the '32 County Sovereignty Movement' shouted 'Brits Out' as Major was accompanied into the City Hall by the Lord Mayor. The Sinn Féin councillors boycotted the event and lodged a formal complaint with the city council about the flying of three Union Jack flags over City Hall.

Inside the City Hall, there was no evidence of protest and the joint conferring ceremony passed off smoothly. Lord Mayor Counihan spoke first and he praised Major and Reynolds for the Downing Street Declaration of 1993, which he said 'led to the establishment of a lasting peace'.[27] He claimed that many before had tried and failed but that Major and Reynolds had successfully persevered. The Lord Mayor ended his speech by appropriately quoting another freeman of Cork, John F. Kennedy, 'peace is a daily process, a weekly, a monthly process, gradually changing opinions, slowly eroding old barriers, quietly building new structures'.[28]

Albert Reynolds was the first to be presented with his freedom casket and then he addressed the large crowd. Next, Thomas McCarthy read a poem that he had composed for the ceremony and it was then the turn of Major to accept his casket and deliver a speech. He said that he was honoured to receive the freedom of Cork city alongside his old friend, Albert.[29]

Major stated that politics was full of advances and setbacks but he was 'utterly confident' that Northern Ireland would not return to the sort of situation that had previously existed.[30]

After the conferring ceremony, Major spoke to reporters and said that the presence of a Union Jack flag flying next to the Irish flag over City Hall was a sign of how far Ireland had come since the Downing Street Declaration.[31] He said that he was not bothered by the protestors outside the venue as he had dealt with 'a lifetime of protests' during his political career.[32] He added, 'I'm utterly unconcerned with the protest. They're just lucky they are in a country in which they can protest freely.'[33]

CONCLUSION

The freedom of Cork remains the greatest honour in the gift of Cork City Council. As highlighted throughout this book there is a rich and colourful history associated with this prestigious award in Cork. Unfortunately, there has been a tendency for controversy in recent years that potentially tarnishes the honour. The nomination of former British Prime Minister John Major in 2008 split the council and saw some councillors not only oppose the proposal but also boycott the subsequent conferring. In 2010, the nomination of Peter Barry was also shrouded in controversy. Lord Mayor Councillor Dara Murphy proposed Barry who he said had served the city with distinction as a TD for Cork between 1969 and 1997 as well as periods as Tánaiste and deputy leader of the Fine Gael party. The nomination was not unanimously agreed and was opposed by six councillors when the vote was called. Even though Fianna Fáil voted in favour, Councillor Terry Shannon subsequently addressed the meeting (26 April 2010) and stated:

> We were under the impression that a gentleman's agreement was in place about giving the freedom of the city. The manner in which this was highly politicised was a disgrace. You, Lord Mayor, went on a solo run. All the rules were broken. We will seek a change in the procedures so that twenty-three votes [three-quarters of council] of members will be required.

Independent Councillor Dave McCarthy criticised the 'horse-trading' that had taken place about the freedom and stated that the honour was too important to be treated in that way.

In recent times, some councillors have argued that the frequency with which the freedom of the city has been granted, over the last decade especially, devalues the honour. There have been suggestions during debates that it would be more appropriate if it was awarded once in the five-year lifetime of a council (Councillor Jonathan O'Brien, 26 April 2010) or once every ten years (Councillor Tim Brosnan, 28 May 2013). The successful nomination by Lord Mayor Councillor John Buttimer for three people to receive the freedom award in 2013 was unprecedented and it will be interesting to see how the freedom of Cork evolves and if tighter protocols will be put in place. Certainly, it is not good practice for the names of possible recipients to be in the public domain before agreement has been reached at council level.

Despite recent controversies there can be no disputing the fact that the list of freemen and freewomen in Cork is a mightily impressive one. The freedom has typically been granted to (a) people who have distinguished themselves on the international stage but who may not have any connection to Cork, or (b) people who may not be widely known but who have made significant contributions to life in Cork. There is equal merit to both categories of recipients.

Cork has witnessed a wide variety of recipients – from theatre (Frank Benson, Frank Duggan, Michael Twomey and Billa O'Connell), from literature (Canon Peadar Ó Laoghaire and Seán Ó Faoláin), from medicine (John Milner Barry and Maurice Hickey), from sport (Con Murphy, Sonia O'Sullivan, Roy Keane and Seán Óg Ó hAilpín), from dance (Michael Flatley) and from social justice (Maureen Curtis-Black and John Bermingham) – not to mention nationalist heroes such as Isaac Butt, Charles Stewart Parnell, John Redmond and Jeremiah O'Donovan Rossa.

The Catholic clergy features prominently on Cork's list and it is worth noting that five of Ireland's nine Presidents have been honoured – Douglas Hyde, Seán T. O'Kelly, Éamon de Valera, Mary Robinson and Mary McAleese (though Hyde was presented with his freedom of the city a full thirty-two years before he became President of Ireland).

Two American Presidents have been made honorary freemen of Cork, Woodrow Wilson and John F. Kennedy, as have two British Prime Ministers, William Gladstone and John Major (though neither was the serving Prime Minister at the time of the award).

In addition, the Cork freedom list boasts two Nobel Peace Prize winners (Woodrow Wilson and John Hume) as well as a winner of the Pulitzer Prize (John F. Kennedy).

There is no doubt that the 'freedom' remains the accolade of accolades in the city of Cork. Long may it continue.

APPENDIX 1

Freedom of Cork City Register complete with citations from 1930

Source: Cork City And County Archives

HONORARY BURGESSES, COUNTY BOROUGH OF CORK, [SEAL OF CORK] REGISTER 1930
BUIRGHÉISIGH ONÓRACHA, BUIRGHEIR CHONNDAETHACH CHORCAIGHE CLÁR 1930

ROLL OF THE HONORARY BURGESSES OF THE CITY OF CORK

The Roll of the Honorary Burgesses admitted prior to 1887 was destroyed in the burning of the Courthouse (1891), and no record is forthcoming of the admission prior to that date of many notable men, amongst others, the late Charles S. Parnell and the late William E. Gladstone. The subsequent Roll was also destroyed in the burning of the Municipal Buildings (December, 1920). Those Admitted since 1887 are as follows:

Hon. Patrick A. Collins, Member of Congress, and General USA Army, enrolled 15 July 1887.

John E. Redmond, Esq., MP Leader of the Irish Parliamentary Party, enrolled 10 January 1902.

Patrick Francis Moran, Cardinal Archbishop of Sydney, enrolled 22 August 1902.

Andrew Carnegie, LL D, Philanthropist, enrolled 5 September 1902.

Vincent Vanutelli, Cardinal Papal Legate, enrolled 5 August 1904.

Jeremiah O'Donovan Rossa, Journalist, enrolled 24 November 1904.

Douglas Hyde, Journalist, enrolled 22 June 1906.

Michael Logue, Cardinal Archbishop of Armagh and Primate of All Ireland, enrolled 12 June 1908.

Hon. Matthew Cumming, President of the Ancient Order of Hibernians, America, enrolled 21 May 1909.

Edward O'Meagher Condon, Captain of the 69th Regiment, USA Army, enrolled 17 September 1909.

Right Hon. Redmond Barry, Lord Chancellor of Ireland, enrolled 20 October 1911.

Peter O'Leary, Canon, PP, enrolled 10 May 1912.

Rt. Hon. Ignatius O'Brien, MA, Lord Chancellor of Ireland, enrolled 25 April 1913.

Rt. Hon. John Campbell, KT, KCMG, GCVO, Lord Lieutenant of Ireland, enrolled 22 January 1915.

Very Rev. Fr Thomas (Dowling), OSFC, Guardian, Holy Trinity Church, Cork, ex-Provincial of the Capuchin Order, Honorary President of the Cork and District Trades and Labour Council, enrolled 10 May 1918.

Kuno Meyer, re-enrolled 14 May 1920, and Order of Council of the 8 January 1915, expunging his name from the roll rescinded.

Dr Woodrow Wilson, President of the United States, enrolled 10 January 1919.

Most Rev. Monsignor Daniel Mannix, DD, LL D, Archbishop of Melbourne, enrolled 6 August 1920.

Most Rev. Dr Spence. Archbishop of Adelaide, enrolled 27 August 1920.

Most Rev. Dr Barry, Coadjutor Archbishop of Hobart, Tasmania, enrolled 10 September 1920.

Rev. Fr Dominick, OSFC, Cork, enrolled 25 February 1922.

Most Rev. Paschal Robinson OFM, 16 July 1930

As a mark of recognition of the great honour bestowed on him by His Holiness, Pope Pius XI, and as a token on the feelings of loyalty and affection entertained by the Lord Mayor, Corporation and Citizens of Cork for the Holy See.
Signed: Fr Paschal Robinson
(signed on the top line where the recipient's name is ordinarily entered. No witnesses noted)

Robert Spence OP Archbishop of Adelaide, Australia, 27 August 1920, conferred 24 November 1930

That the Freedom of the City of Cork be conferred on His Grace, Most Rev. Dr R.N. Spence, OP Archbishop of Adelaide, on the occasion of his visit to his native City, and as a tribute to his adherence to the Cause of Irish Independence – Council, 27 Aug. 1920.
Witnesses: P. O'Dalaigh, Lord Mayor
                     C. Harrington, Town Clerk

Sir Frank Benson, distinguished Shakespearean actor, 31 January 1931

To mark the Farewell Visit of the Distinguished Actor, and in appreciation of his great work on behalf of Art and Drama, and of his long association with the City of Cork.
Signed: Frank Benson
Witnesses: Frank J Daly, for the Lord Mayor
C. Harrington, Town Clerk

His Grace, Most Rev. Dr Finbar Ryan, OP, MA, LL D, 5 October 1937

In recognition of the great honour bestowed on him by His Holiness the Pope in appointing him Coadjutor Archbishop of Port-of-Spain and Archbishop of Gabula.
Signed: Finbar Ryan
Witnesses: James Hickey, Lord Mayor
C. Harrington, Town Clerk

His Excellency Seán T. O'Kelly, President of Ireland, 8 August 1948

That the Freedom of the City of Cork be conferred on His Excellency, Seán T. O'Kelly, President of Ireland, on the Occasion of his first official visit to Cork City.
Signed: Seán T. O'Ceallaigh
Witnesses: Michael Sheehan, Lord Mayor
P. O'Muinechain, City Manager & Town Clerk

His Eminence John Cardinal D'Alton, Archbishop of Armagh & Primate of All Ireland, 16 June 1953

That the Freedom of the City of Cork be conferred on his eminence John Cardinal D'Alton Archbishop of Armagh & Primate of All Ireland, in recognition of his outstanding services to the Church & to the Nation, and as a mark of appreciation of the great honour bestowed upon our Country by His Holiness Pope Pius XII in elevating him to the Sacred College of Cardinals.
Signed: + John Cardinal D'Alton
Witnesses: Patrick McGrath, Lord Mayor
Philip Monahan, City Manager & Town Clerk

His Grace, Most Rev. Dr Richard Cushing, Archbishop of Boston, 26 August 1958

That the Freedom of the City of Cork be conferred on His Grace, Most Rev. Dr Richard Cushing, Archbishop of Boston, in recognition of his practical goodwill towards Ireland and in particular towards the people of the County and City of Cork, and as a token of the affection in which our kith and kin in his Arch-Diocese are held by the Lord Mayor, Corporation and Citizens of Cork.
Signed: Richard J. Cushing
Witnesses: Seán MacCarthaigh, Lord Mayor
P. O'Muineachain, City Manager & Town Clerk

His Eminence Michael Cardinal Browne, OP, 13 August 1962

That the Freedom of the City of Cork be conferred on his eminence Michael Cardinal Browne OP in recognition of the devoted service rendered to the City over the centuries by the order of Preachers, of which he was the distinguished Master General and in appreciation of the honour conferred on him, and through him on the Irish nation by his Holiness Pope John XXII in elevating him as a Prince of The Catholic Church.
Signed: Michael Cardinal Browne OP
Witnesses: Seán Casey, Lord Mayor
Walter McEvilly, City Manager & Town Clerk

John Fitzgerald Kennedy, President of the United States of America, 28 June 1963

That the Freedom of the City of Cork be conferred on the President of the United States of America, John Fitzgerald Kennedy, in token of our pride that this descendant of Irish emigrants should have been elected to such an exalted office, and of our appreciation of his action in coming to visit the country of his ancestors; as a tribute to his unceasing and fruitful work towards the attainment of prosperity and true peace by all the people of the world; and in recognition of the close ties that have always existed between our two countries.
Signed: John F. Kennedy
Witnesses: Seán O'Casey, Lord Mayor
Walter McEvilly, City Manager & Town Clerk

His Eminence William Cardinal Conway, Archbishop of Armagh and Primate of All Ireland, 15 June 1965

That the Freedom of the City of Cork be conferred on His Eminence William Cardinal Conway, Archbishop of Armagh and Primate of All Ireland, in recognition of his eminent services to the Church and to the nation, and of his distinguished achievements as a scholar, theologian and sociologist, and as a mark of appreciation of the honour conferred on him and on Ireland by His Holiness, Pope Paul VI when he elevated him to the Sacred College of Cardinals.
Signed: + William Cardinal Conway
Witnesses: Augustine A. Healy, Lord Mayor
Walter McEvilly, City Manager & Town Clerk

Éamon de Valera, President of Ireland, 31 March 1973

That the Freedom of the City of Cork be conferred on Éamon de Valera, President of Ireland, in appreciation of his lifetime of devoted service to the Irish Nation as patriot, soldier, scholar and statesman and in token of the esteem and affection in which he is held by the people of Cork
Signed: Éamon de Valera
Witnesses: Seán A. O'Leary, Lord Mayor
Patrick Clayton, City Manager & Town Clerk

His Eminence Timothy Cardinal Manning, Archbishop of Los Angeles, 4 December 1973

That the Freedom of the City of Cork be conferred on His Eminence Timothy Cardinal Manning, Archbishop of Los Angeles, in token of our joy and pride at his election to the Sacred College of Cardinals, in recognition of his special care for the underprivileged of his Archdiocese and in appreciation of his abiding affection for and interest in the welfare of the people of the City and County of Cork.
Signed: Timothy Cardinal Manning
Witnesses: Patrick Kerrigan, Lord Mayor
Patrick Clayton, City Manager & Town Clerk

Professor Aloys G. Fleischmann MA, D.MUS; MUS.DOC. (TCD), MRIA, 28 April 1978

That the Freedom of the City of Cork be conferred on Professor Aloys G. Fleischmann MA D.MUS, MUS. DOC. (TCD), MRIA teacher and composer, whose life and energies have been devoted to the development of music and art in the City of Cork, in appreciation of his great and unselfish work and dedication as Director and Organiser of the Cork International Choral Festival, the Cork Orchestral Society and other institutions and of his abiding affection and interest in the welfare of our nation and of the people of the City and County of Cork.
Signed: Aloys G. Fleischmann
Witnesses: Brian C. Sloan, Lord Mayor
            T.J. McHugh, City Manager & Town Clerk

Most Rev. Dr Cornelius Lucey, DD, Ph.D., 19 December 1980

That the Freedom of the City of Cork be conferred on Most Rev. Dr Cornelius Lucey, former Bishop of Cork and Ross in recognition of his outstanding service to the Church and to the City of Cork as Bishop from 1952 to 1980, of his distinguished achievements as a Sociologist renowned for his contributions to major issues of the day and particularly, in the sphere of faith and morals, as the first Irish bishop to inaugurate a Diocesan Foreign Mission by adopting a Parish in Peru as part of his diocese, as a great builder of schools and Churches, as a Pastor who preached the fundamental truths, and as a token of the affection and esteem in which he is held by all the people of the City and County of Cork. For all this and much more, the Lord Mayor, Aldermen and Councillors of the County Borough of Cork consider him worthy to be enrolled in the roll of its Honorary Citizens and so unanimously direct.
Signed: Conchuari Ó'Luasa
Witnesses: Toddy O'Sullivan, Lord Mayor
            T.J. McHugh, City Manager & Town Clerk

Mr John (Jack) Lynch BL, LL D, 19 December 1980

That the Freedom of the City of Cork be conferred on Mr Jack Lynch, BL, LL D, formerly Taoiseach and Head of Successive Governments of the Republic of Ireland from 1966 to 1973 and from 1977 to 1979, one time Chairman of the Council of Ministers of the Council of the European Community, Teachta Dala for the Constituency of Cork City since 1948, Exemplar and upholder of the Democratic Rights of man and rule of law, who devoted himself to the establishment of a better way of life for his fellow countrymen, to the fullest expression of the Irish Ideal and Culture at home and abroad, whose sincerity, dedication and unselfish devotion to his people, his country and his fellow citizens, whose wise counsel, dignified restraint, firmness and humility, at all times, placed him in the fore-front of great leaders and endeared him, not only to those of his friends who knew him best but also to the Nations of the World among whom he is loved and respected and admired; sportsman extraordinary and holder of the greatest awards which can be won in the field of Irish National games. As a Corkman Jack Lynch has brought honour to the City of his birth and has set a goal for all Irishmen to follow for generations to come. For all this and much more the Lord Mayor, Aldermen and Councillors of the County Borough of Cork consider him worthy to be enrolled in the roll of its Honorary Citizens and so unanimously direct.
Signed: Jack Lynch
Witnesses: Toddy O'Sullivan, Lord Mayor
            T.J. McHugh, City Manager & Town Clerk

Honourable Thomas P. O'Neill. Jr – Speaker of the United States House of Representatives, 16 March 1985

That the Freedom of the City of Cork be conferred on the Honourable Thomas P. O'Neill, Jr Speaker of the United States, House of Representatives, in recognition of his outstanding achievements over many years in the political life of his native country, in testimony of the honour which he brings to Ireland, the country of his ancestors, through his love for this country and its people, an affection which he continually demonstrates through his work and actions on our behalf and for his steadfast belief in and concern for democracy at home and in all parts of the world especially where freedom and human rights are under threat. For these reasons and in this historic year when Cork celebrates the 800th anniversary of the grant of its first Charter, the Lord Mayor, Aldermen and Councillors of the County Borough of Cork consider Thomas P. O'Neill, Jr., worthy to be enrolled in the roll of its Honorary Freemen and so direct.
Signed: Thomas P. O'Neill Jr
Witnesses: Liam Burke, Lord Mayor
            T.J. McHugh, City Manager & Town Clerk

Rt. Rev. Monsignor James Dean Bastible, BA, DD, 24 January 1987

That the Freedom of the City of Cork be conferred on Rt. Rev. Monsignor James Dean Bastible, B.A.D.D. in recognition and appreciation of his long and outstanding services to so many voluntary organisations, particularly those organisations involved in the care of the mentally handicapped, disabled and poor of the City, and his magnificent contribution as Chairman for twenty-five years of the Cork Polio and General After-Care Association and as Chairman for twenty-three years of St Patricks Branch, Sick Poor Society; and by honouring Dean Bastible to express the gratitude and appreciation of the citizens for the enormous contribution made by all voluntary organisations to the welfare, health, care and housing of the underprivileged disabled and poor of the community.
Signed: James Bastible, Dean of Cork Diocese
Witnesses: Jerry O'Sullivan, Lord Mayor
            John J. Higgins, City Manager & Town Clerk

Dr Seán Ó Faoláin, 9 July 1988

That the Freedom of the City of Cork be conferred on Dr Seán Ó Faoláin, short story writer, novelist, historian, dramatist, biographer, critic, and man of letters: in recognition of his literary ability and creative imagination, in appreciation of his energetic devotion to his vocation and his outstanding contribution of ten volumes of short stories, three novels, a play, numerous prose works including literary criticism, five biographies as well as travel essays and an autobiographical memoir in acknowledgement of his contribution to the political, social and cultural currents of Irish life and his abiding affection and interest in the welfare of our nation and of the people and city of Cork, in gratitude for his assistance to and encouragement of young writers when as editor of *The Bell* he greatly influenced such writers as Brendan Behan and James Plunkett while publishing the best Irish writers of the time.
Signed: Julia O'Faolain*, Seán O'Faolain
Witnesses: Tom Brosnan, Lord Mayor
            Thomas F. Rice, City Manager and Town Clerk
* The Freedom Register was also signed by the recipient's daughter, reason(s) unknown.

Mary Robinson, Uachtarán na hÉireann, 23 February 1991

That the Freedom of the City of Cork be conferred on Mary Robinson, Uachtarán na hÉireann, in recognition of her outstanding achievements in advancing civil rights and social justice in Ireland; in recognition of her achievement of being the first woman to attain the highest office in the land, that of Uachtarán na hÉireann, and as a token of the high esteem in which she is held by the people of Cork, for all this and much more, the Lord Mayor, Aldermen and councillors of the County Borough of Cork consider her worthy to be enrolled in the Roll of its Honorary Citizens and so direct.

Signed: Mary Robinson
Witnesses: Frank Nash, Lord Mayor
                    Thomas F. Rice, City Manager & Town Clerk

Mr Maurice Hickey MCh. FRCS Surgn, 13 June 1992

That the Freedom of the City of Cork be conferred on Mr Maurice Hickey; in appreciation of his extraordinary contribution to Irish Medical Practice, in recognition of his pioneering work in the field of thoracic surgery, in particular gratitude for his life saving efforts in the campaign against tuberculosis. In admiration for his selfless dedication and great personal kindness to the sick. In respect for a life dedicated to the care of others. As a token of the high esteem and affection in which he is held by the citizens of Cork. For all this and much more, the Lord Mayor, Aldermen and Councillors of the County Borough of Cork consider him worthy to be enrolled in the Roll of its Honorary Citizens and so direct.

Signed: Maurice P. Hickey
Witnesses: Denis Cregan, Lord Mayor
                    Niall Broderick, City Manager & Town Clerk

Rev. Fr Roch Bennett, OFM Cap, 13 June 1992

That the Freedom of the City of Cork be conferred on Fr Roch OFM Cap.: In recognition of his efforts on behalf of the marginalised in Irish Society. In appreciation of his concern for and tireless dedication to the welfare of young people in Cork City. In acknowledgement of his many enterprises which have given productive opportunity to those who otherwise would have been without such. In admiration for his unshakeable belief in the innate worth of every child. As a token of the high esteem and affection in which he is held in the city. For all this and much more, the Lord Mayor, Aldermen and Councillors of the County Borough of Cork consider him worthy to be enrolled in the Roll of its Honorary Citizens and so direct.

Signed: Father Roch OFM Cap (Thomas Bennett)
Witnesses: Denis Cregan, Lord Mayor
                    Niall Broderick, City Manager & Town Clerk

Mrs Maureen Curtis-Black, 19 June 1993

That the Freedom of Cork City be conferred on Mrs Maureen Curtis-Black: In appreciation of her extraordinary commitment to social justice. In admiration of her pioneering work in the establishment of Cork Citizens Advice Bureau and in the development of similar advisory services elsewhere. In recognition of her immense contribution to the welfare of women, particularly those widowed or disadvantaged as manifested in the founding of the Cork Widows Association. In acknowledgement of her courage and role in winning Free Legal Aid for those not in a position to fight for legal entitlement and of the huge national and

international significance of that campaign. In respect for a life dedicated to the service of others, particularly those with no voice. As a token of the high esteem and affection in which she is held in this city. For all this and much more, the Lord Mayor, Alderman and Councillors of the County Borough of Cork consider her worthy to be enrolled in the Roll of its Honorary Citizens and so direct.

Signed: Maureen Curtis-Black
Witnesses: Micheál Martin, Lord Mayor
                    Niall Broderick, City Manager & Town Clerk

Rev. Br. Jerome Kelly, 21 May 1994

That the Freedom of Cork City be conferred on Rev. Brother Jerome Kelly: In appreciation of his remarkable contribution to Irish education over many years. In admiration of his commitment to social justice and his unstinting efforts on behalf of the homeless elderly in Cork. In recognition of his innovative leadership of SHARE, the voluntary housing organisation. In respect for his insistence on everyone's right to dignity in old age. In particular acknowledgement of his encouragement of young people to achieve growth and maturity through the use of their talents in the service of others. As a token of the high esteem and affection in which he is held in this City. For all this and much more the Lord Mayor, Aldermen and Councillors of the County Borough of Cork consider him worthy to be enrolled in the Roll of its Honorary Citizens and so direct.

Signed: Jerome Kelly
Witnesses: John Murray, Lord Mayor
                    Thomas Rice, City Manager & Town Clerk

Mr Con Murphy, 24 June 1995

That the Freedom of Cork City be conferred on Mr Con Murphy: In appreciation of his remarkable contribution to sport and to the Gaelic Athletic Association as player and administrator over many years. In admiration of his personal qualities of integrity, foresight and determination on which were founded many innovative developments within the Gaelic Athletic Association. In respect for his life-long belief in the value of sport as a positive formative influence on the young. In recognition of his love for and commitment to his native Cork and of a lifetime of unselfish service given to the local community. As a token of the high esteem and affection in which he is held in this City. For all this and much more, the Lord Mayor, Aldermen and Councillors of the County Borough of Cork consider him worthy to be enrolled in the Roll of its Honorary Citizens and so direct.

Signed: Conchúr Ó Murchú
Witnesses: Councillor Tim Falvey, Lord Mayor
                    John J. Higgins, City Manager & Town Clerk

Mr John Bermingham, 24 May 1997

That the Freedom of the City of Cork be conferred on John Bermingham in appreciation of his remarkable contribution to the personal growth of persons with mild and profound mental handicap in the City and County of Cork. As a founding member of the Cork Poliomyelitis after Care Association in 1957 he has been continuously involved in directing and expanding the role of that Association. Today known as COPE Foundation it provides a comprehensive service to 1500 persons from the City and County of Cork with mental handicap and a lifetime commitment to the parents of such persons within its care. The comprehensive nature

of services of COPE Foundation is to be seen in its special care unit for severe and profoundly mentally handicapped persons at St Elizabeth's; the sheltered workshops located in towns in the County of Cork and the integrated housing schemes which at this time total 45 dwellings. He has in the course of the past forty years devoted himself to building up an organisation which is predominantly voluntary in its structure and is committed to responding to the needs of special people in our society. For these reasons and at a time when the COPE Foundation is celebrating forty years of commitment to people the Lord Mayor, Aldermen and Councillors of the County Borough of Cork consider John Bermingham worthy to be enrolled in the roll of its Honorary Citizens and so direct.
Signed: John Bermingham
Witnesses: James A Corr, Lord Mayor
                  John J. Higgins, City Manager & Town Clerk

Senator George Mitchell, 28 November 1998

That the Freedom of the City be conferred on Senator George Mitchell: In recognition of his exceptional commitment to the cause of lasting peace, justice, and harmony in Northern Ireland; In appreciation of his willing acceptance of the invitation of President Clinton to find a formula for the ending of violence and community fragmentation; In acknowledgement of his deep concern for the wellbeing and prosperity of all sections of the community; In admiration of his extraordinary commitment as Chairman of the All-Party Talks which led to the historic Good Friday Agreement of 10th April 1998; In honour of his qualities of leadership, negotiation, integrity, wisdom and common sense which made it possible for him to draw together for the first time different and deeply divided political opinions; As a token of the high esteem and affection in which he is held by the people of Cork; For all this and much more, the Lord Mayor, Aldermen and Councillors of the County Borough of Cork consider him worthy to be enrolled in the Roll of its Honorary Citizens and so direct.
Signed: George J. Mitchell
Witnesses: Joe O'Flynn, Lord Mayor
                  Jack Higgins, City Manager & Town Clerk

John Hume MP, MEP, 8 May 2004

That the Freedom of the City be conferred on John Hume MP, MEP, in recognition of his exceptional commitment to the cause of reconciliation on this island and for being a living testament to that fundamental principle of peace – respect for diversity. In recognition of the pivotal role he played in securing the historic Good Friday Agreement of 10th April, 1998 and his unwavering commitment to the Fundamental principles of democracy. In admiration of his qualities as a man of honour, generosity, integrity and courage, but above all else, in recognition of his lifelong commitment to the cause of lasting peace. For his exhortation that we spill sweat together instead of blood and his conviction in the futility of violence; As a token of the high esteem and affection in which he is held by the people of Cork; For all this and more, the Lord Mayor, Aldermen and Councillors of Cork City Council consider him worthy to be enrolled in the Roll of its Honorary Citizens and so direct.
Signed: John Hume
Witnesses: Colm Burke, Lord Mayor
                  Joe Gavin, City Manager

Sonia O'Sullivan, 14 June 2005

That the Freedom of the City be conferred on Sonia O'Sullivan in recognition of her extraordinary achievements in the field of athletics during the course of her remarkable career at both National and International level. For her capacity to uplift her nation with feats of extraordinary brilliance, determination and single-mindedness. In admiration of her courage in the face of adversity. For her unshakeable commitment to competing at the highest level without augmentation and for her devotion to the promotion of athletics particularly among the young. For her Olympian spirit, her indomitable will to succeed and for holding us enthralled by her inspiring feats on the track and field – all wrought from a unique talent and a steadfast resolve. In recognition of her untiring work for humanitarian and charitable causes. As a token of the high esteem and affection in which she is held by the people of Cork; for all this and more the Lord Mayor and Councillors of Cork City Council consider her worthy to be enrolled in the Roll of Honorary Citizens and so direct.
Signed: Sonia O'Sullivan
Witnesses: Seán Ó. Martín, Lord Mayor
                  Joe Gavin, City Manager

Roy Keane, 14 June 2005

That the Freedom of the City be conferred on Roy Keane in recognition of the position which he has occupied for more than a decade at the pinnacle of Premiership and International football and for his contribution to that sport on the local, national and international stage. In admiration for his unwavering commitment to excellence in his chosen sport; for his leadership, skill and courage as captain of both Manchester United and the Irish National Squad. For the exceptional pleasure and pride which he has engendered in the hearts of Irish and most especially Cork men and women during the course of his remarkable career; In recognition of his extraordinary and most often anonymous work for charity. As a token of the high esteem and affection by which he is held by the people of Cork; for all this and more the Lord Mayor and Councillors of Cork City Council consider him worthy to be enrolled in the Roll of Honorary Citizens and so direct.
Signed: Roy Keane
Witnesses: Seán Ó Martín, Lord Mayor
                  Joe Gavin, City Manager

Mary McAleese, Uachtarán na hÉireann, 30 May 2006

That the Freedom of the City be conferred on Mary McAleese, President of Ireland. In recognition of her leadership in promoting greater understanding and building bridges between all the peoples of this island. In recognition of being the first woman to attain a second term in the highest office in the land, that of Uachtarán na hÉireann. In recognition of her outstanding personal and academic achievements, and as a token of the high esteem in which she is held by the people of Cork, for all this and much more, the Lord Mayor and Councillors of Cork City Council consider her worthy to be enrolled in the Roll of Honorary Citizens and so direct.
Signed: Máire Mhic Ghiolla Íosa
Witnesses: Deirdre Clune, Lord Mayor
                  Joe Gavin, City Manager

Michael Flatley, 2 June 2007

That the Freedom of the City be conferred on Michael Flatley. In recognition of his personal achievements as a world-class dancer, musician, performer and as a person of outstanding artistic talent and capability. In recognition of his exceptional vision and achievement of raising the profile of Ireland abroad by bringing Irish Dance and Music to a new level and to a worldwide audience through the phenomenal international success of his shows. In recognition of his pursuit of pushing boundaries and passion for his heritage; and as a token of the high esteem in which he is held by the people of Cork, for all this and much more, the Lord Mayor and Councillors of Cork City Council consider him worthy to be enrolled in the Roll of Honorary Citizens and so direct.

Signed: Michael Flatley
Witnesses: Michael Ahern, Lord Mayor
            Joe Gavin, City Manager

Mr Albert Reynolds and Sir John Major KG Ch., 20 June 2008

That the Freedom of the City be conferred on both Albert Reynolds and Sir John Major. In recognition of their combined contribution to the process which led to the establishment of a lasting democratic solution in Northern Ireland equally respectful of the hopes and aspirations of both communities. In honour of their qualities of leadership, integrity, negotiation, and common sense in so doing. For their statesmanship, diplomacy, energy and commitment to the initiative despite the prevailing climate at the time and their unfailing and unwavering belief in the value of the process. For all this and much more the Lord Mayor and Councillors of the County Borough of Cork consider them worthy to be enrolled in the Roll of its Honorary Citizens and so direct.

Signed: Albert Reynolds, John Major
Witnesses: Donal J. Counihan, Lord Mayor
            Joe Gavin, City Manager

Sr Eucharia Buckley, 22 May 2009

That the Freedom of the City be conferred on Sister Eucharia Buckley. In recognition of her immense contribution to the advancement of religious values and the spiritual and religious well-being of the people of Cork. For her selfless dedication to the service of others and in broader acknowledgement of the role played by religious orders in the development of our society. For this reason and much more the Lord Mayor and Councillors of Cork City Council consider her worthy to be enrolled in the Roll of Honorary Citizens and so direct.

Signed: Sister Eucharia Buckley
Witnesses: Brian Bermingham, Lord Mayor
            D.S. O'Bogaigh, Deputy City Manager

Dean Denis O'Connor, 22 May 2009

That the Freedom of the City be conferred on Dean Denis O'Connor. In recognition of his immense contribution to the advancement of religious values and the spiritual and religious well-being of the people of Cork. For his selfless dedication to the service of others and in broader acknowledgement of the role played by religious orders in the development of our society. For this reason and much more the Lord Mayor and Councillors of Cork City Council consider him worthy to be enrolled in the Roll of Honorary Citizens and so direct.

Signed: Denis O'Connor
Witnesses: Brian Bermingham, Lord Mayor
            D.S. O'Bogaigh, Deputy City Manager

Mr Peter Barry, 11 June 2010

That the Freedom of the City of Cork be conferred on Mr Peter Barry for his lifelong dedication to the service of the citizens of Cork and of Ireland, for his business acumen and philanthropic endeavours, for his statesmanlike representation of Ireland on the International stage and for this steadfast commitment to achieving a peaceful and equitable solution in the North of Ireland through negotiative processes. For all this and much more the Lord Mayor and Councillors of Cork City Council consider him worthy to be enrolled in the Roll of Honorary Citizens and so direct.

Signed: Peter Barry
Witnesses: Dara Murphy, Lord Mayor
            Joe Gavin, City Manager

Seán Óg Ó hAilpín, 27 May 2011

That the Freedom of the City of Cork be conferred on Seán Óg Ó hÁilpín. In recognition of his unwavering commitment to excellence in Gaelic Football and Hurling throughout his career; at school, club, county, provincial and international level. For his generous and genuine commitment to supporting development of hurling and football among the youth of the city and his exemplary role as an ambassador for Irish language and culture. As a token of the high esteem and affection in which he is held by the people of Cork. For all this and much more, the Lord Mayor and Councillors of Cork City Council consider him worthy to be enrolled in the Roll of Honorary Citizens and so direct.

Signed: Seán Óg Ó hAilpín
Witnesses: Michael O'Connell, Lord Mayor
            Tim Lucey, City Manager

Frank Duggan, Michael Twomey, Billa O'Connell, 17 June 2013

That the Freedom of the City of Cork be conferred on Frank Duggan, Michael Twomey and Billa O'Connell. In recognition of their unwavering lifetime contribution to professional and amateur theatre, arts, drama and song in Cork City; for their generosity in mentoring and supporting the development of emerging talent in Cork. For being exemplary national and international ambassadors for Cork through comedy; for their generous contribution to charitable causes throughout the city. As a token of the high esteem and affection in which they are held by the people of Cork; for all this and much more, the Lord Mayor and Councillors of the City of Cork consider them worthy to be enrolled in the Roll of its Honorary Citizens and so direct.

Signed: Frank Duggan, Michael Twomey, Billa O'Connell
Witnesses: John Buttimer, Lord Mayor
            Tim Lucey, City Manager

REFERENCES

The Freedom of the City

1 See http://www.stage.cityoflondon.gov.uk/about-the-city/history-and-future/history-and-heritage/freedom-of-the-city/Pages/default.aspx

2 *Ibid.*

3 John R. Bowen and Conor O'Brien (2005), *Cork Silver and Gold – Four Centuries of Craftsmanship*, Cork: The Collins Press. p.154.

4 The City of New York (2012), *Key to the City of New York*. Available at: http://www.nyc.gov/html/unccp/html/protocol/key.shtml

5 See Aodh Quinlivan (2006), *Philip Monahan, A Man Part – The Life and Times of Ireland's First Local Authority Manager*, Dublin: Institute of Public Administration, pp. 34–35.

6 *The New York Times*, 9 January 1921.

7 'Guess who got the key to Detroit?', CBS News, 11 February 2009 – http://www.cbsnews.com/stories/2003/03/26/iraq/main546287.shtml

8 'Terrell Owens given key to the city of Buffalo' – http://www.youtube.com/watch?v=bnAQNfeRm4w

9 Dublin City Council (2012) *Freedom of the City of Dublin*, Available at: http://www.dublincity.ie/YOURCOUNCIL/LORDMAYORDUBLIN/FREEDOMOFTHECITY/Pages/FreedomoftheCityHome.aspx

10 See http://www.rte.ie/tv/programmes/reeling_in_the_years.html

11 Matthew Potter (2011), *The Municipal Revolution in Ireland – A Handbook of Urban Government in Ireland since 1800*, Dublin: Irish Academic Press, p. 13.

12 *Ibid.*, p. 14.

13 *Ibid.*

14 'Your Council – Charters', Cork City Council website http://www.corkcity.ie/yourcouncil/charters/

15 Matthew Potter, *The Municipal Revolution in Ireland*, p. 15.

16 *Ibid.*

17 *Ibid.*

18 Act of Parliament, Great Britain (1876), Municipal Privileges (Ireland) Act, 39 & 40 Vict. c. 76.

19 Matthew Potter, *The Municipal Revolution in Ireland*, p. 155.

20 Waterford City Council website – http://waterfordireland.tripod.com/freedom_of_the_city.htm

21 Matthew Potter, *The Municipal Revolution in Ireland*, p. 155.

22 Richard Haslam (2003), 'The Origins of Irish Local Government' in M. Callanan and J.F. Keogan (eds.), *Local Government in Ireland: Inside Out*, Dublin: Institute of Public Administration, p. 19.

23 *Ibid.*

24 M.V. Conlon, (1947), 'The Honorary Freemen of Cork, 1690–1946', pp. 74–86, *Journal of the Cork Historical and Archaeological Society*. LII, p. 75.

25 *Ibid.*

26 *Ibid.*

27 From the Richard Dowden papers at the Cork City and County Archive, U140/J/02/04, March–April 1831.

28 M.V. Conlon, (1947), 'The Honorary Freemen of Cork, 1690–1946'.

29 CP/CO/FR Register of Honorary Burgesses.

30 Minute book 11 (CP/CO/M/11) is missing from the Cork City and County Archive.

31 See Cork Corporation minute book CP/CO/M/14 covering the period 12 November 1920 to 28 December 1923, p. 460.

32 See Cork Corporation minute book CP/CO/M36 covering the period June 1986 to January 1988.

33 John R. Bowen and Conor O'Brien, *Cork Silver and Gold – Four Centuries of Craftsmanship*, p. 14.

34 *Ibid.*, p. 154.

35 *Ibid.*

36 M. V. Conlon, (1947), 'The Honorary Freemen of Cork, 1690–1946'.

37 Available at: http://www.christies.com/LotFinder/lot_details.aspx?intObjectID=5516061

38 M. V. Conlon, (1947), 'The Honorary Freemen of Cork, 1690–1946'.

39 John R. Bowen and Conor O'Brien, *Cork Silver and Gold – Four Centuries of Craftsmanship*, p. 155.

40 *Ibid.*

41 Cork Corporation minute books.

42 Robert Day (1899), 'The Freedoms of Cork', *Journal of the Cork Historical and Archaeological Society*, Vol V, p. 244.

43 John R. Bowen and Conor O'Brien, *Cork Silver and Gold – Four Centuries of Craftsmanship*, p. 15.

44 Eileen Moylan (2011), *Eileen Moylan Irish Silversmith*, Available at: http://www.eileenmoylan.com/2011/05/cork-silver-part-1/

45 Chris Carroll (2012), 'Interview on the freedom caskets for the city of Cork', by Pádraig Mac Consaidín, the showrooms of Seán Carroll & Sons, 1 August 2012.

46 *Ibid.*

47 *Ibid.*

48 *Ibid.*

Honorary Burgesses – 1609 to 1841

1 Cork City and County Archives (2007), *List of Freemen of Cork City 1710–1841* transcribed from the existing collection (Ref. U. 11) 'Index/Digest to Council Books of the Corporation of Cork with alphabetical list of Freemen.'

2 Brean Hammond (2010), *Jonathan Swift*, Dublin: Irish Academic Press, p. xiii.

3 *Ibid.*

4 Joseph McMinn (2009), 'Swift, Jonathan', *Dictionary of Irish Biography*, (ed.) James McGuire and James Quinn. Cambridge, United Kingdom: Cambridge University Press. http://dib.cambridge.org/viewReadPage.do?articleId=a8415

5 *Ibid.*

6 *Ibid.*

7 See the website for St Patrick's Cathedral at http://www.stpatrickscathedral.ie/Jonathan-Swift.aspx

8 Brean Hammond, *Jonathan Swift*, p. xv.

9 Joseph McMinn, 'Swift, Jonathan', *Dictionary of Irish Biography*.

10 *Ibid.*

11 Brean Hammond, *Jonathan Swift*, p. xiii.

12 *List of Freemen of Cork City 1710–1841*.

13 Source is the CELT (Corpus of Electronic Texts) website http://www.ucc.ie/celt/online/E700001-004/text001.html

14 Brean Hammond, *Jonathan Swift*, p. xiii.

15 Reproduced from Brean Hammond, *Jonathan Swift* p. 24.

16 Brean Hammond, *Jonathan Swift*, p. xiii.

17 See http://www.passagewestmonkstown.ie/sirius-shaft.asp

18 T. Sheppard (1937), 'The *Sirius*: The First Steamer to Cross the Atlantic', *Mariner's Mirror*, Cambridge, UK: Society for Nautical Research, vol. 23 (January), pp. 84–94.

19 *Ibid.*

20 *Ibid.*

21 *Ibid.*

22 *Ibid.*

23 'Souvenirs of the Sirius', article in *The Irish Times*, 30 December 1905, based on account by William. J. Barry.

24 David Murphy (2009), 'Roberts, Richard', *Dictionary of Irish Biography*, (ed.) James McGuire and James Quinn, Cambridge, United Kingdom: Cambridge University Press. http://dib.cambridge.org/viewReadPage.do?articleId=a7703

25 *Ibid.*

26 *Ibid.*

27 *List of Freemen of Cork City 1710–1841*.

28 *Ibid.*

29 David Murphy (2009), 'Roberts, Richard', *Dictionary of Irish Biography*.

30 See http://www.passagewestmonkstown.ie/sirius-shaft.asp

31 *Ibid.*

32 *Ibid.*

33 *Ibid.*

34 Linde Lunney (2009), 'Brinkley, John', *Dictionary of Irish Biography*, (ed.) James McGuire and James Quinn, Cambridge, United Kingdom: Cambridge University Press. http://dib.cambridge.org/viewReadPage.do?articleId=a0962

35 *Biographical Encyclopaedia of Astronomers* (2007), Thomas Hockey, Editor-in-chief, Virginia Trimble and Thomas R. Williams, Senior Editors, Berlin: Springer-Science + Business Media, p. 170.

36 *Ibid.* – See also 'John Brinkley' in John Venn (1898), *Biographical History of Gonville and Caius College 1349–1897*, vol. ii, pp. 107–108, Cambridge: Cambridge University Press.

37 Information on John Brinkley from Library Ireland website at http://www.libraryireland.com/biography/JohnBrinkley.php

38 *Ibid.*

39 *Ibid.*

40 Information on John Brinkley from the Royal Astronomical Society's Science Photo Library at http://www.sciencephoto.com/media/223752/view

41 Information on John Brinkley from Library Ireland website at http://www.libraryireland.com/biography/JohnBrinkley.php

42 Information on John Brinkley from the Royal Astronomical Society's Science Photo Library at http://www.sciencephoto.com/media/223752/view

43 *Biographical Encyclopaedia of Astronomers* (2007).

44 Linde Lunney, 'Brinkley, John', *Dictionary of Irish Biography*.

45 *Ibid.*

46 *Ibid.*

47 Information on John Brinkley from Library Ireland website at http://www.libraryireland.com/biography/JohnBrinkley.php

48 'Admiral Adam Duncan' from the Clan Duncan Society website, http://www.clan-duncan.co.uk/viscount.html

49 *Ibid.*

50 'Famous Scots – Adam Duncan, 1st Viscount Camperdown', http://www.rampantscotland.com/famous/blfamduncan2.htm

51 *Ibid.*

52 http://www.clan-duncan.co.uk/viscount.html

53 P.K. Crimmin (2008), 'Duncan, Adam, Viscount Duncan (1731–1804)', *Oxford Dictionary of National Biography*, Oxford University Press, 2004; online edn, Jan 2008. http://www.oxforddnb.com/view/article/8211

54 *List of Freemen of Cork City 1710–1841*.

55 http://www.clan-duncan.co.uk/viscount.html

56 P.K. Crimmin, 'Duncan, Adam, Viscount Duncan (1731–1804)', *Oxford Dictionary of National Biography*.

57 As reproduced from BBC website at http://www.bbc.co.uk/arts/yourpaintings/paintings/admiral-adam-duncan-17311804-1st-viscount-duncan-of-camper94518

58 *List of Freemen of Cork City 1710–1841*.

59 John Knox Laughton (2004), 'Beauclerk, Lord Amelius (1771–1846)', rev. Andrew Lambert, *Oxford Dictionary of National Biography*, Oxford University Press. http://www.oxforddnb.com/view/article/1845

60 *Ibid.*

61 Information provided by the National Maritime Museum. See http://collections.rmg.co.uk/collections/objects/14013.html

62 *Ibid.*

63 John Knox Laughton (2004), 'Beauclerk, Lord Amelius (1771–1846)', rev. Andrew Lambert, *Oxford Dictionary of National Biography*, Oxford University Press.

64 As reproduced from BBC website at http://www.bbc.co.uk/arts/yourpaintings/paintings/admiral-lord-amelius-beauclerk-17711846-174847

65 Information from the Trinity College Dublin website, history of the Provost's Office at http://www.tcd.ie/provost/history/former-provosts/f_andrews>php

66 See John Victor Luce (1992), *Trinity College Dublin: The First 400 Years*, Dublin pp. 52–56.

67 *Ibid.*

68 *Ibid.*

69 Linde Lunney, 'Andrews, Francis', *Dictionary of Irish Biography*, (ed.) James McGuire and James Quinn, Cambridge: Cambridge University Press. http://dib.cambridge.org/viewReadPage.do?articleId=a0158

70 See Anne Crookshank and David Webb (1990), *Paintings and Sculptures in Trinity College Dublin*, Dublin, p. 12.

71 Linde Lunney (2009), 'Andrews, Francis', *Dictionary of Irish Biography*.

72 *Ibid.*

73 *Ibid.*

74 *Ibid.*

75 See http://www.tcd.ie/provost/history/former-provosts/f_andrews.php

76 See Dictionary of Canadian Biography Online at http://biographi.ca/009004-119.01-e.php?id_nbr=2500

77 *Ibid.*

78 See John Gideon Millingen (1841), *The History of Duelling*, Volume 2, London: Richard Bentley

79 http://biographi.ca/009004-119.01-e.php?id_nbr=2500

80 *Ibid.*

81 *Ibid.*

82 As reproduced from BBC website at
    http://www.bbc.co.uk/arts/yourpaintings/paintings/
    charles-lennox-17641819-4th-duke-of-richmond-72936

83 Laurence M. Geary (2004), 'Barry, John Milner (1768–1822)',
    Oxford Dictionary of National Biography, Oxford University Press.
    http://www.oxforddnb.com/view/article/1565

84 *Ibid.*

85 *Ibid.*

86 *Ibid.*

87 *Ibid.*

88 *Ibid.*

89 *The Catholic Encyclopaedia* gives Moylan's year of birth as 1739;
    the website of the Diocese of Cork and Ross states it as 1735, as
    does biographer, Angela Bolster.

90 See the *Catholic Encyclopaedia* entry for Francis Moylan at
    http://www.newadvent.org/cathen/10609b.htm

91 *Ibid.*

92 Angela Bolster (2009), 'Moylan, Francis', *Dictionary of Irish
    Biography*, (ed.) James McGuire and James Quinn, Cambridge,
    United Kingdom: Cambridge University Press.
    http://dib.cambridge.org/viewReadPage.do?articleId=a6010

93 *Ibid.*

94 *Ibid.*

95 *List of Freemen of Cork City 1710–1841.*

96 http://www.newadvent.org/cathen/10609b.htm

97 Information from the Diocese of Cork and Ross website at
    http://www.corkandross.org/priests.jsp?priestID=495

98 Angela Bolster (2009), 'Moylan, Francis', *Dictionary of Irish
    Biography*.

99 See Ref. code: U75.

100 Angela Bolster (2009), 'Moylan, Francis', *Dictionary of Irish
    Biography*.

101 *List of Freemen of Cork City 1710–1841.*

102 *Ibid.*

Nationalist Heroes – 1876 to 1921

ISAAC BUTT

1 Alan O'Day (2008), 'Butt, Isaac (1813–1879)', *Oxford Dictionary
   of National Biography*, Oxford University Press, http://
   www.oxforddnb.com/view/article/4222

2 Philip Bull (2009), 'Butt, Isaac', *Dictionary of Irish Biography*,
   edited by James McGuire and James Quinn, Cambridge:
   Cambridge University Press.
   (http://dib.cambridge.org/viewReadPage.do?articleId=a1311)

3 *Ibid.*

4 Alan O'Day, 'Butt, Isaac (1813–1879)', *Oxford Dictionary of
   National Biography*.

5 Philip Bull, 'Butt, Isaac', *Dictionary of Irish Biography*.

6 Alan O'Day, 'Butt, Isaac (1813–1879)', *Oxford Dictionary of
   National Biography*.

7 Philip Bull, 'Butt, Isaac', *Dictionary of Irish Biography*.

8 *Ibid.*

9 *Ibid.*

10 Alan O'Day, 'Butt, Isaac (1813–1879)', *Oxford Dictionary of
   National Biography*.

11 *Ibid.*

12 *Ibid.*

13 *Ibid.*

14 *Ibid.*

15 Philip Bull, 'Butt, Isaac', *Dictionary of Irish Biography*.

16 Alan O'Day, 'Butt, Isaac (1813–1879)', *Oxford Dictionary of
   National Biography*.

17 *Ibid.*

18 *Ibid.*

19 David Thornley (1964), *Isaac Butt and Home Rule*, p. 379,
   London: MacGibbon and Kee

20 *Ibid.* pp. 379–380.

21 *Ibid.*, p. 380.

22 Alan O'Day, 'Butt, Isaac (1813–1879)', *Oxford Dictionary of
   National Biography*.

23 Philip Bull, 'Butt, Isaac', *Dictionary of Irish Biography*.

24 *Ibid.*

25 David Thornley, *Isaac Butt and Home Rule*, p. 380.

26 *Ibid.*

27 Philip Bull, 'Butt, Isaac', *Dictionary of Irish Biography*.

28 *The Irish Times*, 3 October 1876, report entitled 'Mr. Butt
   Admitted a Burgess of Cork'.

29 *Ibid.*

CHARLES STEWART PARNELL

1 F.S.L. Lyons (1977), *Charles Stewart Parnell*, Dublin: Gill &
   Macmillan Ltd., p. 13.

2 F.S.L. Lyons (1965), *Parnell*, Dundalk: Dundalgan Press, p. 3.

3 Seán McMahon (2000), *Charles Stewart Parnell*, Cork: Mercier
   Press, p. 13.

4 John Howard Parnell (1914), *Charles Stewart Parnell – A
   Memoir*, New York: Henry Holt & Company, p. 28.

5 Seán McMahon, *Charles Stewart Parnell*, p. 14.

6 F.S.L. Lyons, *Charles Stewart Parnell*, p. 21.

7 F.S.L. Lyons, *Parnell*, p. 4.

8 Seán McMahon, *Charles Stewart Parnell*, p. 21.

9 F.S.L. Lyons, *Charles Stewart Parnell*, p. 47.

10 *Ibid.*, p. 202.

11 Frank Callanan (2009), 'Parnell, Charles Stewart', *Dictionary
   of Irish Biography*, edited by James McGuire and James
   Quinn, Cambridge: Cambridge University Press, 2009.
   http://dib.cambridge.org/viewReadPage.do?articleId=a7199

12 *Ibid.*

13 Seán McMahon, *Charles Stewart Parnell*, p. 58.

14 Frank Callanan, 'Parnell, Charles Stewart', *Dictionary of Irish
   Biography*.

15 *Ibid.*

16 As cited by Callanan (see above); a new edition of Winston
   Churchill's *Great Contemporaries* was published by ISI Books in
   May 2012.

17 Frank Callanan, 'Parnell, Charles Stewart', *Dictionary of Irish
   Biography*.

18 *Cork Examiner*, 16 April 1880, report entitled 'The Corporation
   and Mr. Parnell MP – Presentation of the Freedom of the City'.

19 *The Irish Times*, 16 April 1880, report entitled 'The Result of the
   Cork Election'.

20 *Cork Examiner*, 16 April 1880.

21 *Ibid.*

22 *Ibid.*

23 *Ibid.*

WILLIAM GLADSTONE

1   BBC News story, 'City marks Gladstone bicentenary, 27 December 2009 http://news.bbc.co.uk/2/hi/uk_news/england/merseyside/8431680.stm

2   Henry Colin Gray Matthew (2011), 'Gladstone, William Ewart (1809–1898)', *Oxford Dictionary of National Biography*, Oxford University Press, 2004; online edition, May 2011 http://www.oxforddnb.com/view/article/10787

3   *Ibid.*

4   *Ibid.*

5   *Ibid.*

6   See 'The Victorian Web', http://www.victorianweb.org/history/pms/gladston.html

7   Henry Colin Gray Matthew, 'Gladstone, William Ewart (1809–1898)', *Oxford Dictionary of National Biography*.

8   'The Victorian Web', http://www.victorianweb.org/history/pms/gladston.html

9   *Ibid.*

10 Richard Shannon (1999), *Gladstone 1809–1865*, London: Hamish Hamilton Ltd., p. 59.

11 'The Victorian Web', http://www.victorianweb.org/history/pms/gladston.html

12 *Ibid.*

13 *Ibid.*

14 *Ibid.*

15 *Ibid.*

16 Henry Colin Gray Matthew (2011), 'Gladstone, William Ewart (1809–1898)', *Oxford Dictionary of National Biography*.

17 *Ibid.*

18 *Ibid.*

19 Paul Bew (2004), 'Parnell, Charles Stewart (1846–1891)', *Oxford Dictionary of National Biography*, Oxford University Press, http://www.oxforddnb.com/view/article/21384

20 Henry Colin Gray Matthew (2011), 'Gladstone, William Ewart (1809–1898)', *Oxford Dictionary of National Biography*.

21 *Ibid.*

22 *Ibid.*

23 *Ibid.*

24 *Ibid.*

25 *Ibid.*

26 *Ibid.*

27 BBC News, see Reference 1 above.

28 John Lawrence Hammond (1938), *Gladstone and the Irish Nation*, London: Longmans, Green and Co., p. 723.

29 *Ibid.* p., 721.

30 Henry Colin Gray Matthew (2011), 'Gladstone, William Ewart (1809–1898)', *Oxford Dictionary of National Biography*.

31 *Ibid.*

32 John Lawrence Hammond (1938), *Gladstone and the Irish Nation*, p. 724.

33 Paul Herbert (1904) (ed.), *Letters of Lord Acton to Mary Gladstone*, London: George Allen, p. 57.

34 BBC News, see Reference 1 above.

35 Henry Colin Gray Mathew (2011), 'Gladstone, William Ewart (1809–1898)', *Oxford Dictionary of National Biography*.

36 *The Irish Times*, 'Mr. Gladstone and the Freedom of Cork', 17 August 1886.

37 *The Irish Times*, 5 October 1886.

38 *Ibid.*

39 *Ibid.*

40 *Ibid.*

41 *Ibid.*

42 *Ibid.*

43 *Ibid.*

ANDREW CARNEGIE

1   Burton Jesse Hendrick (1933), *The Life of Andrew Carnegie*, London: William Heinemann Ltd., p. 41.

2   Biography of Andrew Carnegie, Spartacus Educational http://www.spartacus.schoolnet.co.uk/USAcarnegie.htm

3   *Ibid.*

4   Burton Jesse Hendrick (1933), *The Life of Andrew Carnegie*, pp. 159–160.

5   Biography of Andrew Carnegie, Spartacus Educational.

6   Brendan Grimes (1998), 'Carnegie Libraries in Ireland', *History Ireland*, vol. 6, no. 4.

7   Andrew Carnegie (1889), 'Gospel of Wealth', *North American Review*, June.

8   Biography of Andrew Carnegie, Spartacus Educational.

9   Brendan Grimes, 'Carnegie Libraries in Ireland', *History Ireland*.

10 *Ibid.*

11 *Ibid.*

12 Biography of Andrew Carnegie, Spartacus Educational.

13 *Cork Examiner*, 6 April 1902.

14 *Cork Examiner*, 22 October 1903.

15 *Ibid.*

16 *Ibid.*

17 *Ibid.*

18 *Ibid.*

19 *Ibid.*

JEREMIAH O'DONOVAN ROSSA

1   *The Irish Times*, 1 June 1954, article entitled 'O'Donovan Rossa – The man and the legend' by District Justice M.J. Lennon.

2   Patrick Maume (2009), 'O'Donovan Rossa, Jeremiah', *Dictionary of Irish Biography*, edited by James McGuire and James Quinn, Cambridge: Cambridge University Press http://dib.cambridge.org/quicksearch.do;jsessionid=D4A3C4CAB04DDEA6093A780BE8B91B3A#

3   *Ibid.*

4   *Ibid.*

5   Jeremiah O'Donovan Rossa – Fenian Grave http://www.irishfreedom.net

6   Aodh Quinlivan (2006), *Philip Monahan – A Man Apart: The Life and Times of Ireland's First Local Authority Manager*, Dublin: Institute of Public Administration, p. 9,

7   Patrick Maume (2009), 'O'Donovan Rossa, Jeremiah', *Dictionary of Irish Biography*.

8   *Ibid.*

9   Jeremiah O'Donovan Rossa – Fenian Grave.

10 Patrick Maume, 'O'Donovan Rossa, Jeremiah', *Dictionary of Irish Biography*.

11 *Ibid.*

12 *Ibid.*

13 *Ibid.*

14 *Ibid.*

15 Jeremiah O'Donovan Rossa – Fenian Grave.

16 *Ibid.*

17 Patrick Maume, 'O'Donovan Rossa, Jeremiah', *Dictionary of Irish Biography*.

18 *Ibid.*

19 Patrick Maume, 'O'Donovan Rossa, Jeremiah', *Dictionary of Irish Biography*.

20 *The Irish Times*, 19 August 1981, article entitled 'New stamp commemorates O'Donovan Rossa'.

21 Patrick Maume, 'O'Donovan Rossa, Jeremiah', *Dictionary of Irish Biography*.

22 *Cork Examiner*, 25 November 1904, report entitled 'Cork Corporation and O'Donovan Rossa'.

23 *Ibid.*

24 *Cork Examiner*, 17 December 1904.

25 *Ibid.*

26 *Ibid.*

27 *Ibid.*

DOUGLAS HYDE

1 Cormac Moore (2012), *The GAA v Douglas Hyde – The Removal of Ireland's First President as GAA Patron*, Cork: The Collins Press, p. 5.

2 Gerard Murphy (1949), 'Douglas Hyde 1860–1949', *An Irish Quarterly Review*, vol. 38, no. 151 (September), p. 275.

3 Risteárd Ó Glaisne (1993), 'This is no Political Matter', *An Irish Quarterly Review*, vol. 82, no. 328 (Winter), p. 471.

4 Patrick Maume (2009), 'Hyde, Douglas (de hÍde, Dubhghlas), *Dictionary of Irish Biography*, edited by James McGuire and James Quinn, Cambridge: Cambridge University Press (http://dib.cambridge.org/viewReadPage.do?articleId=a4185)

5 *Ibid.*

6 Gerard Murphy, 'Douglas Hyde 1860–1949', *An Irish Quarterly Review*, p. 276.

7 *Ibid.*

8 Cormac Moore, *The GAA v Douglas Hyde – The Removal of Ireland's First President as GAA Patron*, p. 8.

9 Dominic Ó Dálaigh (1970), 'The Young Douglas Hyde', *Studia Hibernica*, no. 10, pp. 129–130.

10 Patrick Maume, 'Hyde, Douglas (de hÍde, Dubhghlas), *Dictionary of Irish Biography*.

11 Cormac Moore, *The GAA v Douglas Hyde – The Removal of Ireland's First President as GAA Patron*, p. 9.

12 Patrick Maume, 'Hyde, Douglas (de hÍde, Dubhghlas), *Dictionary of Irish Biography*.

13 Cormac Moore, *The GAA v Douglas Hyde – The Removal of Ireland's First President as GAA Patron*, p. 25.

14 *Ibid.* p., 27.

15 Arthur E. Clery (1919), 'The Gaelic League, 1893–1919', *An Irish Quarterly Review*, vol. 8, no. 31 (September), p. 398.

16 Declan Kiberd (1995), *Inventing Ireland: The Literature of the Modern Nation*, London: Random House, p. 145.

17 Patrick Maume, 'Hyde, Douglas (de hÍde, Dubhghlas), *Dictionary of Irish Biography*.

18 *Ibid.*

19 *Ibid.*

20 Declan Kiberd, *Inventing Ireland: The Literature of the Modern Nation*, p. 149.

21 Patrick Maume, 'Hyde, Douglas (de hÍde, Dubhghlas), *Dictionary of Irish Biography*.

22 *Ibid.*

23 *Ibid.*

24 *Ibid.*

25 *Ibid.*

26 Cormac Moore, *The GAA v Douglas Hyde – The Removal of Ireland's First President as GAA Patron*, p. 64.

27 *Ibid.* p., 62.

28 *The Irish Times*, 28 June 1938.

29 Cormac Moore, *The GAA v Douglas Hyde – The Removal of Ireland's First President as GAA Patron*, p. 86.

30 *Ibid.*

31 *Irish Independent*, 14 November 1938.

32 Cormac Moore, *The GAA v Douglas Hyde – The Removal of Ireland's First President as GAA Patron*, p. 3.

33 *Ibid.*

34 Patrick Maume, 'Hyde, Douglas (de hÍde, Dubhghlas), *Dictionary of Irish Biography*.

35 Janet E. Dunleavy and Gareth W. Dunleavy ((1991), *Douglas Hyde: A Maker of Modern Ireland*, Berkeley: University of California Press, p. 430.

36 *The Irish Times*, 13 July 1949.

37 *The Irish Press*, 14 July 1949.

38 Cormac Moore, *The GAA v Douglas Hyde – The Removal of Ireland's First President as GAA Patron*, p. 185.

39 *Cork Examiner*, 23 June 1906.

40 *Ibid.*

41 *Ibid.*

42 *Irish Independent*, 2 August 1906.

43 *Ibid.*

44 *Freeman's Journal*, 2 August 1906.

45 *Ibid.*

46 *Ibid.*

47 *Ibid.*

48 *Ibid.*

KUNO MEYER

1 Aidan Breen (2009), 'Meyer, Kuno', *Dictionary of Irish Biography*, edited by James McGuire and James Quinn, Cambridge: Cambridge University Press http://dib.cambridge.org/viewReadPage.do?articleId=a5810

2 *Ibid.*

3 *Ibid.*

4 *Ibid.*

5 Seán Ó Lúing (1991), *Kuno Meyer, 1858–1919, A Biography*, Dublin: Geography Publications, p. 4.

6 Aidan Breen, 'Meyer, Kuno', *Dictionary of Irish Biography*.

7 Seán Ó Lúing, *Kuno Meyer, 1858–1919, A Biography*, quote on inside cover page.

8 Aidan Breen, 'Meyer, Kuno', *Dictionary of Irish Biography*.

9 *Ibid.*

10 Aodh Quinlivan (2011), 'The Freedom of Cork', a public lecture to mark the seventy-fifth anniversary of the (re)opening of Cork City Hall, 8 September, City Hall, Cork.

11 Aidan Breen, 'Meyer, Kuno', *Dictionary of Irish Biography*.

12 *Ibid.*

13 *Ibid.*

14   *Ibid*.

15   Seán Ó Lúing, *Kuno Meyer, 1858–1919, A Biography*, p. 173.

16   *Ibid*. pp. 173–174.

17   Aidan Breen, 'Meyer, Kuno', *Dictionary of Irish Biography*.

18   Seán Ó Lúing, *Kuno Meyer, 1858–1919, A Biography*, p. 194.

19   Aidan Breen, 'Meyer, Kuno', *Dictionary of Irish Biography*.

20   Seán Ó Lúing, *Kuno Meyer, 1858–1919, A Biography*, p. 195.

21   Aidan Breen, 'Meyer, Kuno', *Dictionary of Irish Biography*.

22   Seán Ó Lúing, *Kuno Meyer, 1858–1919, A Biography*, p. 198.

23   Aidan Breen, 'Meyer, Kuno', *Dictionary of Irish Biography*.

24   Seán Ó Lúing, *Kuno Meyer, 1858–1919, A Biography*, p. 116.

25   *Cork Examiner*, 26 September 1912.

26   Seán Ó Lúing, *Kuno Meyer, 1858–1919, A Biography*, p. 116.

27   *Cork Examiner*, 26 September 1912.

28   *Ibid*.

29   *Ibid*.

30   *The Irish Times*, 9 January 1915.

31   *Ibid*.

32   *The Irish Times*, 15 May 1920.

33   J.P. Duggan article in *The Irish Times*, 12 April 1990, entitled 'Kuno Meyer: Time to make amends?'

CANON PEADAR Ó LAOGHAIRE

1   Douglas Hyde (1920), 'Canon Peter O'Leary and Dr Kuno Meyer', *Studies: An Irish Quarterly Review*, vol. 9, no. 34 (June), pp. 297–301.

2   John A. Murphy (2009), 'Ó Laoghaire, Peadar', *Dictionary of Irish Biography*, edited by James McGuire and James Quinn, Cambridge: Cambridge University Press (http://dib.cambridge.org/viewReadPage.do?articleId=a6390)

3   *Ibid*.

4   Douglas Hyde, 'Canon Peter O'Leary and Dr Kuno Meyer', *Studies: An Irish Quarterly Review*, p. 301.

5   John A. Murphy, 'Ó Laoghaire, Peadar', *Dictionary of Irish Biography*.

6   *Ibid*.

7   Shán Ó Cuív (1954), 'Materials for a bibliography of the Very Reverend Peter Canon O'Leary 1839–1920' supplement to *Celtica*, ii, pt. 2.

8   John A. Murphy, 'Ó Laoghaire, Peadar', *Dictionary of Irish Biography*.

9   *Ibid*.

10   Douglas Hyde, 'Canon Peter O'Leary and Dr Kuno Meyer', *Studies: An Irish Quarterly Review*, p. 300.

11   John A. Murphy, 'Ó Laoghaire, Peadar', *Dictionary of Irish Biography*.

12   Douglas Hyde, 'Canon Peter O'Leary and Dr Kuno Meyer', *Studies: An Irish Quarterly Review*, p. 300.

13   John A. Murphy, 'Ó Laoghaire, Peadar', *Dictionary of Irish Biography*.

14   Declan Kiberd (2001), *Irish Classics*, London: Granta Books, p. 278.

15   *Ibid*.

16   John A. Murphy, 'Ó Laoghaire, Peadar', *Dictionary of Irish Biography*.

17   *Ibid*.

18   Douglas Hyde, 'Canon Peter O'Leary and Dr Kuno Meyer', *Studies: An Irish Quarterly Review*, p. 300.

19   John A. Murphy, 'Ó Laoghaire, Peadar', *Dictionary of Irish Biography*.

20   *Ibid*.

21   *Ibid*. See also Ó Laoghaire's obituary in *The Irish Times*, 23 March 1920.

22   Peter O'Leary (1970), *My Story – A translation of the famous Irish classic* by Cyril T. O Céirn, Cork: Mercier Press, p. 153

23   *Ibid*.

24   *Ibid*.

25   *Cork Examiner*, 26 September 1912.

26   *Ibid*.

27   Peter O'Leary, *My Story*, p. 153.

WOODROW WILSON

1   The Woodrow Wilson Presidential Library & Museum (2012) *About Woodrow Wilson* [Online] Available at: http://www.woodrowwilson.org/about/biography

2   Joseph Nathan Kane (1974), *Facts About The Presidents*, 3rd edition, New York: The H.W. Wilson Company. p. 189.

3   *Ibid*., p. 190.

4   *Ibid*., p. 189.

5   *Ibid*.

6   The Woodrow Wilson Presidential Library & Museum (2012) *About Woodrow Wilson*, [Online] Available at: http://www.woodrowwilson.org/about-woodrow-wilson

7   The White House (2012) *The Presidents*, [Online] Available at http://www.whitehouse.gov/about/presidents/woodrowwilson

8   Wilson, W. (1917) *President Wilson's Address to Congress – April 2, 1917, Addresses of the President of the United States to Congress*, [Online] Available at: http://archive.org/details/presidentwoodrow00unit

9   This image showing President Wilson asking Congress to declare war on Germany is available online at: http://www.emerson kent.com/history/timelines/world_war_I_timeline_1917.htm

10   Thomas A. Bailey (1945) *Woodrow Wilson and the Great Betrayal, New York: Macmillan Company*, pp. 295–296.

11   The White House (2012) *The Presidents*, [Online] Available at: http://www.whitehouse.gov/about/presidents/woodrowwilson

12   Joseph Nathan Kane, *Facts About The Presidents*, p. 189.

13   The Woodrow Wilson Presidential Library & Museum (2012) *About Woodrow Wilson* [Online] Available at: http://www.woodrowwilson.org/about/biography

14   *The Irish Times* (1919) 'President Wilson and Cork – The Freedom of the City', 19 February, p. 5.

15   *The Irish Times* (1919) 'President Wilson and Cork', 16 January, p. 5.

16   Cork Corporation (1919) 'Resolution: Freedom of the City of Cork be conferred on Dr Woodrow Wilson', *Special Meeting of the Cork Corporation 10 January*, Cork Corporation, Cork.

17   *The Irish Times* (1919) 'President Wilson and Cork – The Freedom of the City', 19 February, p. 5.

18   *The Irish Times* (1919) 'Cork Corporation and President Wilson', 13 February, p. 6.

19   *Ibid*.

20   Aodh Quinlivan (2006), *Philip Monahan: A Man Apart – The Life and Times of Ireland's First Local Authority Manager*. Dublin: Institute of Public Administration. p. 1.

MONSIGNOR DANIEL MANNIX

1 Niall Brennan (1965), *Dr Mannix*, London: Angus & Robertson Ltd., p. 1.

2 Jim Griffin (2012), *Australian National University: National Centre of Biography*. Available at: http://adb.anu.edu.au/biography/mannix-daniel-7478

3 Colm Kiernan (1984) *Daniel Mannix and Ireland*, Dublin: Gill & Macmillan, p. 1.

4 *Ibid.*, p. 2.

5 *Ibid.*, p. 10.

6 Jim Griffin, *Australian National University: National Centre of Biography*.

7 The image is available in the National Library of Ireland Catalogue at: http://catalogue.nli.ie/Record/KE_179

8 Colm Kiernan, *Daniel Mannix and Ireland*, p. 67.

9 Jim Griffin, *Australian National University: National Centre of Biography*.

10 Colm Kiernan, *Daniel Mannix and Ireland*, p. 93.

11 Jim Griffin, *Australian National University: National Centre of Biography*.

12 *Ibid.*

13 Colm Kiernan, *Daniel Mannix and Ireland*, p. 225.

14 *Cork Examiner* (1920) 'Archbishop Mannix's Visit – Questions in Commons', 23 July, p. 4.

15 *The Irish Times* (1920) 'Archbishop Mannix', 9 August, p. 5.

16 Jim Griffin, *Australian National University: National Centre of Biography*.

17 Aodh Quinlivan (2006), *Philip Monahan: A Man Apart – The Life and Times of Ireland's First Local Authority Manager*. Dublin: Institute of Public Administration. p. 67.

18 *Cork Examiner* (1925), 'Archbishop Mannix – Freedom of Cork Presented', 29 October, p. 7.

19 Aodh Quinlivan, *Philip Monahan: A Man Apart – The Life and Times of Ireland's First Local Authority Manager*, p. 234.

20 *Cork Examiner*, 'Archbishop Mannix – Freedom of Cork Presented'.

21 *Ibid.*

22 *Ibid.*

23 *Ibid.*, p. 8.

24 Colm Kiernan, *Daniel Mannix and Ireland*, p. 202.

Catholic Clergy and Statesmen – 1922 to 1989

SIR FRANK BENSON

1 See Pete Orford (2011), '"Capable, but uninspired": Evaluating Frank Benson's Hesitant/Heroic History Cycles', *Shakespeare Bulletin*, Vol. 29, No. 2, pp. 133–163, Johns Hopkins University Press.

2 John Peter Wearing (2011), 'Benson, Sir Frank Robert (1858–1939)', *Oxford Dictionary of National Biography*, Oxford University Press, 2004; online edition 2011, http://www.oxforddnb.com/view/article/30714

3 *Ibid.*

4 *Ibid.*

5 Ann Pennington (1988), 'Sir Frank Benson', available at: http://www.alresfordhistandlit.co.uk/Alresford%20Displayed/52%20Sir%20Frank%20Benson.pdf

6 *Ibid.*

7 John Peter Wearing, 'Benson, Sir Frank Robert (1858–1939)', *Oxford Dictionary of National Biography*.

8 *Ibid.*

9 *Ibid.*

10 *Ibid.*

11 *Ibid.*

12 *Ibid.*

13 *Ibid.*

14 *Ibid.*

15 *Ibid.*

16 *The Irish Times* (1928), 'Sir Frank Benson: Actor and Sportsman' by 'Muman', 6 December 1928

17 Pete Orford, 'Capable, but uninspired', p. 133.

18 John Peter Wearing, 'Benson, Sir Frank Robert (1858–1939)', *Oxford Dictionary of National Biography*.

19 *Ibid.*

20 Pete Orford, 'Capable, but uninspired', p. 133.

21 John Peter Wearing, 'Benson, Sir Frank Robert (1858–1939)', *Oxford Dictionary of National Biography*.

22 *Ibid.*

23 Ann Pennington, 'Sir Frank Benson'.

24 John Peter Wearing, 'Benson, Sir Frank Robert (1858–1939)', *Oxford Dictionary of National Biography*.

25 *Ibid.*

26 Ann Pennington, 'Sir Frank Benson'.

27 *Ibid.*

28 John Peter Wearing, 'Benson, Sir Frank Robert (1858–1939)', *Oxford Dictionary of National Biography*.

29 *Ibid.*

30 *The Irish Times* (1928), 'Sir Frank Benson: Actor and Sportsman' by 'Muman', 6 December 1928.

31 *Cork Examiner* (1930), 'Sir F. Benson – Civic Honour to be Conferred', Monday 27 January 1930, p. 6.

32 *Ibid.*

33 *Ibid.*

34 *The Irish Times* (1931), 'Cork Honours Sir Frank Benson', 23 January 1931.

35 *Ibid.*

36 *Ibid.*

37 *Ibid.*

38 *Ibid.*

SEAN T. O'KELLY

1 O'Kelly had vivid memories of the funeral of Charles Stewart Parnell (freeman of the city of Cork in 1880) passing his home on Berkeley Road where mourners passed from midday to eight o'clock that evening.

2 Kevin Kenna (2010), *The Lives and Times of The Presidents of Ireland*, Dublin: The Liffey Press. p. 29.

3 *Ibid.*, p. 30.

4 *Ibid.*, p. 30.

5 *Ibid.*, p. 30.

6 *Ibid.*, p. 31.

7 *Ibid.*, pp. 33–34.

8 *Ibid.*, p. 37.

9 *Ibid.*, p. 37.

10 *Ibid.*, p. 38.

11 *Ibid.*, p. 39.

12 O'Kelly was also appointed Chairman of the Foreign Relations Committee that was sent to Paris to lobby President Woodrow Wilson (freeman of the city of Cork in 1919) and others for international recognition for the independent Dáil.

13 Kevin Kenna, *The Lives and Times of The Presidents of Ireland*, p. 40.

14 Aodh Quinlivan (2006), *Philip Monahan – A Man Apart: The Life and Times of Ireland's First Local Authority Manager*. Dublin: Institute of Public Administration, p. 142.

15 Kevin Kenna, *The Lives and Times of The Presidents of Ireland*, p. 32.

16 *The Irish Times* (1934), 'Death of Mrs Seán T. O'Kelly', 28 July 1934, p. 4.

17 *The Irish Times* (1945), 'President Will Have No Policy', 30 April 1945, p. 5.

18 *The Irish Times* (1945), 'Mr. Seán T. O'Kelly Elected President of Ireland', 23 June 1945, p. 10.

19 Kevin Kenna, *The Lives and Times of The Presidents of Ireland*, p. 50.

20 *Ibid.*, p. 53.

21 *The Washington Post* (1959), 'Joint Session Hails O'Kelly's Address', 19 March 1959, p. 19.

22 Kevin Kenna, *The Lives and Times of The Presidents of Ireland*, p. 56.

23 *Ibid.*

24 *Cork Examiner* (1947), 'Freedom of Cork for President', 26 November 1947, p. 4.

25 *The Irish Times* (1948), 'President's Gift to Irish Red Cross Society', 10 September 1948, p. 3.

26 *Cork Examiner* (1948), 'President Receives Freedom of Munster Capital', 9 September 1948, p. 5.

27 *Ibid.*, p. 7.

28 *Ibid.*

29 *Ibid.*

CARDINAL JOHN D'ALTON

1 Miranda Salvador, *The Cardinals of the Holy Roman Church*, John D'Alton section at http://www2.fiu.edu/~mirandas/bios-d.htm

2 *The Irish Times* (1946), 'Dr D'Alton to be Archbishop', 26 April.

3 Rev. Bernard J. Canning (1987), *Bishops of Ireland 1870–1987*, Donegal: Donegal Democrat Co.

4 *The Irish Times*, 'Dr D'Alton to be Archbishop'.

5 Diarmaid Ferriter (2009), 'D'Alton, John Francis', *Dictionary of Irish Biography*, (ed.) James McGuire and James Quinn, Cambridge: Cambridge University Press, 2009 http://dib.cambridge.org/viewReadPage.do?articleId=a2358

6 *Ibid.*

7 Diarmaid Ferriter (2009), 'D'Alton, John Francis', *Dictionary of Irish Biography*.

8 Rev. Bernard J. Canning, *Bishops of Ireland 1870–1987*.

9 Diarmaid Ferriter (2009), 'D'Alton, John Francis', *Dictionary of Irish Biography*.

10 Miranda Salvador, *The Cardinals of the Holy Roman Church*.

11 Diarmaid Ferriter, 'D'Alton, John Francis', *Dictionary of Irish Biography*.

12 *Ibid.*

13 Rev. Bernard J. Canning, *Bishops of Ireland 1870–1987*.

14 *Ibid.*

15 *Cork Examiner* (1953), 'Freedom of Cork for Cardinal', 29 April, p. 5.

16 *Cork Examiner* (1953), 'Cork Gives Great Welcome to Cardinal D'Alton', 17 June.

17 *Ibid.*

18 *The Irish Times* (1953), 'Cardinal D'Alton Gets Freedom of Cork', 17 June.

19 Diarmaid Ferriter, 'D'Alton, John Francis', *Dictionary of Irish Biography*.

20 *Ibid.*

21 *Ibid.*

22 Rev. Bernard J. Canning, *Bishops of Ireland 1870–1987*.

23 *Ibid.*

24 *Ibid.*

JOHN FITZGERALD KENNEDY

1 Carter Smith (2005), 'John Fitzgerald Kennedy', in *Presidents – All You Need to Know*, New York: Hylas Publishing, p. 220.

2 Ryan Tubridy (2010), *JFK in Ireland – Four Days That Changed a President*, London: HarperCollins Press, p. 10.

3 Robert Dallek (2003), *John F. Kennedy – An Unfinished Life*, London: Penguin Books, pp. 26–27.

4 *Ibid.* pp. 27–28, from a conversation with Kennedy's 1960 biographer, James MacGregor Burns.

5 Robert Dallek, *John F. Kennedy – An Unfinished Life*, p. 27.

6 Ryan Tubridy, *JFK in Ireland – Four Days That Changed a President*, p. 11.

7 *Ibid.*

8 Robert Dallek, *John F. Kennedy – An Unfinished Life*, p. 35.

9 Ryan Tubridy, *JFK in Ireland – Four Days That Changed a President*, p. 11.

10 Robert Dallek, *John F. Kennedy – An Unfinished Life*, p. 41.

11 Ryan Tubridy, *JFK in Ireland – Four Days That Changed a President*, p. 12.

12 Robert Dallek, *John F. Kennedy – An Unfinished Life*, p. 45.

13 *Ibid.*, p. 65.

14 Carter Smith, 'John Fitzgerald Kennedy', in *Presidents – All You Need to Know*, p. 220.

15 Robert Dallek, *John F. Kennedy – An Unfinished Life*, p. 83.

16 Ryan Tubridy, *JFK in Ireland – Four Days That Changed a President*, p. 24.

17 Joan and Clay Blair Jr (1974), *The Search for JFK*, New York: Berkeley, p. 356.

18 Carter Smith, 'John Fitzgerald Kennedy', in *Presidents – All You Need to Know*, p. 220.

19 Robert Dallek, *John F. Kennedy – An Unfinished Life*, p. 133.

20 *Ibid.*, p. 135.

21 *Ibid.*, p. 182.

22 *Ibid.*, p. 194.

23 *Ibid.*, p. 213.

24 *Ibid.*

25 Ryan Tubridy, *JFK in Ireland – Four Days That Changed a President*, p. 38.

26 *Ibid.*

27 The Nixon-Kennedy debates on history.com at: http://www.history.com/topics/kennedy-nixon-debates

28 Robert Dallek, *John F. Kennedy – An Unfinished Life*, p. 336.

29 *Ibid.*

30 'Life of John F. Kennedy' from the website of the John F. Kennedy Presidential Library and Museum, at: http://www.jfklibrary.org/JFK/Life-of-John-F-Kennedy.aspx?p=4

31 *Ibid.*

32 Thomas Reeves (1991), *A Question of Character: A Life of John F. Kennedy*, London: Arrow Books.

33 Ryan Tubridy, *JFK in Ireland – Four Days That Changed a President*, p. 41.

34 *Ibid.*

35 Carter Smith, 'John Fitzgerald Kennedy', in *Presidents – All You Need to Know*, p. 220.

36 'Life of John F. Kennedy' from the website of the John F. Kennedy Presidential Library and Museum.

37 John F. Kennedy Presidential Library and Museum, The Kennedy Legacy Exhibit.

38 Robert Dallek, *John F. Kennedy – An Unfinished Life*, p. 702.

39 'Life of John F. Kennedy' from the website of the John F. Kennedy Presidential Library and Museum.

40 Ryan Tubridy, *JFK in Ireland – Four Days That Changed a President*, pp. 274–275.

41 *Cork Examiner* (1963), 'Pres. Kennedy Asked To Go To Cork', 15 June, p. 9.

42 *Cork Examiner* (1963), 'Kennedy's Irish Visit', 20 May, p. 10.

43 *Cork Examiner* (1963), 'Top Kennedy Men For Cork This Week', 27 May, p. 1.

44 *Cork Examiner* (1963), 'Freedom of Cork To Be Offered To Pres. Kennedy', 29 May, p. 9.

45 *Cork Examiner* (1963), 'Salinger and US Envoy in Cork Today', 14 June, p. 1.

46 *Cork Examiner* (1963), 'Kennedy Visit Plans Finalised', 15 June, p. 1, p. 9.

47 *Cork Examiner* (1963), '900 Gardaí will be on duty in Cork', 16 June.

48 *Cork Examiner* (1963), 'Kennedy Visit Plans Finalised', 15 June, p. 1, p. 9.

49 *Cork Examiner* (1963), 'Kennedy Will Fly To Cork In Jet Helicopter', 'Kennedy's Visit to South', 21 June, p. 1, p. 12.

50 *Cork Examiner* (1963), 'The Special Kennedy Touch Was Soon Applied', 29 June, p. 9.

51 *The Irish Times* (1963), 'Rose petal showers as Cork greets honorary freeman', by Michael Foy and Noel Conway, 29 June.

52 *Ibid.*

53 *Ibid.*

54 *Ibid.*

55 *Ibid.*

56 Maurice N. Hennessy (1967), *I'll Come Back in the Springtime*, London: Sphere Books, p. 68.

57 Ryan Tubridy, *JFK in Ireland – Four Days That Changed a President*, p. 169.

58 *Ibid.*

59 *Cork Examiner* (1963), 'Tumultuous Cork Reception', 29 June 1963 p. 11.

60 Ryan Tubridy, *JFK in Ireland – Four Days That Changed a President*, p. 172.

61 *Cork Examiner* (1963), 'Cork's New Freeman Regarded as a Great Irishman', 29 June.

62 Ryan Tubridy, *JFK in Ireland – Four Days That Changed a President*, p. 172.

63 *Cork Examiner* (1963), 'Cork's New Freeman Regarded as a Great Irishman'.

64 *The Irish Times* (1963), 'Rose petal showers as Cork greets honorary freeman'.

65 Ryan Tubridy, *JFK in Ireland – Four Days That Changed a President*, p. 173.

66 *Ibid.*

67 *The Irish Times* (1963), 'Rose petal showers as Cork greets honorary freeman'.

68 *Ibid.*

69 John F. Kennedy Presidential Library and Museum (2013), John F. Kennedy Speeches; Speech to the Irish Institute NYC 12 January 1957, available at: http://www.jfklibrary.org/Research/Research-Aids/JFK-Speeches/Irish-Institute-NYC_19570112.aspx

70 John F. Kennedy Presidential Library and Museum (2013), John F. Kennedy Speeches; President John F. Kennedy 22 November 1963, available at: http://www.jfklibrary.org/Research/Research-Aids/JFK-Speeches/Austin-TX-Undelivered_19631122.aspx

ÉAMON DE VALERA

1 Tim Pat Coogan (1993), *De Valera: Long Fellow, Long Shadow*, London: Hutchinson p. 3.

2 *Ibid.*, pp. 4–6.

3 *Ibid.*, p. 6 and p. 7.

4 *Ibid.*, p. 19 and p. 20.

5 *Ibid.*, p. 16 and p. 20.

6 Seán Farragher (2003), 'Éamon de Valera and Blackrock 1898–1921', in Gabriel Doherty and Dermot Keogh (eds.), *De Valera's Irelands*. Cork: Mercier Press, p. 30.

7 Tim Pat Coogan, *De Valera; Long Fellow, Long Shadow*, p. 3.

8 *Ibid.*, pp. 27–29.

9 *Ibid.*, p. 31.

10 *Ibid.*, p. 35.

11 *Ibid.*, p. 35, pp. 40–41.

12 *Ibid.*, p. 50.

13 *Ibid.*, p. 53, p. 59.

14 Michael McInerney (1976), 'Controversial giant of modern Ireland', in an *Irish Times* publication *Éamon de Valera: 1882–1975*. Dublin: The Irish Times Limited, p. 17.

15 *Ibid.*, p. 17.

16 *Ibid.*, p. 27.

17 Tim Pat Coogan, *De Valera; long fellow, long shadow*, pp. 140–144.

18 Aodh Quinlivan (2006), *Philip Monahan – A Man Apart: The Life and Times of Ireland's First Local Authority Manager*. Dublin: Institute of Public Administration. p. 1.

19 Michael McInerney, 'Controversial giant of modern Ireland', p. 32.

20 *Ibid.*, p. 37.

21 *Ibid.*, p. 51.

22 *Ibid.*, pp. 53–55.

23 Ronan Fanning (2011) *Éamon de Valera, ('Dev')*. [Online] Available at: www.treaty.nationalarchives.ie/wp-content/uploads/2011/11/De-Valera.pdf p.10.

24 *Ibid.*

25 *Ibid.*, p. 15.

26 *Ibid.*, p. 16.

27 Tim Pat Coogan, *De Valera; Long Fellow, Long Shadow*, p. 610.

28 John A. Murphy (1983), 'The achievement of Éamon de Valera', in J.P. O'Carroll and John A. Murphy (eds.), *De Valera and his times*, Cork: Cork University Press, p. 9.

29 Sinnott, R. (2010), 'The Electoral System', in J. Coakley and M. Gallagher (eds.) *Politics in the Republic of Ireland*. 5th edn. New York: Routledge, pp. 113–114.

30 Ronan Fanning, *Éamon de Valera, ('Dev')*, p. 20.

31 Tim Pat Coogan, *De Valera; Long Fellow, Long Shadow*, p. 681.

32 Dick Brazil (1972), 'Contrast in city's welcome to new Freeman', *Cork Examiner*, 2 April, p. 7.

33 *Ibid.*

34 *Ibid.*

35 *Ibid.*

36 George Cronin (1972), 'President gets standing ovation', *Cork Examiner*, 2 April, p. 7.

37 *Ibid.*

38 *Ibid.*

39 *Ibid.*

40 Dick Brazil, 'Contrast in city's welcome to new Freeman', p. 7.

ALOYS FLEISCHMANN

1 See Joseph P. Cunningham and Ruth Fleischmann (2010), *Aloys Fleischmann (1880–1964) – Immigrant Musician in Ireland*. Cork: Cork University Press.

2 Mentioned by Charles Acton in his feature article on Aloys Fleischmann, *The Irish Times*, 19 April 1980.

3 Joseph P. Cunningham and Ruth Fleischmann, *Aloys Fleischmann (1880–1964) – Immigrant Musician in Ireland*, p. 107.

4 Mary Leland (1978), 'Profile of Aloys Fleischmann', *The Irish Times*, 29 April.

5 Joseph P. Cunningham and Ruth Fleischmann, *Aloys Fleischmann (1880–1964) – Immigrant Musician in Ireland*, p. 2.

6 *Ibid.*

7 Ruth Fleischmann (2010), 'Profile of Aloys Fleischmann Sr', *The Fleischmanns – A Remarkable Cork Family*. Cork: Cork City Libraries, pp. 23–24.

8 Séamas de Barra (2010), 'Profile of Aloys Fleischmann Jr', *The Fleischmanns – A Remarkable Cork Family*. Cork: Cork City Libraries, p. 31.

9 Charles Acton in his feature article on Aloys Fleischmann, *The Irish Times*, 19 April 1980.

10 *Ibid.*

11 Obituary of Professor Aloys Fleischmann, *The Irish Times*, 22 July 1992.

12 Obituary by Séamas de Barra in *New Music News*, September 1992.

13 *Ibid.*

14 Séamas de Barra (2010), 'Profile of Aloys Fleischmann Jr', *The Fleischmanns – A Remarkable Cork Family*, pp. 40–41.

15 *Ibid.*

16 *Ibid.*

17 *Ibid.*

18 Quoted in Séamas de Barra (2010), 'Profile of Aloys Fleischmann Jr', *The Fleischmanns – A Remarkable Cork Family*, p. 43.

19 Obituary of Professor Aloys Fleischmann, *The Irish Times*, 22 July 1992.

20 Séamas de Barra (2010), 'Profile of Aloys Fleischmann Jr', *The Fleischmanns – A Remarkable Cork Family*, p. 44.

21 Maureen Fox (1978), 'Fleischmann made Freeman', report in *Cork Examiner*, Saturday 29 April, p. 1.

22 *Ibid.*

23 *Ibid.*

24 *Ibid.*

25 *Ibid.*

BISHOP CORNELIUS LUCEY

1 Dick Hogan (1980), 'Lynch and Bishop given freedom of Cork', *The Irish Times*, 20 December.

2 Diarmaid Ferriter (2009), 'Lucey, Cornelius', *Dictionary of Irish Biography*, (ed.) James McGuire and James Quinn, Cambridge, United Kingdom: Cambridge University Press, (http://dib.cambridge.org/viewReadPage.do?articleId=a4909)

3 *Ibid.*

4 *Ibid.*

5 Diocese of Cork and Ross, http://www.corkandross.org/priests.jsp?priestID=398

6 Diarmaid Ferriter (2009), 'Lucey, Cornelius', *Dictionary of Irish Biography*.

7 *Ibid.*

8 *Ibid.*

9 *Ibid.*

10 Diocese of Cork and Ross.

11 *Ibid.*

12 Diarmaid Ferriter, 'Lucey, Cornelius', *Dictionary of Irish Biography*.

13 Diocese of Cork and Ross.

14 Diarmaid Ferriter, 'Lucey, Cornelius', *Dictionary of Irish Biography*.

15 Diocese of Cork and Ross.

16 Diarmaid Ferriter, 'Lucey, Cornelius', *Dictionary of Irish Biography*.

17 *Ibid.*

18 *Ibid.*

19 Dermot Keogh (1994), *Twentieth-Century Ireland: Nation and State*, Dublin: Gill & Macmillan, p. 217 (with reference to the report of the Commission on Emigration and Other Population Problems).

20 Diarmaid Ferriter, 'Lucey, Cornelius', *Dictionary of Irish Biography*.

21 *Ibid.*

22 *Ibid.*

23 *Ibid.*

24 Bernard Canning (1987), *Bishops of Ireland 1870–1987*, Donegal: Donegal Democrat Co., pp. 256–257.

25 Fr James Good (2008), 'Setting the Record Straight', *The Irish Catholic*, 7 August 2008.

26 *Ibid.*

27 See Fr James Good, 'Setting the Record Straight', The Irish Catholic, and Diarmaid Ferriter, 'Lucey, Cornelius', *Dictionary of Irish Biography*.

28 See 'Bishop Lucey Park' in Cork Past & Present at: http://www.corkpastandpresent.ie/places/grandparade/bishopluceypark/

29 Diarmaid Ferriter, 'Lucey, Cornelius', *Dictionary of Irish Biography*.

30 Canon Denis O'Connor, as quoted in the Diocese of Cork and Ross website.

31 Cork Corporation minute book for 1980.

32 *Ibid.*, p. 488.

33 Dick Hogan, 'Lynch and Bishop given freedom of Cork', *The Irish Times*.

34 Cork Corporation minute book for 1980.

35 Denis Reading (1980), 'City proudly honours two great citizens', *Cork Examiner*, 20 December, p. 1.

36 Cork Corporation minute book for 1980, p. 489.

37 *Ibid*. Also, see *Cork Examiner*, 'No place like Cork', 20 December 1980, back page.

38 Cork Corporation minute book for 1980, p. 489.

39 *Ibid*., p. 490.

40 *Ibid*.

41 *Ibid*.

42 *Cork Examiner* (1980), 'No place like Cork', 20 December, back page.

JACK LYNCH

1 Dermot Keogh (2009), *Jack Lynch – A Biography*, Dublin: Gill & Macmillan, p. 2.

2 National Census (1911) [Online], Available at http://www.census.nationalarchives.ie/reels/nai001872186/

3 Dermot Keogh, *Jack Lynch – A Biography*, p. 2.

4 *Ibid*., p. 5.

5 T.P. O'Mahony (1991), *Jack Lynch – A Biography*, Dublin: Blackwater Press. p. 31.

6 *Ibid*., p. 29.

7 Dermot Keogh, *Jack Lynch – A Biography*, p. 7.

8 T. Ryle Dwyer (2001), *Nice Fellow: a biography of Jack Lynch*, Cork: Mercier Press. p. 15.

9 Dermot Keogh, *Jack Lynch – A Biography*, p. 12.

10 *Ibid*., p. 14.

11 *Ibid*., pp. 14–15.

12 Jack Lynch (1979) ,'My life and times', *Magill*, November, pp. 36–37.

13 Dermot Keogh, *Jack Lynch – A Biography*, p. 18.

14 *Irish Independent* (1939), 'Britain and France declare war: Reich will not capitulate Fuehrer says', 4 September, p. 1.

15 Liam O'Tuama (2000), *Jack Lynch: Where he sported and played*. Dublin: Blackwater Press. pp. 173–174.

16 *The Irish Times* (1939), 'Hurling final played in thunderstorm: Kilkenny gain their twelfth title', 4 September, p. 11.

17 Dermot Keogh, *Jack Lynch – A Biography*, p. 19.

18 *Ibid*., pp. 23–25.

19 Dave Hannigan (2005), *Giants of Cork Sport*, Cork: Evening Echo, p. 60.

20 Croke Park (2013), *Exhibitions: Medal Collections*, [Online]. Available at: http://www.crokepark.ie/gaa-museum/exhibitions/collections/medal-collections

21 Cork City Libraries (2013), Cork Past and Present, [Online]. Available at: http://www.corkpastandpresent.ie/mapsimages/corkphotographs/michaelolearyphotos/corkbuttermarket/

22 Dermot Keogh, *Jack Lynch – A Biography*, pp. 26–27.

23 *Ibid*. pp. 30–31.

24 *The Irish Times* (1948), 'New Ministers Begin Their Tasks: Opposition Activity', 20 February, p. 1.

25 *The Irish Times* (1951), 'Dissolution', 5 May, p. 7.

26 *The Irish Times* (1951), 'Mr. de Valera is elected by 74 votes to 69: new government has the smallest majority on record', 14 June, p. 1.

27 Dermot Keogh, *Jack Lynch – A Biography*, pp. 40–41.

28 *Ibid*., p. 42.

29 *Ibid*., pp. 46–49.

30 *Ibid*., pp. 50–56.

31 *Ibid*., pp. 70–79.

32 *The Irish Times* (1965), 'Dáil will elect Taoiseach to-day', 21 April, p. 1.

33 *The Irish Times* (1965), 'Pen-pictures of Ministers', 22 April, p. 6.

34 Dermot Keogh, *Jack Lynch – A Biography*, pp. 96–99.

35 *Cork Examiner* (1966), 'Cork enthusiastic welcome for new Taoiseach', 14 November, p. 1.

36 Dermot Keogh, *Jack Lynch – A Biography*, p. 10.

37 J. Horgan, (1966), 'Cork takes Lynch (again) to its heart: a full blooded welcome', *The Irish Times*, 14 November, p. 11.

38 Dermot Keogh, *Jack Lynch – A Biography*, p. 476.

39 *Ibid*., pp. 476–477.

40 *Ibid*., pp. 125–126.

41 *The Irish Times* (1971), 'Uproar at Fianna Fáil Árd-Fheis: Scuffles between Lynch and Boland supporters', 22 February, p. 7.

42 Dermot Keogh, *Jack Lynch – A Biography*, pp. 478–479.

43 *Ibid*., p. 486.

44 *The Irish Times* (1979), 'More of a convulsion', 9 November, p. 11.

45 Dermot Keogh, *Jack Lynch – A Biography*, p. 445.

46 From speech by Lord Mayor Alderman Toddy O'Sullivan at Lynch's conferring ceremony, 19 December 1980, Cork Corporation minute book.

47 *Ibid*.

48 *Ibid*.

49 From speech by Jack Lynch at freedom conferring ceremony, 19 December 1980, Cork Corporation minute book, p. 493.

50 *Ibid*.

51 *Ibid*.

52 *Ibid*.

53 *Cork Examiner* (1980), 'No place like Cork', 20 December.

THOMAS 'TIP' O'NEILL

1 Tip O'Neill with William Novak (1987), *Man of the House: The Life and Political Memoirs of Speaker Tip O'Neill*, New York: Random House. p. 7.

2 Bill Clinton (1994), *Statement by the President*, [Press release], 6 January, Available at: http://clinton6.nara.gov/1994/01/1994-01-06-statement-on-death-of-tip-o-neill.html

3 Tip O'Neill with William Novak (1987), *Man of the House*, p. 8.

4 Boston College (2002) *Thomas P. O'Neill Junior and Boston College*, Available at: http://www.bc.edu/content/bc/libraries/about/exhibits/burnsvirtual/oneill/2.html

5 Boston College (2002) *Thomas P. O'Neill Junior and Boston College*, Available at: http://www.bc.edu/content/bc/libraries/about/exhibits/burnsvirtual/oneill/3.html

6 Tip O'Neill with William Novak (1987), *Man of the House*, p. 23.

7 *Ibid*., p. 26.

8 Boston College (2002) *Thomas P. O'Neill Junior and Boston College*, Available at: http://www.bc.edu/content/bc/libraries/about/exhibits/burnsvirtual/oneill/4.html

9 Tip O'Neill with William Novak (1987), *Man of the House*, p. 178.

10 Boston College (2002) *Thomas P. O'Neill Junior and Boston College*, Available at: http://www.bc.edu/content/bc/libraries/about/exhibits/burnsvirtual/oneill/4.html

11 Bill Clinton, *Statement by the President*.

12 Denis Reading and Maurice Gubbins (1985), 'A Sentimental Journey to Freedom', *Cork Examiner*, 18 March, p. 7.

13 *Ibid*.

14 Denis Reading and Maurice Gubbins (1985), 'Joining the Famous Five', *Cork Examiner*, 18 March, p. 7.

15   Denis Reading and Maurice Gubbins, 'A Sentimental Journey to Freedom', p. 7.

16   Denis Reading and Maurice Gubbins, 'Joining the Famous Five', p. 7.

17   Denis Reading and Maurice Gubbins, 'A Sentimental Journey to Freedom', p. 7.

SEÁN Ó FAOLÁIN

1   This forms part of the full citation for Ó Faoláin in the Cork Corporation freedom register.

2   In his 1994 biography of Ó Faoláin, *A Life*, Maurice Harmon says that he was born on 22 February; however, in Harmon's 2009 biography for the *Dictionary of Irish Biography*, he gives the date of birth as 23 February.

3   Maurice Harmon (1994), *Seán Ó Faoláin – A Life*, London: Constable, p. 15.

4   *Ibid.*

5   Seán Ó Faoláin (1993), *Vive Moi!*, London: Sinclair-Stevenson, p. 3.

6   Maurice Harmon (2009), 'O'Faolain, Sean', *Dictionary of Irish Biography*, (ed.) James McGuire and James Quinn, Cambridge, United Kingdom: Cambridge University Press. http://dib.cambridge.org/viewReadPage.do?articleId=a6736

7   *Ibid.*

8   Seán Ó Faoláin, *Vive Moi!* p. 91.

9   Maurice Harmon, 'O'Faolain, Sean', *Dictionary of Irish Biography*.

10   Maurice Harmon, *Seán Ó Faoláin – A Life*, p. 46.

11   *Ibid.*

12   *Ibid.*, p. 47.

13   *Ibid.*

14   Maurice Harmon, 'O'Faolain, Sean', *Dictionary of Irish Biography*.

15   *Ibid.*

16   Maurice Harmon, *Seán Ó Faoláin – A Life*, p. 70.

17   Maurice Harmon, 'O'Faolain, Sean', *Dictionary of Irish Biography*.

18   Maurice Harmon, *Seán Ó Faoláin – A Life*, p. 89.

19   Maurice Harmon, 'O'Faolain, Sean', *Dictionary of Irish Biography*.

20   Maurice Harmon, *Seán Ó Faoláin – A Life*, p. 100.

21   Seán Ó Faoláin, *Vive Moi!* p. 295.

22   *Ibid.*, p. 295.

23   Maurice Harmon, 'O'Faolain, Sean', *Dictionary of Irish Biography*.

24   Maurice Harmon, *Seán Ó Faoláin – A Life*, p. 143.

25   Maurice Harmon, 'O'Faolain, Sean', *Dictionary of Irish Biography*.

26   Seán Ó Faoláin, *Vive Moi!* p. 337.

27   Maurice Harmon, 'O'Faolain, Sean', *Dictionary of Irish Biography*.

28   *Ibid.*

29   Maurice Harmon, *Seán Ó Faoláin – A Life*, p. 280.

30   John Spain (2013), Review of *Trespassers*, *Irish Independent*, 6 April.

31   Julia Ó Faoláin (2013), *Trespassers: A Memoir*, London: Faber and Faber, as quoted in *The Irish Times*, 9 March 2013.

32   Dick Hogan (1988), 'Cork freedom for Seán Ó Faoláin', *The Irish Times*, 11 July.

33   Peter Cluskey (1988), 'Freedom of City for Ó Faoláin', *Cork Examiner*, 11 July.

34   *Ibid.*

35   *Ibid.*

High Achievers – 1990 to 2013

MARY ROBINSON

1   Olivia O'Leary and Helen Burke (1998), *Mary Robinson – The Authorised Biography*, London: Hodder & Stoughton, p. 10.

2   *Ibid.*, p. 14.

3   *Ibid.*, p. 19

4   Chancellor biography from Trinity College website at http://www.tcd.ie/chancellor/biog/

5   Biography of Robinson by David McWilliams on RTÉ website at http://www.rte.ie/tv/irelandsgreatest/maryrobinson.html

6   Olivia O'Leary and Helen Burke, *Mary Robinson – The Authorised Biography*, p. 310.

7   *Ibid.*, p. 42.

8   Chancellor biography from Trinity College website at http://www.tcd.ie/chancellor/biog/

9   Biography of Robinson by David McWilliams on RTÉ website at http://www.rte.ie/tv/irelandsgreatest/maryrobinson.html

10   Olivia O'Leary and Helen Burke, *Mary Robinson – The Authorised Biography*, p. 310.

11   Chancellor biography from Trinity College website at http://www.tcd.ie/chancellor/biog/

12   *Ibid.*

13   See Robinson's election history on ElectionsIreland.org at http://electionsireland.org/candidate.cfm?ID=3142

14   Olivia O'Leary and Helen Burke, *Mary Robinson – The Authorised Biography*, p. 315.

15   Irish Marketing Surveys Poll conducted for Independent Newspapers.

16   Olivia O'Leary and Helen Burke, *Mary Robinson – The Authorised Biography*, p. 135.

17   *Ibid.*, p. 139.

18   Tim Pat Coogan (2003), *Ireland in the Twentieth Century*, London: Hutchinson, p. 622.

19   Olivia O'Leary and Helen Burke, *Mary Robinson – The Authorised Biography*, p. 3.

20   *Ibid.*

21   Peter Gleeson (1991), 'No lavish fête for Robinson', *Cork Examiner*, 23 February, p. 11.

22   Ann Mooney (1991), '1,000 attend lavish event', *Cork Examiner*, 25 February, p. 11.

23   Ann Mooney (1991), 'Mary notches up another first', *Cork Examiner*, 25 February 1991, p. 1.

24   Ann Mooney (1991), '1,000 attend lavish event', *Cork Examiner*, 25 February, p. 11.

25   *Ibid.*

26   *Ibid.*

27   Dick Cross (1991), 'President laughs her way into Cork's heart', *Irish Independent*, 25 February, p. 5.

28   *Ibid.*

29   Ann Mooney (1991), '1,000 attend lavish event', *Cork Examiner*, 25 February, p. 11.

30   Dick Cross (1991), 'President laughs her way into Cork's heart', *Irish Independent*, 25 February, p. 5.

31   *Ibid.*

32 Miriam Donohue (1991), 'City with a unique spirit', *Cork Examiner*, 25 February, p. 11.

33 *Ibid*.

34 *Ibid*.

MAURICE HICKEY

1   Turlough O' Riordan (2011), 'Hickey, Maurice Desmond', *Dictionary of Irish Biography*, (ed.) James McGuire and James Quinn, Cambridge, United Kingdom: Cambridge University Press, 2011
    http://dib.cambridge.org/viewReadPage.do?articleId=a9421

2   *Ibid*.

3   *Ibid*.

4   *Ibid*.

5   *Ibid*.

6   *Ibid*.

7   From speech by Maurice Hickey at his freedom of the city conferring ceremony, 13 June 1992, as contained in the Cork Corporation minute book for 1992.

8   *The Irish Times* (2005), ''A giant of Irish medicine and the leading chest surgeon of his time', 21 May, p. 12.

9   *Ibid*.

10 *Ibid*.

11 From speech by Maurice Hickey at his freedom of the city conferring ceremony.

12 Turlough O' Riordan, 'Hickey, Maurice Desmond', *Dictionary of Irish Biography*.

13 From speech by Maurice Hickey at his freedom of the city conferring ceremony, 13 June 1992.

14 *The Irish Times* (2005), ''A giant of Irish medicine and the leading chest surgeon of his time'.

15 Turlough O' Riordan, 'Hickey, Maurice Desmond', *Dictionary of Irish Biography*.

16 *Ibid*.

17 *Ibid*.

18 *The Irish Times* (2005), ''A giant of Irish medicine and the leading chest surgeon of his time'.

19 Turlough O' Riordan, 'Hickey, Maurice Desmond', *Dictionary of Irish Biography*.

20 *Ibid*.

21 *Ibid*.

22 *The Irish Times* (2005), ''A giant of Irish medicine and the leading chest surgeon of his time'.

23 Turlough O' Riordan, 'Hickey, Maurice Desmond', *Dictionary of Irish Biography*.

24 From speech by the Lord Mayor Councillor Denis Cregan at the Maurice Hickey freedom of the city conferring ceremony, 13 June 1992, as contained in the Cork Corporation minute book for 1992.

25 *Ibid*.

26 From speech by Maurice Hickey at his freedom of the city conferring ceremony.

27 *Ibid*.

MAUREEN CURTIS-BLACK

1   *The Irish Times* (1999), 'Maureen Curtis Black – Appreciation', 23 March.

2   Sandra McAvoy (1994), 'A Woman of Vision', *Wise Women – A Portrait*, Cork: Bradshaw Books, p. 3.

3   *Ibid*., pp. 3–4.

4   *The Irish Times*, 'Maureen Curtis Black – Appreciation'.

5   *Ibid*.

6   *Ibid*.

7   Sandra McAvoy, 'A Woman of Vision', *Wise Women – A Portrait*, pp. 4–5.

8   *Ibid*., p. 5

9   *The Irish Times*, 'Maureen Curtis Black – Appreciation'.

10 *Ibid*.

11 Sandra McAvoy, 'A Woman of Vision', *Wise Women – A Portrait*, p. 6.

12 *Ibid*., p. 7

13 *Ibid*.

14 *The Irish Times*, 'Maureen Curtis Black – Appreciation'.

15 Sandra McAvoy, 'A Woman of Vision', *Wise Women – A Portrait*, p. 8.

16 *The Irish Times*, 'Maureen Curtis Black – Appreciation'.

17 Sandra McAvoy, 'A Woman of Vision', *Wise Women – A Portrait*, p. 8.

18 *Ibid*., p. 10.

19 *Ibid*.

20 *The Irish Times*, 'Maureen Curtis Black – Appreciation'.

21 Sandra McAvoy, 'A Woman of Vision', *Wise Women – A Portrait*, p. 10.

22 T.P. O'Mahony (1993), 'A commitment to justice', *Cork Examiner*, 21 June.

23 *Ibid*.

24 *Ibid*.

25 *Ibid*.

26 *Ibid*.

27 *Ibid*.

28 *Ibid*.

GEORGE MITCHELL

1   Biography of George Mitchell on Academy of Achievement website http://www.achievement.org/autodoc/page/mit0bio-1

2   Interview with George Mitchell in Dublin, 7 June 2002, by Academy of Achievement, video and audio versions available at http://www.achievement.org/autodoc/page/mit0int-1

3   Biography of George Mitchell on Academy of Achievement website, as per 1 above.

4   Interview with George Mitchell in Dublin.

5   Biography of George Mitchell on Academy of Achievement website.

6   Interview with George Mitchell in Dublin.

7   Biography of George Mitchell on Academy of Achievement website.

8   *Ibid*.

9   Interview with George Mitchell in Dublin.

10 See entry for George Mitchell in the *Gale Encyclopaedia of Biography*.

11 Biography of George Mitchell on Academy of Achievement website.

12 *Ibid*.

13 *Ibid*.

14 Interview with George Mitchell in Dublin.

15 George Mitchell (1999), *Making Peace*, London: William Heinemann, p. i.

16 *The Guardian* Politics Blog (2009), http://www.guardian.co.uk/politics/blog/2009/jan/23/george-mitchell-interview

17 George Mitchell, *Making Peace*, p. 187.

18 *Ibid.*, p. 188.

19 Biography of George Mitchell on Academy of Achievement website.

20 *Ibid.*

21 *Ibid.*

22 *Ibid.*

23 George Mitchell, *Making Peace*, p. 188.

24 Barry Roche (1998), 'Special kind of homecoming', *The Examiner*, 30 November.

25 *Ibid.*

26 *Ibid.*

27 *Ibid.*

28 *Ibid.*

29 *Ibid.*

30 Barry Roche (1999), 'Mitchell says son's birth inspired him to persevere when tensions were high', *The Examiner*, 30 November.

JOHN HUME

1 Barry White (1984), *John Hume – Statesman of the Troubles*, Belfast: The Blackstaff Press, p. 5.

2 John Hume (1996), *Personal Views: Politics, Peace and Reconciliation in Ireland*, edited by Jack Van Zandt and Tom McEnery, Dublin: Town House, p. 1.

3 *Ibid.*, p. 4.

4 Barry White, *John Hume – Statesman of the Troubles*, p. 11.

5 *Ibid.*, p. 26.

6 John Hume, *Personal Views*, p. 5.

7 *Ibid.*, p. 5.

8 *Ibid.*, p. 6.

9 Interview with John Hume by Academy of Achievement, video and audio versions available at http://www.achievement.org/autodoc/page/hum0int-3

10 Biography of John Hume on the Academy of Achievement website at http://www.achievement.org/autodoc/page/hum0bio-1

11 *Ibid.*

12 Barry White, *John Hume – Statesman of the Troubles*, p. 68.

13 *Ibid.*, p. 72.

14 Interview with John Hume by Academy of Achievement.

15 Biography of John Hume on the Academy of Achievement website.

16 *Ibid.*

17 Interview with John Hume by Academy of Achievement, video and audio versions available at http://www.achievement.org/autodoc/page/hum0int-3

18 Barry White (1984), *John Hume – Statesman of the Troubles*, p. 231.

19 Biography of John Hume on the Academy of Achievement website.

20 John Hume (1996), *Personal Views*, p. 43.

21 Biography of John Hume on the Academy of Achievement website.

22 *Ibid.*

23 *Ibid.*

24 John Coakley (2010), 'Northern Ireland and the British dimension', pp. 383–406 in J. Coakley and M. Gallagher (eds.), *Politics in the Republic of Ireland* (5th edition), Dublin: PSAI Press, p. 392.

25 *Ibid.*, p. 402.

26 Tim Pat Coogan (2003), *Ireland in the Twentieth Century*, London: Hutchinson, p. 690.

27 Biography of Hume by Miriam O'Callaghan on RTÉ website at http://www.rte.ie/tv/irelandsgreatest/johnhume.html

28 Biography of John Hume on the Academy of Achievement website.

29 See BBC news report at http://www.bbc.co.uk/news/uk-northern-ireland-foyle-west-18733621

30 Eoin English (2004), 'Hume "humbled" to accept Freedom of Cork', *Irish Examiner*, 10 May.

31 Niall O'Connor (2004), 'Hume calls for "certificate of Irishness"', *The Irish Times*, 10 May.

32 Eoin English, 'Hume "humbled" to accept Freedom of Cork'.

SONIA O'SULLIVAN

1 Tina Ryan (2007), 'Inspirational athlete: Sonia O'Sullivan, middle distance runner', *Teaching Expertise* (interview), http://www.teachingexpertise.com/articles/inspirational-athlete-sonia-osullivan-2731

2 *Ibid.*

3 Sonia O'Sullivan with Tom Humphries (2008), *Sonia, My Story*, London: Penguin, p. 15.

4 *Ibid.*, p. 14.

5 *Ibid.*, p. 15.

6 *Ibid.*, pp. 11–12.

7 *Ibid.*, p. 56.

8 *Ibid.*, p. 46.

9 *Ibid.*, p. 75.

10 *Ibid.*, p. 105.

11 *Ibid.*

12 *Ibid.*, p. 108.

13 *Ibid.*, p. 112.

14 *Ibid.*, p. 158.

15 *Ibid.*, p. 166.

16 Ewan MacKenna interview (2013), 'A one-track mind no more', *Irish Examiner*, 13 April.

17 Sonia O'Sullivan with Tom Humphries, *Sonia, My Story*, pp. 204–205.

18 Graham Lynch (2005), 'Freedom of the City', *Inside Cork*, 16 June.

19 Noel Baker (2005), 'Humble words from mighty stars', *Irish Examiner*, 15 June, p. 11.

20 *Ibid.*

21 Graham Lynch (2005), 'Freedom of the City', *Inside Cork*.

22 From Theo Dorgan's poem, 'Running with the Immortals', recited at Sonia O'Sullivan's conferring ceremony on 14 June 2005.

ROY KEANE

1 Dave Hannigan (2005), 'Roy' pp. 63–72 in *Giants of Cork Sport*, Cork: Evening Echo Publications, p. 63.

2 Roy Keane with Eamon Dunphy (2002), *Keane – The Autobiography*, London: Penguin Group, pp. 1–2.

3 *Ibid.*, p. 8

4 Dave Hannigan, *Giants of Cork Sport*, p. 67.

5 *Ibid.*, p. 68.

6 Roy Keane with Eamon Dunphy, *Keane – The Autobiography*, p. 19.

7 Dave Hannigan, *Giants of Cork Sport*, p. 66.

8 Roy Keane with Eamon Dunphy, *Keane – The Autobiography*, p. 35.

9 Dave Hannigan, *Giants of Cork Sport*, p. 66.

10 Roy Keane with Eamon Dunphy, *Keane – The Autobiography*, p. 38.

11 *Ibid.*, pp. 49–50.

12 *Ibid.*, p. 79.

13 *Ibid.*, p. 81.

14 *Ibid.*

15 *Ibid.*, p. 90.

16 Alex Ferguson (1999), *Managing My Life*, London: Hodder & Stoughton.

17 From fundraising speech at Rockmount AFC by Keane, as at http://www.goal.com/enie/news/3942/ireland/2012/05/14/3102016/roy-keane-manchester-united-lied-and-insulted-me-when-i-left

18 Dave Hannigan, *Giants of Cork Sport*, p. 70.

19 Graham Lynch (2005), 'Freedom of the City', *Inside Cork*, 16 June.

20 Noel Baker (2005), 'Humble words from mighty stars', *Irish Examiner*, 15 June, p. 11.

21 Miriam Lord (2005), 'Feeling free and easy, Sonia and Roy are given the run of their city', *Irish Independent*, 15 June.

22 Noel Baker, 'Humble words from mighty stars', p. 11.

23 *Ibid.*

24 *Ibid.*

MARY MCALEESE

1 Ray Mac Mánais (2004), *The Road from Ardoyne – The Making of a President*, Kerry: Brandon, p. 32.

2 *Ibid.*, p. 47.

3 *Ibid.*, p. 57.

4 Biography of McAleese on Áras an Uachtaráin website at http://www.president.ie/past_presidents/mary-mcaleese-2/

5 Ray Mac Mánais, *The Road from Ardoyne – The Making of a President*, p. 64.

6 Rob Kevlihan (2012), *Aid, Insurgencies and Conflict Transformation: When Greed is Good*, London: Routledge, p. 31.

7 Mary McAleese (1993), interview with Fionnuala O'Connor for *In Search of a State: Catholics in Northern Ireland*, as reproduced in *The Field Day Anthology of Irish Writing* (2002), Cork: Cork University Press, p. 1521.

8 *Ibid.*, p. 1520.

9 Ray Mac Mánais, *The Road from Ardoyne – The Making of a President*, p. 172.

10 See McAleese's Dáil electoral performance on ElectionsIreland.org at http://www.electionsireland.org/result.cfm?election=1987&cons=104

11 Biography of McAleese on Áras an Uachtaráin website at http://www.president.ie/past_presidents/mary-mcaleese-2/

12 *Ibid.*

13 Ray Mac Mánais, *The Road from Ardoyne – The Making of a President*, p. 339.

14 From article by Emily O'Reilly in *Magill* (1999) entitled, 'Mary, Mary, Quite Ordinary', as reproduced in *The Field Day Anthology of Irish Writing*, p. 301.

15 See 1997 presidential election results on ElectionsIreland.org at http://electionsireland.org/result.cfm?election=1997P&cons=194

16 As quoted by McAleese during her inauguration speech of 11 November 1997, as reproduced in *President Mary McAleese – Building Bridges: Selected Speeches and Statements* (2011), Dublin: The History Press Ireland, p. 19.

17 *Ibid.*

18 *Ibid.*, p. 22.

19 Jeffrey VanderWilt (2002), *Communion With Non-Catholic Christians: Risks, Challenges, and Opportunities*, Liturgical Press, p. 51.

20 *Ibid.*

21 Garry O'Sullivan and Sarah MacDonald (2012), 'McAleese reveals attack by disgraced cardinal', *Irish Independent*, 6 October.

22 *Ibid.*

23 As quoted by McAleese during her re-inauguration speech of 11 November 2004, as reproduced in *President Mary McAleese – Building Bridges: Selected Speeches and Statements*, p. 97.

24 Mary McAleese (2011), 'My personal thanks to Ireland', *The Irish Times*, 10 November.

25 Biography of McAleese on Áras an Uachtaráin website at http://www.president.ie/past_presidents/mary-mcaleese-2/

26 From speech by Lord Mayor Councillor Deirdre Clune at the McAleese conferring ceremony on 30 May 2006, from the Cork City Council archived news section at: http://www.corkcity.ie/news/archivednews2006/mainbody,153,en.html

27 *Ibid.*

28 From speech by President McAleese at her conferring ceremony on 30 May 2006, from the Cork City Council archived news section.

29 Eoin English (2006), 'McAleese granted freedom of Cork', *Irish Examiner*, 31 May, p. 13

30 From speech by President McAleese at her conferring ceremony on 30 May 2006, from the Cork City Council archived news section.

31 *Ibid.*

32 *Ibid.*

MICHAEL FLATLEY

1 Michael Flatley with Douglas Thompson (2006), *Lord of the Dance*, Basingstoke: Pan Macmillan, p. 9.

2 *Ibid.*

3 *Ibid.*, p. 53.

4 See Michael Flatley biography from 'The Biography Channel' at http://www.thebiographychannel.co.uk/biographies/michael-flatley.html

5 Michael Flatley with Douglas Thompson, *Lord of the Dance*, p. 59.

6 See Michael Flatley biography from 'The Biography Channel'.

7 *Ibid.*

8 From speech by Lord Mayor Councillor Michael Ahern at Flatley's freedom of city conferring ceremony, 2 June 2007, Cork City Council minute book for 2007.

9 Michael Flatley with Douglas Thompson, *Lord of the Dance*, p. 103.

10 *Ibid.*

11 See Michael Flatley biography from 'The Biography Channel'.

12 Michael Flatley with Douglas Thompson, *Lord of the Dance*, p. 121.

13 Jean Butler as quoted in *Sunday Mirror* on 25 August 1996; see also *Lord of the Dance*, p. 125.

14   See Michael Flatley biography from 'The Biography Channel'.

15   *Ibid*.

16   Michael Flatley with Douglas Thompson, *Lord of the Dance*, p. 207.

17   *Ibid*., p. 210.

18   See Michael Flatley biography from 'The Biography Channel'.

19   Michael Flatley with Douglas Thompson, *Lord of the Dance*, p. 292.

20   Cornelia Lucey (2007), 'Flatley freedom has its limits', *Irish Examiner*, 4 June, p. 5.

21   *Ibid*.

22   *Ibid*.

23   *Ibid*.

24   From speech by Lord Mayor, Councillor Michael Ahern, at Flatley's freedom of city conferring ceremony, 2 June 2007, Cork City Council minute book for 2007.

25   *Ibid*.

26   Cornelia Lucey (2007), 'Flatley freedom has its limits'.

27   From Flatley's acceptance speech at his conferring ceremony, from the archived news section of the Cork City Council website at http://www.corkcity.ie/news/archivednews2007/ mainbody,6837,en.html

JOHN MAJOR

1   Keith Laybourn (2002), 'John Major', in *Fifty Key Figures in Twentieth-Century British Politics*, London: Routledge, p. 179.

2   Michael Foley (2002), *John Major, Tony Blair and a Conflict of Leadership*, Manchester: Manchester University Press, p. 10.

3   *Ibid*.

4   *Ibid*.

5   *Ibid*., p. 11.

6   Keith Laybourn, 'John Major', in *Fifty Key Figures in Twentieth-Century British Politics*, p. 179.

7   Michael Foley, *John Major, Tony Blair and a Conflict of Leadership*, p. 11.

8   *Ibid*.

9   Biography of Sir John Major at http://www.johnmajor.co.uk/bio.html

10   Michael Foley, *John Major, Tony Blair and a Conflict of Leadership*, p. 12.

11   *Ibid*.

12   *Ibid*.

13   *Ibid*., p. 13.

14   Margaret Thatcher (1993), *The Downing Street Years*, London: HarperCollins, pp. 757–758.

15   Biography of Sir John Major.

16   Michael Foley, *John Major, Tony Blair and a Conflict of Leadership*, p. 15.

17   *Ibid*.

18   Keith Laybourn, 'John Major', in *Fifty Key Figures in Twentieth-Century British Politics*, p. 181.

19   Biography of Sir John Major.

20   Keith Laybourn, 'John Major', in *Fifty Key Figures in Twentieth-Century British Politics*, p. 181.

21   *Ibid*., p. 182.

22   Michael Foley, *John Major, Tony Blair and a Conflict of Leadership*, p. 150.

23   'Major and Currie had four-year affair', BBC News, 28 September 2002, http://news.bbc.co.uk/2/hi/uk_news/politics/2286008.stm

24   Eoin English (2008), 'Council split over Major and Reynolds', *Irish Examiner*, 13 May.

25   *Ibid*.

26   *Ibid*.

27   Eoin English (2008), 'Peace process built to last, say Major and Reynolds', *Irish Examiner*, 21 June.

28   *Ibid*.

29   *Ibid*.

30   *Ibid*.

31   Eoin English (2008), 'Major heralds Union Jacks as sign of progress', *Irish Examiner*, 21 June.

32   *Ibid*.

33   *Ibid*.

INDEX

Illustrations are indicated by page numbers in **bold**.

THE FREEDOM OF CORK: A CHRONICLE OF HONOUR